W9-CEZ-574

FLORIDA STATE
UNIVERSITY LIBRARIES

APR 0 2 2001

TALLAHASSEE, FLORIDA

COMPETITION, REGULATION AND THE PRIVATISATION
OF BRITISH RAIL

Op de vrome, de glorieuze en onsterfelijke herinnering
van Kolonel Puf Puf

Competition, Regulation and the Privatisation of British Rail

JON SHAW
Department of Geography
University of Aberdeen

Ashgate

Aldershot • Burlington USA • Singapore • Sydney

HE
3020
.B76
S53
2000

© Jon Shaw 2000

All rights reserved. No part of this publication may be reproduced, stored in a retrieval system, or transmitted in any form or by any means, electronic, mechanical, photocopying, recording or otherwise without the prior permission of the publisher.

Published by
Ashgate Publishing Ltd
Gower House
Croft Road
Aldershot
Hants GU11 3HR
England

Ashgate Publishing Company
131 Main Street
Burlington, VT 05401-5600 USA

Ashgate website: http://www.ashgate.com

British Library Cataloguing in Publication Data
Shaw, Jon
    Competition, regulation and the privatisation of British
    Rail. - (Transport and mobility)
    1. British Rail - History 2. Privatisation - Great Britain
    3. Competition - Great Britain
    I. Title
    385.1'0941

Library of Congress Control Number: 00-135326

ISBN 0 7546 1483 2

Printed and bound in Great Britain by
Antony Rowe Ltd, Chippenham, Wiltshire

Contents

List of Figures

List of Tables

List of Abbreviations

ASI	Adam Smith Institute
ATOC	Association of Train Operating Companies
BG	British Gas
BR	British Rail
BRB	British Railways Board
BREL	British Rail Engineering Limited
BRIS	British Rail Infrastructure Services
BRML	British Rail Maintenance Limited
BT	British Telecom
CCICM	Controlled Competition in Contestable Markets
CE	Chief Executive
CEGB	Central Electricity Generating Board
CI	Compulsory Interavailability
CPS	Centre for Policy Studies
CRD	Conservative Research Department
DETR	Department of the Environment, Transport and the Regions

DoT	Department of Transport
DTI	Department of Trade and Industry
ECML	East Coast Main Line
EWS	English, Welsh and Scottish Railway
GDP	Gross Domestic Product
GNER	Great North Eastern Railway
ITT	Invitation to Tender
LTS	London, Tilbury and Southend Railway
MBO	Management Buy-out
MEBO	Management/Employee Buy-out
MD	Managing Director
MMC	Monopolies and Mergers Commission
MoC	Moderation of Competition
MP	Member of Parliament
MSR	Mode of Social Regulation
NAO	National Audit Office
NFC	National Freight Corporation
NRES	National Rail Enquiry Service
Offer	Office of Electricity Regulation
Ofgas	Office of Gas Supply

OforQ	Organising for Quality
Oftel	Office of Telecommunications
Ofwat	Office of Water Services
OIG	Objectives, Instructions and Guidance
OPRAF	Office of Passenger Rail Franchising
ORCATS	Operational Research Computer Allocation of Tickets to Services
ORR	Office of the Rail Regulator
PSBR	Public Sector Borrowing Requirement
PSO	Public Service Obligation
PSR	Public Service Requirement
REC	Regional Electricity Company
ROSCO	Rolling Stock Leasing Company
RPI	Retail Price Index
RPPF	Rail Passenger Partnership Fund
SR	Southern Region
TOC	Train Operating Company
WAGN	West Anglia Great Northern Railway

Acknowledgements

I must first and foremost thank Richard Gibb and Clive Charlton for all their help and guidance during the writing of this book. The text would not have been completed – or even started, given that they secured the necessary research funding from the Department of Geographical Sciences at the University of Plymouth – without their exceptional efforts.

I am also grateful to Ian Bailey, Steve Bennett, Mark Cleary, John Farrington, Sir Christopher Foster, Phil Goodwin, Chris Price, Peter White, Christian Wolmar and some in government and the rail industry who must remain anonymous for their comments and advice on various earlier drafts. Their attention to detail and critical appraisal of the work has immeasurably improved its quality, although of course the usual disclaimer still applies.

Brian Rogers, Tim Absalom, Ian Stokes and Jamie Quinn no doubt found my scribbling rather tiresome but still managed to turn it into artwork. Kate Hopewell provided excellent secretarial support.

Thanks to my parents, Richard and Barbara, and also to Tim, Roland, Matt, Mike, James, Tony, Amanda, Dave and Sam, Stu, Shea and some of those already mentioned above for the swift halves – not to mention preposterous pub crawls – whilst I was researching and writing the book. The warm welcome and encouragement from my new friends and colleagues in Aberdeen helped ensure that the final preparations went smoothly.

Some of chapters three and seven of this book have appeared in revised form elsewhere and I am extremely grateful to the copyright holders, PricewaterhouseCoopers and Taylor and Francis, for allowing the partial reproduction of the work.

Finally, very many thanks indeed to the respondents, who agreed to be interviewed at length about their involvement in, and perceptions of, the rail privatisation process. Their insights were invaluable and I hope they are fairly and accurately represented.

Foreword

BRIAN GRAHAM AND RICHARD KNOWLES
Series Editors

The inception of this series marks a major resurgence of geographical research into transport and mobility. Reflecting the critical importance of the dynamic relationships between transport and socio-spatial change, this work includes research on:

- the impacts of liberalisation, privatisation, competition and globalisation on transport policies, networks and strategies
- traffic generation and diversion and the economic impacts of large-scale infrastructure projects such as the Channel Tunnel
- the assessment of environmental sustainability concerns about increasing mobility, dispersal of activity sites and the dependence of transport on fossil fuels and its associated air pollution
- transport, gender and welfare issues
- the relationships between transport and leisure
- congestion and capacity constraints in transport systems.

This monograph series complements the international, quarterly research journal, *Journal of Transport Geography* (launched in 1993) and *Modern Transport Geography* (eds Brian Hoyle and Richard Knowles, 2nd ed., 1998 on behalf of the TGRG). Together, these three outlets act as a forum for cutting-edge research into transport and mobility, and for innovative and decisive debates on the formulation and repercussions of transport-policy making.

1 Introduction

1.1 The privatisation of British Rail

The dominant political ideology in Britain during the 1980s and early 1990s was that of the New Right, whose economic beliefs, based upon neoliberalism, prioritised reducing public sector involvement in society and the economy by promoting a 'free' market driven by competition (Barry, 1987; Farnham and Horton, 1993; Green, 1987; Hayes, 1994). For this and other reasons, the privatisation of public sector industries was of central importance to successive Conservative governments in the 1979-1997 period and the most recent major divestiture was that of British Rail (BR).

The Conservatives argued that selling BR was necessary in order to "see better use made of the railways, greater responsiveness to the customer and a higher quality of service and better value for money for the people who travel by rail" (Department of Transport (DoT), 1992a), but they acknowledged that rail privatisation was likely to be more complex than many earlier divestitures. Although BR was one of the most technically efficient railways in western Europe (Nash and Preston, 1994), its passenger operations still made heavy losses. Many of BR's routes, although unprofitable, were seen as socially and politically necessary and any method of sale would need to maintain pre-privatisation service levels and therefore incorporate a means of providing the private sector with continuing subsidies from the state. Moreover, experience from previous sell-offs had convinced ministers that the liberalisation of BR's market was essential if the potential benefits of privatisation were to be realised. A key objective of the Major administration was therefore to end BR's monopoly and introduce a competitive structure into the railway industry. The White Paper *New Opportunities for the Railways* (DoT, 1992a), published in July 1992, committed the government to radically restructuring BR in advance of privatisation. The method of divestiture adopted, the 'track authority' model, would resolve the subsidy question by franchising passenger rail services and would promote competition by splitting BR into 92 companies to create an internal market (DoT, 1996).

Academic interest in the BR sell-off has been widespread. Various studies have traced the evolution of policy from empirical and theoretical perspectives, whilst others have provided generalised policy analyses or focused upon specifics such as the economics of rail privatisation.[1] The centrality of market liberalisation to the government's plans has also prompted a considerable amount of research. Studies in the early 1990s reviewed *ex ante* the theoretical prospects for, and implications of, competition between passenger operators (Dnes 1993; Jones *et al.*, 1993; Preston, 1997; Shires *et al.*, 1994a; Starkie, 1993; Williams, 1992) whilst Bradshaw (1997), Charlton *et al.* (1997) and Gibb *et al.* (1998) have described *ex post* and in general terms where competition has materialised in the railway industry.

But despite the rapidly expanding literature on rail privatisation, there remain omissions and considerable scope for original investigation into the subject. This is particularly true with regard to railway competition and there is a need to further develop academic understanding of the policy adopted to promote it. Although the above studies have contributed significantly to current knowledge, they have tended to assess the policy either in terms of economic theory or without extending their analyses much beyond the bounds of the railway industry. Little attempt has been made to examine the evolution of railway competition policy, or to discuss it in the wider context of political economy. Moreover, none of the studies has examined the outcome of this competition policy in any significant detail. Concern has instead revolved around general concepts rather than comprehensive reviews of specifics. Finally, those studies which review the policy's prospects of promoting competition in the future are now somewhat dated and need revisiting in the light of recent events.

This book therefore focuses on the policy adopted to promote competition in the British railway industry at the time of its privatisation. The research was designed in light of gaps in the literature and seeks to answer numerous research questions, including: Why did competition become central to the Conservatives' rail privatisation plans? How did policy makers' wish to liberalise BR influence the policy advanced in *New Opportunities for the Railways*? Where do opportunities for competition now exist and are they being exploited by the private sector? What are the future prospects for railway competition? Has the policy been, or is it likely to be, a success? This book attempts to address these questions by drawing upon the experiences of key personnel involved in framing, executing and operating within the policy to augment existing secondary data. It draws heavily upon more than 60 interviews with former Secretaries and Ministers of State for Transport, senior and mid-level civil servants, government advisors, industry experts, British Railways Board (BRB) members and employees, industry regulators, franchise bidders and senior managers within the 'new' railway. Verbatim quotations are used throughout the book to enliven the text and support the arguments advanced therein, although most are presented anonymously to honour a condition upon which interviews were granted.

1.2 Aims and objectives of the book

The central aim of this study is to evaluate the extent to which the promotion of competition was an appropriate policy goal in the privatisation of British Rail. In pursuit of this aim, the book critically evaluates the evolution, outcomes and future prospects of the policy adopted to liberalise BR's market and closely examines the translation of neoliberal political philosophy into practical policy measures. As such, there are three key objectives:

- To establish why and how the liberalisation of the passenger train market became an important goal of rail privatisation policy;
- To assess the outcome of rail privatisation policy in terms of the extent to which the passenger rail market has been liberalised;
- To review the future prospects for competition developing between passenger train operators.

Although the potential for competition was introduced throughout much of the rail industry at the time of privatisation, this study focuses specifically upon competition among passenger train operators.[2] The passenger railway was chosen as the principal object of study because of its relative importance to policy makers. As one commentator has observed, producing change in the delivery of passenger, rather than freight, services was uppermost in ministers' minds when they sold the railways (Clarke, 2000) and in this sense it is appropriate to review the passenger business before embarking upon a study of other industry components.

It is also important to stress that an exhaustive analysis of railway competition in terms of its impact upon service output is not attempted. It is not the case, therefore, that operators' efficiency, investment records and quality and frequency of service are scrutinised for comparison with pre-privatisation levels. Rather, the book seeks to identify the circumstances in which competitive opportunities are now available in the new railway structure, whether or not they are being exploited and why. The rationale supporting this line of investigation is that many of the opportunities for competition are subtle and/or complex – indeed, some were still being discovered by train operators when respondents were being interviewed – and these should probably be identified and understood before any large-scale survey of their impact upon service output can begin. Moreover, many were in a rather embryonic stage of development when data were being collected and no reasonable judgement about their impacts could have been made after such a short period of time. The central aim of the book does not demand a comprehensive review of the impact of service competition. Focus here is on the *viability* of promoting competition as a goal of rail privatisation policy, i.e. whether or not the railway industry is capable of supporting competition as an organising principle and why.

1.3 Scope of the book

The privatisation of BR followed the sales of numerous British transport concerns. Transport, particularly since World War Two, was perceived to be an industry which required the control and supervision of the state (Lowndes, 1997), but the Conservatives under Thatcher were more inclined to believe that the "best way to ensure the public interest is to promote free competition between the providers and free choice between the users" (Conservative Party, 1977: 364). The first Thatcher administration sold the National Freight Corporation (NFC) to a management buy-out team and liberalised the long distance coach industry. BR's Hovercraft, Hotels and Holidays businesses were also disposed of. Subsequent transport privatisations included those of Sealink, British Airways, the British Airports Authority and the National and Scottish Bus Companies.[3]

Primarily because of the nature of their business, the transport companies sold by the Conservatives share key characteristics with BR. This is particularly true of the bus industry. Not only does it require continuing subsidy to fund its loss-making yet socially necessary services, but ministers also perceived the need to introduce service competition between operators. Both the National and Scottish Bus Companies were fragmented and the successor businesses were transferred to the private sector by competitive tender. Furthermore, the market was liberalised by way of the '42-day rule', which entitled new operators to compete with incumbents provided they gave six weeks' notice of their proposals (White and Farrington, 1998). Thus, from having been a statutory monopoly, the bus industry was restructured to allow competition *for* the market, through competitive tendering, and competition *in* the market, as a result of the 42-

day rule. The privatised railway industry was also restructured to accommodate both these forms of competition.

It is perhaps logical to assume that the model adopted to privatise BR was a direct descendant of that used for the disposal of the bus companies, but chapter three explains that this may not, in fact, be the case (see also Charlton *et al.*, 1997; Helm, 1996; Mountford, 1996). The track authority model of rail privatisation was originally suggested in the mid-1980s (Gylie, 1984; Starkie, 1984), but became influential after a variant had successfully been applied to the privatisation of the Central Electricity Generating Board (CEGB), part of a 'network' industry. Such industries – examples are telecommunications, gas, water and electricity – were viewed by some policy makers as analogous to BR in that they have a network element: wires, pipes or, in the case of BR, track. The track authority model adopted to restructure BR can be seen as further experimentation with the method used to sell the CEGB and, in this sense, is based upon a model of privatisation adopted for a network industry rather than companies in the transport sector.

In the light of these issues, the book is structured as follows. Chapter two examines the privatisation of the network industries. It outlines the key assumptions of neoliberal thought and explores the interaction between privatisation policy and abstract theoretical ideals. The network industry sell-offs are assessed in terms of the extent to which they promoted a 'free' market driven by competition, whilst the chapter's conclusions establish the political and economic contexts in which ministers considered the privatisation of BR.

The remainder of the book documents and critically assesses the privatisation of BR in terms of the aims and objectives stated above. Chapter three traces the evolution of rail privatisation policy and establishes why and how the promotion of competition between passenger train operators became an important policy goal. The chapter shows that debates over rail privatisation within the Conservative Party can be traced back to the late 1960s and that BR was considered as a candidate for divestiture throughout most of the 1980s. Potential policy options advanced from both within and outside of government are explained and events leading up to the adoption of the track authority model are reviewed. Finally, the chapter outlines the structure of the 'new' railway industry and identifies key shortcomings in the policy contained in *New Opportunities for the Railways*.

Chapters four to six assess the extent to which the passenger rail market has been liberalised. The analysis begins by addressing the passenger rail franchising process, or competition *for* the market. Chapter four examines the private sector's attitude towards the BR sale in the early 1990s and explains its potential impact on the outcome of rail privatisation policy. The development of franchising policy is discussed in chapter five in this context. The degree to which competition for the market developed among franchise bidders is assessed and various reasons as to why this was so are suggested. Finally, rail franchising's contribution to attaining the neoliberal policy aims outlined in chapter two is considered.

Chapter six is concerned with competition *in* the market, or 'on rail' competition between train operators. Interviews for this chapter were undertaken in early 1998, four years after the railway industry was restructured, and results presented in the chapter pertain to that period. The chapter first reviews debates surrounding the appropriateness of on-rail competition and highlights several weaknesses in the case for such a policy. The opportunities for competition in the passenger rail market are then identified and compared with those which the government originally envisaged. The chapter concludes by comparing the policy outcome of rail privatisation with those of the telecommunications, gas and water industry divestitures in the 1980s.

Finally, chapter seven summarises the findings of the above chapters, before moving on to evaluate the prospects for competition developing between passenger rail operators in the future. Overall conclusions pertaining to the central aim of the book are presented in a discussion which re-evaluates, in view of potential future trends, the fundamental themes addressed throughout the book.

Notes

1.   On policy evolution: Gibb *et al.*, 1996; Grantham, 1998; Knill and Lehmkuhl, 1998; Truelove, 1991; Zahariadis, 1995, 1996.   General critiques, see, for example: Bradshaw, 1996a; Curwen, 1997; Freeman and Shaw, 2000; Glaister and Travers, 1993; Knowles, 1998; Nash, 1993; Nash and Preston, 1993; Welsby and Nicholls, 1999. On the economics of rail privatisation, see, for example, Bradshaw, 1996b; Else, 1993; Foster, 1994; Harris and Godward, 1997; Helm, 1996; Jones *et al.*, 1993; Nash and Preston, 1992; Powell, 1997; Preston, 1996; Shires *et al.*, 1994a; Stittle, 1996; White, 1998. These and other studies are discussed later in the book.

2.   In its broadest sense, the passenger rail industry includes infrastructure (track, bridges, signalling), the ownership of rolling stock, heavy maintenance depots and so on. However, as chapter three will show, BR was fragmented to such an extent that 'Train Operating Companies' (TOCs) now do little more than their name suggests. They own neither infrastructure nor rolling stock and must buy in almost all of the services upon which they depend. It is competition between these TOCs with which this book is primarily concerned.

3. The current Labour administration, elected in May 1997, is continuing the policy of privatisation in the transport industry. It has announced that the National Air Traffic Service and parts of the London Underground are to be sold off, although the precise form of each sale is yet to be determined.

2   Privatisation and the Network Industries

2.1 Introduction

The sale of BR was the last in a series of network industry privatisations undertaken by Conservative governments in the period 1979-1997. When ministers considered various means of divesting the rail industry and establishing a competitive regime therein, their decisions were in large part informed by experience gained from the sale of the electricity industry (see chapter one). For this reason it is appropriate to place the forthcoming assessment of rail privatisation policy in the context of issues arising from other network industry privatisations. In turn, these issues are discussed with regard to the theoretical assumptions upon which privatisation itself is based. Why and how did a policy of privatisation arise in the first place? Why was competition considered to be so important? What was the outcome of the network industry privatisations and what lessons were learnt as the programme developed? This chapter will address such questions.

As chapter one pointed out, the privatisation programme was a part of the New Right's neoliberal economic philosophy, which prioritised reducing public sector involvement in the economy by promoting a competitive, free market (Barry, 1987; Farnham and Horton, 1993). Although it began slowly, the programme was later endorsed enthusiastically by the Conservatives, with one policy advisor even suggesting that denationalisation would help ministers succeed in "halving the size of the state sector" (Mount, quoted in Letwin, 1988: 11). At first glance, as Graham and Prosser (1988) point out, the policy of privatisation would appear to have contributed significantly to reducing the role of the government and replacing it with market forces: by the mid 1990s, more than two thirds of the state's industrial sector – 50 major businesses – were sold, raising over £65 billion in sale receipts; around one million jobs were transferred from the public to the private sector; and almost one in four adults, compared to less than one in ten in 1979, became shareholders as a result of privatisations (Conservative Party, 1996).

In reality, however, such figures are misleading and in certain cases, most notably the network industries, privatisation has done far less than they suggest to reduce the state's role in industrial affairs. The monopolies enjoyed by the utilities whilst they were in the public sector were, to a large extent, conferred upon the private sector following divestiture. In the absence of market forces to protect consumers, the Conservatives were forced to create a host of regulatory mechanisms and institutions in order to prevent the utilities from abusing their monopoly powers. Although utility privatisation reduced the physical *size* of the state's industrial role, it is questionable how far its *influence* was diminished.

This chapter introduces the theoretical assumptions which underpin privatisation and discusses their influence over initial policy formulation. It seeks to explain why the network industries were sold as "virtual monopolies" throughout the 1980s (Moore, 1985a: 94), considers the nature and scope of utility regulation and assesses the extent to which the state maintained a continuing role in the companies' affairs. The privatisation of British Telecom (BT) is used as a case study, although references are made to British Gas (BG) and the water industry where appropriate. Finally, the chapter concludes by reviewing the key issues which arose from the privatisation of the utilities throughout the 1980s and suggests that they prompted a notable reorientation of policy in the 1990s which resulted in market liberalisation being accorded a new priority in the privatisation of BR.

2.2 Neoliberalism

Neoliberalism draws upon the works and ideas of economists (Friedman, 1962, 1980; Hayek, 1944, 1960, 1976), public choice theorists (Buchanan *et al.*, 1978; Mueller, 1979; Niskanen, 1971) and political scientists (Lindblom, 1977). It emphasises the importance of three key concepts: individual liberty, a minimal role for the state in society and the 'free' market. The first of these ideas is held most sacred, with the other two being seen as essential to its existence and defence (Atkinson and Savage, 1994; King, 1987). As Ashford (1991: 185) summarises, neoliberalism "argues that the consequences of allowing individuals the freedom to pursue their own interests... will generally be more beneficial than government action."

Following a brief overview of its history, this section discusses each of neoliberalism's three main concepts. What follows is intended neither as a critique nor a definitive review of neoliberalism, as such discussions are beyond the scope of this chapter (although see Barry, 1983, 1987; Gray, 1995; Hayes, 1994; King, 1987; Peck and Tickell, 1994). Rather, the aim here is to provide an understanding of the theoretical basis from which the policies analysed in this book arose.

Free to choose

Neoliberalism is a restatement of classical liberal values (Gray, 1995; Green, 1987). The roots of classical liberalism stem from the individualistic beliefs of radical Protestants in the seventeenth century, which maintained that everyone should be free to choose their own path to eternal salvation rather than be bound by the wishes of the church (Bradley, 1985; Hardin, 1993). Since that time, liberals have fought to protect the status of the individual confronted with the demands of larger social groups: they have supported movements to emancipate people from political, economic and other constraints upon their activities and they have campaigned for a society which is open, tolerant and diversified, rather than paternalist and authoritarian (Eccleshall, 1994). Despite a commitment to the sanctity of the individual, liberals are not anarchists and have always recognised the need to set certain, defined, limits to people's freedom in order to prevent them from abusing it and harming others. As *The Economist* (1996a: 20) notes, "perhaps the individual is the best judge of his own interest, perhaps not; but, unless the well being of others is jeopardised, he should be the judge."

Although its defining characteristic is a commitment to individual liberty, it is insufficient simply to refer to neoliberalism as the 'philosophy of freedom' because there are ambiguities associated with the concept. To illustrate, many interventionists would claim to support a 'free' society, yet they disagree with neoliberals about many fundamentals (Farnham and Horton, 1993; Gray, 1995; King, 1987). Such ambiguities are best resolved by drawing a distinction between two kinds of freedom, positive and negative. The former relates to interventionist notions of liberty, whereas the latter describes the neoliberal conception. Positive freedom is a *moral* concept. It suggests that individuals have the right to expect a given standard of material wealth to enable them to participate fully within society

(Heald, 1983). Social matters such as poverty, ill-health and poor education are identified as coercive factors in addition to harm imposed by other individuals. As a consequence, it is argued that the state should provide social services such as education and healthcare and establish a redistributive wealth allocation system capable of achieving a 'just' apportionment of income (*The Economist*, 1996a). Positive freedom is so-called because it provides individuals with opportunities which the state is duty-bound to enhance and secure – positive outcomes are not the sole responsibility of the individual (Heald, 1983).

In contrast, the negative conception of freedom employed by neoliberals overlooks material considerations entirely and is concerned solely with minimising harm, or 'coercion', from other human beings. Hayek (1960: 20-21) accords coercion a highly specific definition, arguing that it is:

> ...such control of the environment or circumstances of a person by another that, in order to avoid greater evil, he is forced to act not according to a coherent plan of his own but to serve the ends of another. Except in the sense of choosing the lesser evil in a situation forced on him by another, he is unable either to use his own intelligence or knowledge to follow his own aims and beliefs. Coercion is evil precisely because it thus eliminates an individual as a thinking and valuing person and makes him a bare tool in his achievement of the ends of another.

Because Hayek believes coercion to be a personal attribute, manifested solely by other individuals, his conception makes no mention of the range of *physical* options available to someone at any given time (King, 1987). This allows him to contend that where individuals are not controlled by others, but in fact have no real choices available to them, they are still free. This point is illustrated with reference to a rock climber:

> Freedom refers solely to a relation of men to other men and the only infringement on it is coercion by men. This means, in particular, that the range of physical possibilities from which a person can choose at a given moment has no direct relevance to freedom. The rock climber on a difficult pitch who sees only one way out to save his life is unquestionably free, though we would hardly say he has any choice (Hayek, 1960: 12).

Thus negative freedom carries with it no worth or value in any moral sense and, unlike its positive counterpart, does not assure individuals of any material opportunities. Negative freedom requires only that individuals are able to act for a purpose of their own choosing. Whether or not individuals achieve their goals, or even have a selection of realisable goals from which to choose, is irrelevant from Hayek's standpoint (Newman, 1984). In this sense wealth inequalities within society, for example, are not viewed as assaults on freedom because they do not preclude choice, however unpalatable it may be. As Joseph and Sumption (1977: 49 and 52) point out with "impeccable liberal logic" (Hayes, 1994: 34):

> ...a person who cannot afford to buy food may well have a justifiable grievance... but it would be wrong to describe his grievance as lack of freedom... [L]iberty is liberty, not something else. And a slave is a slave, you do not set him free by feeding him.

The state and the market

The role of the state is central to maintaining and defending a neoliberal free society, because governments can promote liberty through the enforcement of law. To Hayek (1960), the law upholds impartial rules of just conduct, which are based on the traditions and customs of a society. As such, the law is not a tool with which the government can or should secure its own objectives – instead, it represents end-independent values which delimit the scope of freedom and protect the realm of private activity (Hayes, 1994). One person's freedom to murder his neighbour must be sacrificed in order to preserve the freedom of the neighbour to live; likewise, "my freedom to move my fist must be limited by the proximity of your chin" (Friedman, 1962: 26). The law provides individuals with known and predictable rules around which to build their lives and, because everything which is not prohibited by law is allowed, the existence of a vast number of diverse individual purposes is recognised and facilitated (Hayek, 1960).

Beyond law enforcement, however, neoliberals are deeply sceptical of the state because they also regard it as the greatest potential threat to the freedom it promotes (Atkinson and Savage, 1994). The relationship between the state and individuals is viewed as personal in character – decisions are taken by individuals on behalf of other individuals – and a virtually unlimited scope exists for a government to coerce its citizens. For example, every time a government programme is implemented, it necessarily involves a subjective (coercive) allocation of resources which benefits some at the expense of others. Although it is acknowledged that each new programme may harm individuals only a little, it is argued by Hayek (1944) that the cumulative effect will inevitably be totalitarianism, the widespread coercion of all.

Neoliberals therefore favour the free market as the most effective means of organising economic and social affairs to protect individual liberty (Lindblom, 1977). The market is embraced almost uncritically because, unlike those of the government, its mechanisms are viewed as being entirely impersonal. The market itself has no ends and purposes and market phenomena are merely what emerge from the actions of individuals pursuing *their own* ends and purposes by voluntarily exchanging private property. Goods and services are thus allocated 'objectively' according to supply and demand (Hayek, 1976). The need for coercive, statutory co-ordination of economic and social affairs is negated because markets "harmonise as far as possible diverse individual purposes and leave maximum scope for non-conformity, voluntary experimentation and personal fulfilment" (Harris, 1978: 240-241). The market system works so well, according to neoliberals, because it allows risk-taking entrepreneurs to seek profit whilst simultaneously benefiting others, the so-called *invisible hand* principle (Smith, quoted in Friedman, 1980).

In the same way that the state upholds the rule of law in relation to non-market transactions, so it also should in the economic sphere. Thus, the law should enforce contracts, protect private property, prevent fraud, inhibit restrictive practices and grant people authority to control their own labour (Lindblom, 1977). In addition, and of specific relevance to this book, the law has a role to play in promoting competition. Competition is seen as a spur to increase the efficiency, quality and diversity of services offered to consumers. It is also believed to prevent coercion by maximising choice: the consumer is protected from coercion by the seller because of the presence of other sellers from whom he can buy and the seller is protected from coercion by the consumer because of other consumers to whom he can sell (Friedman, 1962). If entrepreneurs become monopolists, they could become inefficient and, more worryingly from the neoliberal point of view, coerce consumers because the latter lose their ability to engage in voluntary transactions.

Hayek (1960) argued that market imperfections such as monopolies will arise, but that they are acceptable so long as market entry is not restricted – especially by the government – because monopolists will be subject to *potential* competition. For Friedman, however, this position is too simplistic. He notes that if a monopolist is large enough, it can engage in anti-competitive practices, such as heavy internal cross-subsidisation, to prevent market entry and maintain its market dominance (see section 2.4). Friedman (1962: 132) stresses that, because of monopolists' effect upon liberty, not only must governments not restrict market entry, but they must also uphold vigorous anti-trust laws as a "first and most urgent necessity." That said, Friedman accepts that some industries do possess unavoidable 'natural' monopoly characteristics. Natural monopoly occurs where a single firm can produce total industry outputs more efficiently than two or more firms (Yarrow, 1994). A traditional example has been a utility: the cost of building, say, a second national grid to compete with the existing one would be prohibitive. In such situations, Friedman (1962) concludes that the natural monopoly should be conferred upon a private sector firm subject to regulatory control.

Neoliberals concede that the state also has a limited market role pertaining to the provision of public goods. King (1987) defines these as goods and services which have the characteristics of indivisibility (their use cannot be meaningfully divided among individuals) and nonexcludability (individuals or groups cannot be excluded from using them). An example is national defence. As Friedman (1962: 23) points out, "I cannot get the amount of national defense I want and you [cannot get] a different amount." Externalities, such as pollution, are also categorised as public goods. Car owners do not necessarily intend to pollute the environment, but they inescapably force everyone to exchange clean air for dirty (Pearce *et al.*, 1989). In this example, the government might insist that certain anti-pollution measures are adhered to by motorists.

Although they accept the case for governmental provision of public goods, neoliberals remain suspicious of such action even in this diminutive incarnation. In addition to concerns regarding freedom, Friedman (1962, 1980) asserts that, because it is not subject to market forces such as profit, risk and competition, the public sector lacks motivation to satisfy consumers and will therefore perform inefficiently. Furthermore, Buchanan *et al.* (1978) contend that public servants seek to manipulate governmental activities to maximise their own interests rather than those of consumers. Such bureaucratic self-interest is regarded as particularly dangerous because it can result in a stealthy and rapid expansion of the state's activity beyond that which is judged appropriate (Friedman, 1980). Accordingly, neoliberals seek to extend the rule of law to circumscribe government activity constitutionally (Hayes, 1994). In this way it is argued that, with the few exceptions noted above, the politicisation of society can be prevented and its citizens do not have to surrender their liberty by "putting [their] heads under a yoke imposed by bureaucratic bunglers" (*The Economist*, 1919: 472).

Philosophy into policy

The defining characteristic of neoliberalism is its commitment to a negative conception of individual liberty and how it is believed that this is best defended and maintained by limiting the role of the state and maximising that of the competitive, free market. But these abstract concepts are of limited value without some indication of how they might be translated into practical policy measures. Hayek (1960) urged that government policies should primarily have regard to promoting freedom through the minimisation of coercion. By neoliberal standards, the state in the late 1970s constituted a powerful coercive force. The welfare state consensus, based on Keynesian economic principles, had involved successive administrations assuming a prominent responsibility for economic and social planning. By 1979, nationalisation programmes had brought the major basic industries – coal, steel, gas, electricity, healthcare, the airlines, the buses and the railways – under the government's control and many of these were statutory monopolies; around seven million people were employed in the public sector and many millions more in the private sector were dependent upon government contracts, funding or subsidies for their employment; other government schemes, particularly those in the welfare state, had grown rapidly and state spending as a proportion of gross domestic product (GDP) stood at 40.5 per cent (Veljanovski, 1987; Farnham and Horton, 1993). Policies designed to promote freedom would therefore need to reverse the trend of government intervention in the economy and society by transferring power from the state back to 'liberated', 'risk-taking', 'competitive' individuals. Key among these policies was the privatisation of state-owned industry.

2.3 Neoliberalism and the initial development of privatisation policy

Privatisation has been variously defined (see, for example, Beesley and Littlechild, 1983; Wiltshire, 1987). In essence, it is the transfer of at least part of the operations of a state-owned enterprise to private control (Heald, 1983). As Pirie (1988) points out, privatisation can be accomplished in numerous different ways, although the three most practised have been:

denationalisation, which involves the direct sale of public assets; *contracting out*, where the production of state-financed goods and services is franchised to private firms, usually for a finite period; and *liberalisation*, which requires the abolition of statutory monopoly to promote competition in markets previously characterised by restricted entry (Kay and Silbertson, 1984; Kay and Thompson, 1986). Each of these policy strands has been pursued separately – for example, the denationalisation of BT in 1984, the contracting out of municipal services throughout the 1980s and the liberalisation of long distance coach services in 1980 (Foster, 1992; Vickers and Yarrow, 1988; White 1995) – or together, as was the case with the privatisation of BR in the mid 1990s (Gibb *et al.*, 1996).

Supporters of privatisation now offer political and economic experience, as well as theoretical assertions, to justify pursuing the policy. In terms of politics, studies have shown that people who bought shares in denationalised companies, or council houses under the 'Right to Buy' scheme, have been, in the short term at least, more likely to vote for the government in office (Saunders, 1991). In addition, revenue raised from privatisation can be used – in some cases explicitly – to fend off tax increases or public expenditure reductions (Jenkins, 1995; Segall, 1998). From an economic perspective, private firms have often performed more efficiently than their nationalised counterparts when subjected to market disciplines and 'freed' from government involvement in their day to day operations (*The Economist*, 1995a).

The attention paid to the political and economic experience of privatisation has resulted in some authors downplaying the role of neoliberal theory in the development of privatisation policy. Kay and Thompson (1986: 18) refer to the latter as being "in search of a rationale," and Jenkins (1995: 24) suggests that the Conservatives' initial endorsement of privatisation was "hardly a ringing ideological crusade." Atkinson and Savage (1994: 7), whilst acknowledging the influence of neoliberalism within the academic community, have questioned whether the theories of Hayek, Friedman and Buchanan had "real effects upon 'pragmatic' politicians such as Thatcher who were primarily concerned with achieving and retaining power." Farnham and Horton (1993) rightly point out that it would be naive to assume that the Conservatives were hijacked by neoliberal radicalism throughout their time in office and, as this chapter will show, key neoliberal goals were undoubtedly marginalised as privatisation policy unravelled in practice. Nevertheless, the influence of neoliberalism on the initial development of privatisation policy during the 1970s should not be dismissed (Atkinson and Savage, 1994). Key to this argument, of course, is that the Conservatives did not *have* much political and economic experience of privatisation at that time. Although a handful of small concerns, such as the Thomas Cook travel agency, had been sold by previous administrations, nothing approaching a sustained programme of divestiture had ever been attempted.

The ratchet effect and the welfare state consensus

Support within the Conservative Party for a sustained programme of privatisation began to materialise in the late 1960s (Conservative Research Department (CRD), 1968), although it was concentrated initially around a small group of politicians on the Right of the Party. Keith Joseph in particular became obsessed with the 'ratchet effect' of British politics – essentially, that the influence and power of the state was continuously increasing because new Conservative governments were unwilling to reverse nationalisations undertaken by previous Labour ones (Joseph, 1976). In 1968, a confidential report of the Policy Group on Nationalised Industries, chaired by Nicholas Ridley, explicitly objected to public sector corporations and went on to suggest a policy strategy which amounted to the beginnings of a coherent privatisation programme:

> We have listed a number of small concerns which should be denationalised – £60 million worth – and these should be tackled at once. Steel, the airlines and road haulage represent £900 million worth of assets. We believe it is possible to sell them back... [but denationalisation] should be a continuing process of which our proposals are only the first stage (CRD, 1968: iv and 20).

Following Ridley's report, Conservative MP Rhodes Boyson edited a book, *Goodbye to Nationalisation,* which argued that public sector industries had been a political and social failure and that there was a need to return them to a market-orientated framework (Boyson, 1971). Suggestions were made regarding how this might be done (see Lewis, 1971), although they were not elaborated upon in any great detail and Foster (1992: 108) has accused *Goodbye to Nationalisation* as being "less than penetrating in its arguments." Nevertheless, Boyson's book can be regarded as important if only because it was one of the first public expositions of large-scale privatisation from a Conservative MP.

The official Conservative Party position on denationalisation in the early 1970s was not swayed by right-wing fringe opinion. The 1970-74 Heath administration was committed to the welfare state consensus and the 1970 *Campaign Guide* (Conservative Party, 1970), although emphasising the belief that political interference in the affairs of public corporations was deleterious, was unsympathetic to a sustained programme of privatisation. A noticeable shift in the Party's official stance did not occur until the election of Thatcher as leader in 1975. Shortly after becoming Conservative Party leader, Thatcher attended a policy seminar at the CRD in London. During the seminar, a researcher presented a paper which argued that the Party believed in, and should continue subscribing to, the welfare state consensus. However, before the researcher had finished,

> ...the new Party leader reached into her briefcase and took out a book. It was Friedrich von Hayek's *The Constitution of Liberty*. Interrupting our pragmatist, she held the book up for us all to see. 'This,' she said sternly, 'is what we believe,' and banged Hayek down on the table (Ranelagh, 1991: ix).

Official Conservative Party literature published between 1975 and 1979 (see, for example, Conservative Party, 1976a, 1976b, 1979a; Fowler, 1977; Howe *et al.*, 1977) began to emphasise key neoliberal ideas. Echoing Joseph's earlier concerns regarding the ratchet effect, the Conservative Right warned that the decades of welfare state consensus had resulted in governments making unacceptable infringements upon individual liberty and that nationalisation was in large part responsible for this (Johnson, 1978). Official party statements restated the key themes of *The Constitution of Liberty* (Hayek, 1960): "[We] need to enlarge freedom of choice for the individual by reducing the power of the state" (Conservative Party, 1979a: 1); "Our purpose is to restore and defend individual freedom and individual responsibility" (Conservative Party, 1976b: 1). Johnson (1978) asserted, quoting Hayek (1944), that Britain was driving at speed along the road to serfdom. Central to the case for privatisation was that it would apply the brakes:

> We shall [restore individual freedom] by reducing the proportion of the nation's wealth consumed by the state [and] by taking the first steps towards making this country a nation of worker-owners (Conservative Party, 1976b: 1).

The long term aim must be to reduce the preponderance of state ownership and to widen the base of ownership in our community. Ownership by the state is not the same as ownership by the people (Howe *et al.*, 1977: 47).

The Conservative Right also began to draw upon the work of Buchanan (1978) and Friedman (1962) to justify its support for privatisation. First, the nationalised industries were portrayed as being run for the benefit of politicians and bureaucrats rather than consumers (Veljanovski, 1987). For instance, as the Conservatives suspected in opposition and were to find when they took office in 1979, many of the profitable corporations were required to forego important capital investment programmes because their cash surpluses were siphoned off by government to help fulfil its macroeconomic objectives (Heald and Steel, 1981). Second, because some of the nationalised industries were monopolies and none were subject to true market forces, it was argued that they were complacent, inefficient and offered poor standards of service (Conservative Party, 1974, 1977). As such, emphasis was placed upon the need for the privatisation programme to foster a competitive free market by removing as far as possible state involvement in industry. A statement of transport policy, *The Right Track*, is a case in point:

Conservatives reject the idea that transport ought to be regarded primarily as a social service to which the taxpayer must be forced to contribute huge and continuing subsidies in order to secure social and political objectives selected by government... [T]he best way to ensure the public interest is to promote free competition between the providers and free choice between the users (Conservative Party, 1977: 364).

That said, a confidential report leaked to *The Economist* in 1978 accepted as had Friedman that some industries, particularly the utilities, were natural monopolies and were likely to remain so (Veljanovski, 1987).

Thus it can be argued that the Conservative Right approached the 1979 general election with limited practical experience of privatisation, but with some expectation derived from neoliberal ideology that it should deliver enhanced individual freedom by: a) promoting competition, rather than monopoly, in an industry's market to allow voluntary exchange between individuals and b) genuinely reducing the powers of the state to manage an industry and the production/distribution of its goods and services.[1] In addition, promoting competition and downsizing the state were expected to stimulate industrial efficiency, encourage risk-taking and refocus corporate activities on the interests of consumers. It is important to note, therefore, that although each of the three means of privatisation listed above – asset transfer, contracting out and liberalisation – can be executed separately, an effective combination of these might be necessary to achieve a *genuine* reduction in the power of the state over an industry. To illustrate, simply transferring the assets of a monopolist would do nothing to liberalise the market in which it operated and could necessitate a continuing role for government as an industry regulator.

Early policy implementation

Given Thatcher's "vehement... wish to roll back the borders of the public sector" (Foster, 1992: 109) and the enthusiasm of the Conservative Right for privatisation, it is perhaps surprising that the Party's 1979 manifesto (Conservative Party, 1979b) was distinctly circumspect on the matter. Indeed, the word 'privatisation' did not appear and with regard to industry pledges were made only to sell shares in the NFC, to relax bus-licensing controls and to reconsider the ownership of British Aerospace, British Shipbuilders and the British National Oil Corporation (BNOC). The Queen's speech of 1979 was vague, outlining only "proposals [to] reduce the extent of nationalised and state ownership and increase competition" (quoted in McLachlan, 1983: 21).

Two key reasons seem to explain why the manifesto did not reflect the Conservative Right's enthusiasm for privatisation. First, the concept was at this stage still unpopular with the majority of the population (Heath *et al.*, 1985). Opposition was also forthcoming from public sector industry, Conservative backbenchers and especially some quarters of the civil service, who regarded privatisation as dangerously radical (Foster, 1992). Thatcher, despite her often belligerent outward appearance, was politically cautious (Jenkins, 1995) and was determined not to lose the election before it even took place. As Howe (1994: 254) recalled, Thatcher "had been fearful that a more extensive catalogue might frighten the floating voter." Although the privatisation programme gained momentum throughout the 1980s, Thatcher's political caution, as chapter three will show, was to resurface during debates over the BR sell-off.

Second, the Conservatives had not actually formulated privatisation policy in any great detail during their time in opposition. Although the Party's right wing had embraced privatisation as a corollary of neoliberal theory, a blueprint regarding how it could actually be executed in practice – which companies could be sold and how, for example – had not been produced. Oliver Letwin, one of Thatcher's policy advisors, admitted in 1988 that although,

> ...we had a fundamental distrust in the state running things... we had no coherent policy. It was not the case that we knew that privatisation would bring in millions of new shareholders. It was not the case that we knew all these shareholders would benefit from premiums. It was not the case that we knew companies would do better in the private sector. Almost nothing that has happened since was known in advance (quoted in Foster, 1992: 109).

The combination of widespread opposition and the lack of a policy blueprint resulted in the privatisation programme developing slowly during Thatcher's first term in office. A dedicated Cabinet committee, E (DL) (Economic (Disposal)), was set up although Thatcher remained cautious. According to Ridley (1991: 83), the Prime Minister would not risk embarking upon a major privatisation programme because "she didn't want to stir up the lobbies in the public sector. She felt we could come to that in a few years' time." As a result, the first industries to be privatised were the most convenient to dispose of – such as those which had only recently been nationalised – not necessarily the most strategically important. Shortly after the election, five per cent of British Petroleum (BP) was sold, which reduced the government's share to 46 per cent and thereby officially returned the company to the private sector (Letwin, 1988). Before the election in 1983, a further nine firms had been sold by asset transfer to the private sector (see Table 2.1). The industrial privatisations of the early 1980s were complemented by the initiation of the 'Right to Buy' scheme, which entitled sitting tenants to purchase their council houses at a discounted rate, and the contracting out of local authority services such as street cleaning and refuse collection (Bishop and Kay, 1988). Liberalisation of the long-distance coach industry also took place following the 1980 Transport Act (White, 1995).

Table 2.1   Companies privatised by asset transfer during the first Thatcher administration

Date	Company sold	Proceeds (£m)
November 1979	BP	290
June 1980	Fairey Engineering	22
June 1980	Ferranti	54
February 1981	British Aerospace	149
November 1981	Cable & Wireless	224
February 1982	Amersham International	63
February 1982	National Freight Consortium	7
February 1983	Associated British Ports	22
March 1983	International Aeradio	60
March 1983	British Rail Hotels	45

Sources: Bishop and Kay, 1988; Wright and Thompson, 1994.

2.4 Privatising the network industries

The Conservative Party's 1983 election manifesto announced that the privatisation programme would be extended to embrace the utility industries. The utilities were significantly different in character to those companies previously divested. First, they were much bigger. The subsequent sale of BT, for example, would at the time represent the largest transfer of assets from the public to the private sector in world history (Veljanovski, 1987). Second, they traded as vertically integrated monopolies. As already noted, it had been assumed that almost all of the utilities' business constituted natural monopoly because competition was only feasible if second networks were constructed (Harrison, 1982). By the early 1980s, however, technological developments allowed this assumption to be challenged and it was realised that any number of different companies could in fact compete via the same pipes or wires to supply consumers with gas, electricity or telecommunications services.   Thus, although the networks themselves remained natural monopolies, the rest of the utilities' activities were exposed as a collection of *artificial* monopolies.   Ministers acknowledged this (Moore, 1983a) and implied that, if re-elected, they would seek to break them:

Our aim is that BT should become a private sector company... [but] merely to replace state monopolies by private ones would be to waste a historic opportunity... we shall continue our programme to expose state-owned industries to competition (Conservative Party, 1983: 292).

Following the Conservatives' 1983 election victory, the minister then in charge of privatisation, John Moore, added that: "the long term success of the privatisation programme will stand or fall by the extent to which it maximises competition. If competition cannot be achieved, an historic opportunity will have been lost" (Moore, 1983b: 92).

The simplest way to liberalise statutory monopolies is to remove legal barriers to market entry. The 1982 Oil and Gas (Enterprise) Act and the 1983 Energy Act had undertaken this for the gas and electricity industries respectively and allowed competing energy suppliers to gain access to the nationalised distribution networks. However, as Veljanovski (1989) points out and as Friedman (1962) had predicted (see section 2.2), competition failed to materialise because the Acts made no attempt to restrict the nationalised industries from engaging in anti-competitive practices. Both BG and the electricity industry manipulated their accounting procedures to make it economically unattractive for potential new suppliers to enter their markets. In the case of telecommunications, ministers had commissioned a report (Beesley, 1981) which concluded that BT should be forced to sell spare capacity on its network to potential competitors. Reactions to this suggestion were mixed. Although generally favoured by users' groups, BT and the trade unions were hostile, with the Post Office Engineering Union noting that Beesley's work "was widely criticised as being rushed and inadequate in its evidence and conclusions" (quoted in Harrison, 1982: 17). In the event, the 1981 Telecommunications Act maintained BT's call monopoly but introduced some competition into 'fringe' areas of its activities such as equipment supply. A promise was made to review this decision in 1989 (Foster, 1992).

The sale of British Telecom

A chance for the Conservatives to conduct an early re-evaluation of this policy came with the decision to sell BT. The failure of previous legislation to affect the gas and electricity monopolies led Treasury ministers, in particular Nigel Lawson, to press for a different method of breaking BT's monopoly. One such method would have been to complement the removal of entry barriers with a strengthening of competition law to prevent BT from abusing its position, but Lawson favoured a more radical alternative – a full-scale reorganisation of the telecommunications industry (Jenkins, 1995). A logical outcome of Lawson's idea would have been to split BT into a number of enterprises. One would have retained control of the network and thus kept its natural monopoly status, whilst others would have competed amongst each other to provide telecommunications and related services to the public. Academics such as Kay and Silbertson (1984: 15) sided with Lawson and urged the Conservatives to take their commitment to competition seriously. Aside from considerations of liberty, evidence had emerged to suggest that the key to improving industrial performance was not a simple change of ownership, as might have been concluded from the earlier divestitures, but competition. Thus, as Kay and Silbertson (1984: 15) argued, it was imperative to break BT's monopoly because "the benefits of privatisation are likely to be small, or non-existent, in the absence of measures to create a more competitive environment within which the newly-privatised concerns will operate." Although they acknowledged that the Conservatives would encounter resistance if they tinkered with the structure of BT, not least from vested interests such as management and the trade unions, Kay and Silbertson suggested that a competitive environment would be easier to create before privatisation than after.

In the event, ministers made only minor revisions to the competition policy they had announced in 1981. BT was sold as a "virtual monopoly" guaranteed by statute for at least six years (Moore, 1985a: 94) and only one competitor, Mercury Communications, was allowed to enter the market. Mercury had been licensed to build its own long distance network in 1982, but from 1984 it was allowed access to BT's network in an attempt to generate some realistic competition (in order to prevent BT from engaging in anti-competitive practices, its access charges were made subject to independent regulation).[2] Mercury's disadvantage, however, was huge. Although it was hoped that the company would be carrying around five per cent of total telecommunications traffic from the outset, it in fact took until 1991 to reach this figure and even by 1996 around 10 per cent of residential and business customers were unable to access the Mercury network (Foster, 1992; Conservative Party, 1996).

Why should the Conservatives, driven by a philosophy of "personal freedom, individuality, choice and opportunity" (Conservative Party, 1984: 1), choose to divest one of its largest industrial concerns as a virtual monopoly? Thatcher (1993: 67) suggests that a full-scale reorganisation of

BT would have been delayed to an unacceptable degree by obstacles such as the lack of modern accounting and management systems. Thompson (1990) and Marsh (1991) suggest in addition that BT's management did not favour a break up and advised Thatcher that it would not be in the industry's interests. Thus it was concluded that, although overlooking competition, a monopoly sale was advantageous in that it could be achieved quickly and with relative ease:

> If it was a choice between having the ideal circumstances for privatisation, which might take years to achieve, and going for a choice within a politically determined timescale, the second was the preferable option (Thatcher, 1993: 676).

To an extent this version of events seems plausible. Restructuring BT would, based on subsequent experience, have taken two or three years and a lack of management co-operation would have created a host of difficulties for ministers in a range of areas from technical advice to public relations. Given that the privatisation of BT was breaking significant new ground, it might seem reasonable that the Conservatives should not create unnecessary obstacles for themselves in a prominent policy area. Whilst these considerations may have been influential, however, further evidence suggests that they were not decisive. It is likely that ministers' primary motivation for selling BT as a monopoly was tied up with the circumstances in which the wider decision to privatise the company had been taken – and these were financial (*The Economist*, 1995b).

The early results of the privatisation process had been encouraging from the viewpoint of the Conservative Right. The policy was seen as having reduced or virtually eliminated the government's powers to control the divested companies.[3] As a result of their new-found 'freedom', the companies had become more competitive and achieved major efficiency gains. The NFC, for example, increased its profitability sevenfold (Vickers and Yarrow, 1988; Grimstone, 1990). The perceived success of the early divestitures was to convert many Conservative backbenchers, who had initially regarded privatisation with some scepticism, to the Right's ideological cause and the policy's radical image with civil servants and voters was also softened considerably. Yet although this precedent was necessary in helping ministers prepare for the ambitious programme of sell-offs which was to follow, it was certainly not sufficient. Prominent authors now argue that the Conservatives were driven into large-scale privatisation not just by ideology, but also by fiscal necessity (Foster, 1992; Jenkins, 1995).

During her first term in office Thatcher had learnt that in addition to rolling back the frontiers of the state and increasing competition, privatisation could reap a number of other benefits. Key among these was that its proceeds could be used as a politically convenient way of restoring order to public finances (Mitchell, 1990). The Conservatives had committed themselves to reducing the Public Sector Borrowing Requirement (PSBR) in their 1979 election manifesto as part of their wider neoliberal policy agenda (Conservative Party, 1979) but, partly because of pledges to increase spending on defence and health and partly because of rising unemployment, they had found themselves unable to curtail public expenditure. Indeed, rather than falling, public expenditure actually rose from 40.5 per cent of gross domestic product (GDP) in 1978/79 to 43.5 per cent in 1982/83 (Veljanovski, 1987).

Once in office, some senior Conservatives began to realise that sales proceeds from privatisations could take the place of reductions in public expenditure as a means of cutting public borrowing. The then Chancellor of the Exchequer, Sir Geoffrey Howe (1994: 254), has admitted that, in the early 1980s, "the sensible disposal of public sector assets had grown in urgency, not least as a short-term way of helping reduce the PSBR." A further consideration was the investment requirements of some of the nationalised industries. BT, for example, needed vast sums to modernise its network in the face of increasing demand, but this could not be publicly funded without severely affecting the PSBR.[4] The most pragmatic way around this problem was to sell BT and other companies in a similar position and let the private sector find the investment capital (Foster, 1992).

Early privatisations had impacted only modestly on public finances (see Table 2.1), but the potential contribution of BT was huge – the company was valued at around £5.5 billion. BT's high market value was connected to its significant market dominance, however, and had the Conservatives broken BT into a host of competing parts the sale price would have fallen and its contribution to reducing the PSBR would have been less significant (*The Economist*, 1995b; Veljanovski, 1989). Smaller companies would also, it was feared, have been less well placed to raise the necessary investment funds. Brittan (1984: 113) asserts that it is "ludicrous to suppose that major industrial decisions such as whether to denationalise the telephone system," were taken to massage public finances. Nevertheless, there is a strong case to be made for interpreting the monopoly sale of BT as a pragmatic solution to an economic problem. Given the expanding PSBR and the realisation that this could be tackled by privatisation, it seems likely that financial advantage was the most important consideration in both the sale of BT and the failure to meaningfully liberalise its market. It is perhaps ironic that the cash surpluses of privatisation – just as those of nationalisation beforehand – had come to make such a major contribution towards fulfilling the Conservatives' macroeconomic objectives.

British Gas and the water industry

Following the sale of BT, ministerial statements regarding competition in the utilities became contradictory. On the one hand, in response to charges similar to that presented above, the importance of market liberalisation was re-emphasised. John Moore noted that:

> [Labour] argue that we are selling off assets because we desperately need the money. Nothing could be further from the truth... [O]pening up nationalised industry to competition [i.e. by licensing Mercury] is not about balancing the books. It is about choice (Moore, 1985b: 1).

On the other hand, it was admitted that BT faced practically no competition and privatising BG and the water industry as monopolies was advocated. Revising earlier claims that the utilities' monopolies were in large part artificial, Moore (1985a: 95) now suggested they were natural and argued that it would be "wasteful or impractical to break them up." Subsequent policy developed adopting this latter view. BG was sold as a statutory monopoly in 1986 and, although some competition existed from the electricity industry (Adamson *et al.*, 1991), any threat of competitive entry into the gas market, however unlikely, was removed. The water industry was restructured before privatisation, but little genuine competition resulted because a series of regional monopolies was created.[5] Arguments advanced by opponents of liberalisation claimed that contemporary technology, in both the water and gas industries, was insufficient to allow competing suppliers access to the domestic markets, although the validity of such claims is difficult to determine because ministers did not extensively investigate the range of options available.[6]

It has already been noted that the simple transfer of a monopoly from the public to the private sector, aside from doing nothing to liberalise the market, necessitates an industry role for the state as a regulator to prevent the monopolist from abusing its position. Section 2.2 pointed out that theorists such as Friedman (1962) do not object to governmental regulation of natural monopoly because they recognise that consumer protection measures are necessary where competition is impractical. However, the regulation of artificial monopolies – of which many of BT's activities were examples – exceeds that which is acceptable for most neoliberals because it results in unnecessary state activity. As Littlechild (1983: 7) points out, competition is believed "indisputably [to be] the most effective means – perhaps ultimately the only effective means – of protecting consumers against monopoly power. Regulation is... not a substitute for competition." Nevertheless, in the absence of competition the Conservatives were forced to devise suitable regulation prior to the divestiture of the utilities and a dedicated regulatory body was assigned to each utility.[7]

2.5 Regulation and surrogate competition

An all encompassing definition of regulation has eluded politicians and scholars alike, although Hancher and Moran (1989) suggest two uses of the term which predominate over all others. First, regulation *theory* is a political-economy approach to the theorisation of capital accumulation, often advanced from a neo-marxist perspective (Aglietta, 1979, Lipietz, 1993; Jessop, 1997). It integrates the patterns of production, consumption and exchange (the regime of accumulation) with the role of political and social relations (the mode of social regulation) which serve to secure the integrity and cohesion of the accumulation process (Tonts and Jones, 1996). The principal contribution of regulation theory is its conception, based on the integration of political, economic and social relations, of capitalist industrial society being founded on a regulatory system or form of governance which guarantees the reproduction of the regime of accumulation (Michalak, 1994).

Second, and of specific relevance here, *statutory* regulation describes a specific framework of legal and/or administrative rules determining acceptable courses of action to be followed by economic agents (Hancher and Moran, 1989).[8] Various ways exist of achieving such regulation, from the one extreme of flexibility or procedural formality, to the other of legislation enforceable through the courts. Foster (1992) notes that a useful distinction within statutory regulation is that between *economic* regulation, which is primarily concerned with monopoly and competition and *social* regulation, which revolves around safety and environmental issues, notions of 'fairness' and product quality. Both economic and social regulation were used in combination to provide the utilities with a form of 'surrogate' competition, that is to say the regulation was designed to replicate the effects of actual competition by forcing prices down and efficiency up (*The Economist*, 1995c).

Economic regulation

Unlike in the United States, where utilities have been in the private sector for a considerable time, the economic regulation of industry was long-neglected in Britain (the railways were regulated in the 19th and early to mid 20th centuries – see Parris, 1965 – but, following nationalisation, the practice was largely abandoned). Economic regulation in the USA follows the 'rate of return' model, which limits the profits a firm can make to an agreed rate of return on its employed capital. Various weaknesses were identified with this type of regulation, not least that it often leads to over-capitalisation and regulatory capture (see, for example, Thompson, 1990) and this experience led the Conservatives to seek an alternative. A report, *The regulation of British Telecommunications' profitability* (Littlechild, 1983), was commissioned to address the issue and suggested a novel price-capping mechanism, RPI minus 'x'. This requires regulated firms to restrict their price increases to a fixed level below the rate of inflation for a given number of years. In this way, firms are incentivised to increase efficiency as they are allowed to retain any profits they make within their price cap over the specified period. The difference between rate of return regulation, which revolves around profit, and RPI minus 'x', which focuses on price, is fundamental. As Hillman and Braeutigam (1989: 37) point out:

> A shift from profit to price level regulation effects a shift of risks and benefits between the firm and its consumers... [P]rofit level regulation assigns to consumers the risks of cost increases and the benefits of cost reductions, while price level regulation reassigns them both to the firm.

Littlechild suggested that only the monopoly elements of BT's business – for example, local calls, connection charges and rentals – should be subject to RPI minus 'x' and that areas where the potential for competition existed – in particular, long-distance calls – should not. Although the logic of his position might have suggested the need for a range of individual price caps, one for each monopoly service, potential complexities led him to recommend a tariff 'basket', within which BT's monopoly elements should be placed and whose *average* price level must not rise over RPI minus 'x'. The tariff basket approach was adopted but, perhaps illustrating ministers' apprehension regarding the size of the competitive threat posed by Mercury, long-distance calls were included (Foster, 1992).

RPI minus 'x' was retained as the means of economic regulation for BG and the water industry, although the formula was modified slightly to account for certain costs which were regarded as being subject to fluctuation beyond management control. These costs – North Sea gas in the case of BG and unpredictable government commitments to, for example, EU anti-pollution directives in the water industry – are passed directly on to consumers. The revised formula for the gas industry was RPI minus 'x' plus 'y' (where 'y' was the cost of North Sea gas), whereas for the water industry it became RPI plus 'k' (where 'k' represented the sum required for new investment 'y' less the efficiency gains 'x') (Helm, 1987; Beesley and Littlechild, 1989). Such modifications tend to compromise the fundamental difference between rate of return regulation and RPI minus 'x', however, because they re-assign costs to the consumer. Because BG can pass on the cost of any North Sea gas contract to consumers, it need not concern itself with securing the best price for that gas. Likewise, the water industry is not forced to 'shop around' among suppliers when it undertakes government-required enhancement schemes. Of course, it could be argued that the 'y' and 'k' factors were necessary regulatory characteristics in the gas and water privatisations in order to introduce a degree of stability into the industries. Equally, though, they might be interpreted as further evidence of the Conservatives' desire to maximise sales revenues because the new factors removed considerable financial risks for potential investors.

The impact of RPI minus 'x' regulation on the utilities' efficiency was mixed and of particular disappointment to ministers was the fact that some public sector monopolies began outperforming their privatised counterparts. *The Economist* (1995b) notes, for example, that BG managed to increase its productivity by only 0.4 per cent per year between 1989 and 1994, compared to the Post Office's annual improvement of over three per cent and BR's of around one per cent during that period.

Social regulation

Social regulation has been imposed upon the utilities both through conditions in their licences and action by their respective regulators. BT, BG and the water industry are all required to satisfy certain safety requirements, in particular regarding the well-being of their workers, and fulfil environmental responsibilities where appropriate. The water industry, for example, is obliged to provide unpolluted water and the Director General of Ofgas is required to promote, as far as possible, the efficient use of energy (Foster, 1992). The utilities' licences also stipulate that a 'fair' level of service should be provided for consumers. Such an obligation is not concerned with notions of social justice in the sense that utility prices should in some way seek to redistribute income (Oftel, 1986; Burns *et al.*, 1995). Instead, because monopolists are in a position to deprive consumers of their only means of obtaining a particular good, the utilities are generally required to provide universal service without discriminating their prices, terms or conditions. Finally, certain customer groups, such as the disabled or poor, have been protected. BT, for example, must provide various services for the deaf and blind at no extra cost and has agreed to provide rebates on line rental for those with low bills.

Explicit provisions to regulate service quality were not included in plans to privatise BT and BG. Ministers' initial lack of attention in this area is perhaps surprising given that deteriorating service quality is a potential side-effect of the RPI minus 'x' method of economic regulation. As Foster (1992) observes, once an 'x' value has been fixed, a firm must cut costs in order to maintain its profitability and a simple way to achieve this is by lowering its output standards. Immediately after privatisation, BT stopped publishing performance data it had been required to disseminate as a public corporation and public sentiment – in the absence of hard data – suggested a decline in service standards. An Oftel investigation confirmed this to be the case and BT was required to accept some financial liability if it failed to provide certain services to a given standard (Rovizzi and Thompson, 1992). Complaints about BG's service standards also increased following privatisation (Chapman, 1990) and, in the light of this experience, quality of service regulation including a financial liability scheme was formally established prior to the divestiture of the water industry (see Table 2.2).

Table 2.2   **Summary of quality of service regulation in the water industry (certain complexities are omitted here for the sake of clarity)**

Service	Performance level	Payment if not achieved
Appointments to visit customer	(i) Specify morning or afternoon on relevant day	£10
	(ii) Keep specified appointment	£10
Responding to written account queries	Within 20 working days	£10
Responding to requests to change payment methods or arrangements if it is not possible to meet the request	Within 10 working days	£10
Responding to written complaints:		
(a) No further action necessary	(i) Substantive reply within 10 working days	£10
(b) Further action	(ii) Holding reply within 10 working days and substantive reply within 20	£10
Warning notices of a planned interruption to water supply	At least 24 hours' notice to be given for interruptions lasting more than 4 hours	£10
Restoring supplies:		
(a) Planned interruptions	By the time specified in a warning notice	£10
(b) Unplanned interruptions (e.g. bursts)	(i) Within 48 hours for strategic main	£10, plus £10 for each additional 24 hours
	(ii) Within 24 hours in all other cases	£10, plus £10 for each additional 24 hours
Installing a meter at customer's request	Within 15 working days of payment	£10
Flooding from sewers	No waste water to enter customer's building	Refund of year's sewage charges (up to a maximum of £1,000)

Source: Gray and Ramanadham, 1994.

The continuing role of the state

It is not the purpose of this chapter to assess the efficacy of the above regulatory mechanisms and institutions in terms of their consumer protection outcomes (a thorough review can be found in Lowndes, 1997). Rather, emphasis here is placed upon the consequences of such regulation in terms of the state's continuing role in the utilities' affairs. It was suggested earlier that key objectives of privatisation identified by the Conservatives were to reduce the powers of the state to control an industry and to promote competition. Senker (1989: 179) has claimed that the utility privatisations represented a "triumph of ideology over economics," implying the above objectives were fulfilled, although it is difficult to see how he arrives at this conclusion. As Kay and Thompson (1986: 31) point out:

> Privatisation in the United Kingdom... increasingly [came] to emphasise the virtues of denationalisation over, and even at the expense of, the promotion of competition... The conflict between privatisation and liberalisation... is no longer a conflict but a rout.

In the absence of meaningful competition, the state could not withdraw in any simple sense from the privatised sectors. The introduction of regulatory mechanisms to act as surrogate competition represented continued statutory involvement in the affairs of the utilities despite a change of ownership. Quality of service regulation represented control over the production of goods and services, for example, in the same way that universal service obligations amounted to a degree of control over their distribution. Thompson (1990) suggests that privatisation swapped a previously 'close' form of intervention – nationalisation – for intervention 'at a distance' – regulation. Yet there is a sense in which Thompson might be understating his case. According to Foster (1992: 124), the system of regulation adopted following privatisation was not at all distant; in fact, it was more systematic and penetrating than that which it superseded. Regulation under nationalisation was "rubbed smooth to achieve consensus, ...reflected mainly administrative and some political considerations, quickly ran into difficulties and ended by pleasing no-one." Certainly, the constitutional relationship between the government and its public corporations was such that effective regulation was difficult to enact. In a speech in 1981, Howe (quoted in Foster, 1992: 114) explained that the government was empowered only to issue instructions of a 'general character,' and that,

...any specific command like 'make sure the 8.15am from Victoria runs on time' would be legally unenforceable. The government's only real weapon is the threat to reduce or cut off external funds. This is far too drastic to be effective. It is like equipping traffic wardens with anti-tank guns but depriving them of the right to leave parking tickets.

Privatisation gave ministers the opportunity to address this constitutional loophole. The regulatory briefs of Oftel, Ofgas and Ofwat were very much moulded by objectives and guidance issued by central government acting in the light of previous experience (Jenkins, 1995; Thompson, 1990) and regulators were given powers to address specific areas of poor utility performance. Moreover, despite the technical independence of the regulators, the utilities were not protected from potential and actual governmental interference in their affairs. Because the Conservatives retained the right to change the regulators' briefs through legislation, ministers could overrule, say, an Oftel decision regarding the appropriate value for 'x' in the RPI minus 'x' formula. As Veljanovski (1987) points out, this introduced a degree of uncertainty into the utilities' businesses and gave ministers potential influence over the companies' profitability, share prices, investment plans and so on. Evidence also indicates that governmental pressure was sometimes used to 'inform' the regulators' day to day decisions. For example, following Ofwat's decision to force a price reduction in the south west of England, it was Conservative ministers and politicians who claimed credit for having brought this about (Jenkins, 1995). On a separate occasion, Nicholas Ridley (1991: 83) boasted that "the utilities which we have privatised... are more easily controlled when they are in the private sector."

At stake in the utility privatisations was the *form* of government intervention rather than its existence (Kay and Vickers, 1988; Thompson, 1990). Hancher and Moran (1989: 131), in a general discussion about deregulation, suggest that what begins as an intent to withdraw from the intervention arena often results in "not so much a change in the content of rules, or a departure from regulatory objectives, [but simply] an adjustment to the means of enforcement." Letwin (1988) concurs, noting in relation to the context of this chapter that the state retained powerful control over the network industries following their divestiture. The privatisation of the utilities throughout the 1980s was as much – if not more – of an exercise in the formulation of regulatory mechanisms and institutions as it was an attempt to promote competition and reduce state control over the utility industries.

2.6 Utility privatisation reviewed – lessons for the 1990s

This chapter has examined the development of utility privatisation policy throughout the 1980s. It began by reviewing the key characteristics of neoliberalism and argued that, despite some authors' tendency to downplay the theory's role in privatisation policy development, its influence – at least initially – should not be dismissed. It was suggested that the Conservative Right had some expectation that privatisation would enhance individual liberty, the fundamental concern of neoliberal theory, by: a) promoting competition, rather than monopoly, in an industry's market to allow voluntary exchange between individuals and b) genuinely reducing the powers of the state to control an industry and the production/distribution of its goods and services. In addition, market liberalisation and state downsizing were expected to result in improved industrial efficiency, innovation and customer care.

Gamble (1994) rightly points out that the 1980s did not see the unfolding of a New Right ideological masterplan. Key neoliberal goals were undoubtedly marginalised as privatisation policy unravelled in practice and this is evidenced by the privatisation of the network industries as regulated monopolies. When BT, BG and the water industry were divested, the Conservatives failed to liberalise their markets meaningfully and, as a result, were forced to create regulatory mechanisms and institutions to prevent the utilities from abusing their positions. Such regulation resulted in a significant and continuing role for the state in the utilities' affairs despite the transfer of ownership to the private sector. Evidence also showed that aspects of the utilities' performance, in the absence of competition, had not matched the expectations of regulators. In some cases, the efficiency gains achieved by the privatised utilities had not matched those of their public sector counterparts.

A policy shift

It was against this background that ministers considered the privatisation of the electricity industry. The Conservatives' 1987 election manifesto (Conservative Party, 1987) stressed the importance of freedom and individualism and asserted that these could be achieved by checking state power. With specific reference to forthcoming privatisations, the manifesto noted that: "competition forces the economy to respond to the needs of the consumer. It promotes efficiency, holds down costs, drives companies to innovate and ensures that customers get the best value for money" (Conservative Party, 1987: 30).

Although this statement was a move away from John Moore's previous assertion that market liberalisation might not be practical or desirable in the case of the utilities (see section 2.4), previous experience suggested that a shift in policy would not be forthcoming – the rhetoric of competition had not prevented BT, BG and the water industry being sold as regulated monopolies. In a notable reorientation of policy, however, plans were unveiled in 1988 to liberalise the electricity generating industry before divestiture at the turn of the decade (Veljanovski, 1989).

The electricity industry can be divided into three components: generation, transmission (the network element) and supply. Prior to divestiture, the Central Electricity Generating Board controlled generation and transmission and 12 Area Boards supplied electricity to customers via their own local distribution systems discrete from the transmission network. Industry restructuring did not provide for much immediate competition among the Area Boards, with only the largest customers set to benefit from a choice of supplier, although plans to relax market entry in the future were advanced (see below). The principal achievement of the electricity divestiture was to remove the transmission component from the CEGB's control (to become National Grid) and to further split the CEGB into two generating companies (see Figure 2.1).[9] Coupled with the removal of entry restrictions, this restructuring created a genuinely competitive generating industry. Because National Grid was separated from the CEGB, the potential for any one generator to deny others access to the network, as had happened following the 1983 Energy Act, was removed. By 1993, 14 licences had been issued to new generators (Littlechild, 1993). As a result, the need for surrogate competition was eliminated and, with the exception of anti-trust measures to prevent discriminatory practice from National Grid, the industry is now free from statutory economic and social regulation. The privatisation of the electricity generators therefore not only achieved a transfer of ownership, but also liberalised the market and reduced the degree of state control over the industry.

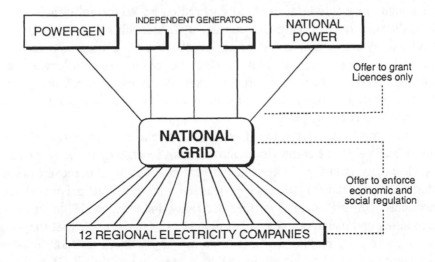

Figure 2.1   The structure of the privatised electricity industry in England and Wales

The electricity generating industry has not been the only utility market which has seen significant liberalisation in the 1990s. The 'duopoly policy' in telecommunications, which had restricted entry beyond BT and Mercury, was ended in 1991. The gas supply market was liberalised in 1996, when a pilot scheme in south west England allowed all business and domestic customers to choose from a range of suppliers – competition has now been extended throughout the country (*The Guardian*, 1997a) – and the electricity supply industry was made fully competitive during 1998 (*The Guardian*, 1997b). Considerable efficiency gains and customer service improvements have resulted in all these industries following the introduction of competition (Lowndes, 1997; Offer, 1999; Ofgas, 1999).

The liberalisation of the telecommunications and gas industries did not result from an enforced reorganisation of either BT or BG. Instead, network ownership has remained with the former utility monopolies.[10] Following the model employed when Mercury was connected to BT's network in 1984 (see section 2.4), Oftel and Ofgas have been charged with the additional responsibility of ensuring non-discriminatory access for potential competitors. In the electricity industry, the Area Boards (now termed Regional Electricity Companies (RECs)) have retained ownership of their local distribution networks and thus Offer has a similar task. Whilst this extra regulatory activity undoubtedly increased governmental influence over the utility industries, it is in fact consistent with neoliberal ideology because it essentially constitutes a kind of anti-trust law. Over time, and as actual competition increases, the aim is that the regulators can cease many activities *in*consistent with the free market, in particular those designed to act as surrogate competition (although at the time of writing there is little evidence of this taking place).

It is not clear why the Conservatives chose to re-emphasise the ideological values of competition and freedom when they came to privatise the electricity industry. After all, the reasons cited by Thompson (1990), Marsh (1991) and Thatcher (1993) as to why BT was privatised as a monopoly applied equally to the electricity industry in 1988: 'modern' accounting and management systems did not exist in the sense that they were incapable of underpinning a restructured industry without revision; top-level management argued passionately against a break-up of the CEGB, with the plans ultimately leading to the resignation of its chairman, Walter Marshall (Jenkins, 1995); and the sell-off plans were advanced with a similar amount of parliamentary time remaining before a general election was required. Nevertheless, as Thatcher (1993: 684) recalls, she "again and again insisted that whatever structure [was created had to] provide genuine competition."

One explanation is that the limitations of transferring public monopolies into the private sector had become unacceptable to many Conservatives and a desire to secure genuine movement towards market liberalisation had developed within the Party. Backbench MPs, many of whom were initially sceptical of the privatisation programme, had come to embrace it with a high degree of ideological fervour and one noted that, "what Conservative members want is competition" (*Hansard*, 1986: Col. 6). Some ministers shared this view and Cecil Parkinson, the Secretary of State for Energy, was convinced that the lack of competition and continuing government involvement in the telecommunications and gas markets was responsible for BT and BG's limited efficiency gains and poor customer service. He had "very strong views" that the Conservatives should "never again 'do a BT.'" Parkinson's appointment enhanced the credibility of Lawson's original case for competition (see section 2.4) and resulted in a forceful argument for market liberalisation being presented to the Cabinet. (As will be shown further in chapter three, Parkinson seemed to enjoy considerable influence over Thatcher regarding privatisation policy.)

A second explanation relates to finance. Section 2.4 argued that the need to address a burgeoning PSBR resulted in BT being privatised as a monopoly in order to maximise sales proceeds. By 1988, following several years of strong economic growth, the PSBR as a percentage of GDP had fallen considerably and the importance of privatisation revenue as a means of 'balancing the books' had subsided (see Figure 2.2). As Pliatzky (quoted in Mitchell, 1990: 24) observes, it was increasingly felt in the Treasury that "the objective of reducing public expenditure... [could] be achieved without bringing privatisation receipts into the reckoning." As such the Conservatives were accorded an opportunity to experiment with restructuring the CEGB notwithstanding the lower income the Treasury would receive from the sale of a liberalised industry. There is a strong possibility that such economic considerations, just as they had in previous utility divestitures, proved decisive in determining the method used to privatise the CEGB. In the light of previous experience, it seems unlikely that backbench pressure and the appointment of Cecil Parkinson, even in combination, would have resulted in a genuine move towards market liberalisation had ministers still needed to maximise revenue from the sale.

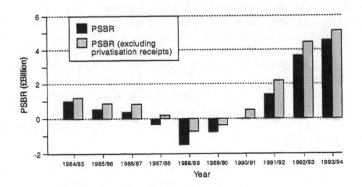

Figure 2.2   **PSBR, 1984/85 – 1993/94, showing the effect of privatisation revenue**

Source: CSO Financial Statistics, 1992, 1995.

The Conservatives' renewed commitment to promoting competition continued in earnest throughout the mid 1990s. After the liberalisation of the telecommunications, gas and electricity supply industries, the next large network industry privatisation was that of British Rail. This was announced in 1992, at a time when the economy had relapsed into recession and the state of government finances had worsened considerably (see Figure 2.2). Nevertheless, ministers announced their determination that BR should not be privatised as a monopoly like BT, BG and the water industry had been. Instead, they insisted that competition should be introduced into almost every aspect of railway operation and that BR should accordingly be restructured along the lines of the electricity generating industry (Gibb *et al.*, 1998). The next chapter documents the evolution of the policy which was designed to do this.

Notes

1. It is important to recognise that the government will always retain a degree of control over any enterprise. Companies are subject to law, taxes, safety legislation and so on. Although neoliberal purists might argue that many safety laws are superfluous – choice is said to protect the consumer and the worker (see Friedman, 1962; 1980) – the Conservatives never claimed that they accepted this line of thought.

2. The newly-created Office of Telecommunications performed this task.

3. In reality, it was not always the case that the government foreswore as much control as it might have done. Golden Shares, for example, were often retained to prevent 'undesirable' (i.e. foreign) takeovers or to restrict third parties' voting rights (see Graham and Prosser, 1994; Howe, 1994). Nevertheless, ministers could no longer control the management of the companies, or influence production/distribution matters.

4. This was because of the so-called Ryrie rules, named after Sir William Ryrie, the civil servant then in charge of public expenditure. The rules stated that any borrowing by nationalised industries remained public sector borrowing because the risk ultimately lay with the government.

5. Although technically this provided scope for some direct competition around the 'borders' and some indirect competition by way of 'emulation' (see chapter six), the principal theoretical benefit of this restructuring was that it would ease the regulator's task by providing yardsticks for him to judge comparative performance. However, as Foster (1992) argues, comparisons have proved difficult because the greatly varying characteristics of each company have resulted in considerable differences in costs and other measures of efficiency (although see Williams, 1992).

6. One civil servant interviewed for this book, who was directly involved in selling both industries, claimed that competition in the domestic market would have been feasible.

7. BT is regulated by the Office of Telecommunications (Oftel); BG by the Office of Gas Supply (Ofgas); the water industry by the Office of Water Services (Ofwat); and the electricity suppliers by the Office of Electricity Regulation (Offer).

8. The two interpretations of regulation – theory and statutory – are by no means separate and distinct. As Leyshon (1992: 250) notes, the form of "systemic equilibrium in operation at any one time will influence the drafting and administration of a system of legal rules and guidelines which are used to define the range of permissible practices open to economic agents."

9. The two generating companies were later to become three as financial difficulties arose over the nuclear generators (see Bowdery, 1994). It is also important to note that the industry description given here relates to England and Wales only. Scotland and Northern Ireland have their own, slightly different, industry organisation (see Electricity Association, 1998).

10. BG has split into BGplc (network) and Centrica (supply), although they are still owned by the same holding company.

3 New Opportunities for Britain's Railways

3.1 Introduction

The Conservatives' proposals for rail privatisation were formally unveiled in the 1992 White Paper *New Opportunities for the Railways* (DoT, 1992a). As chapter one pointed out, selling BR had been regarded by some as potentially troublesome because it differed from the other network industries in several important respects. Most importantly BR, unlike the utilities, was heavily dependent upon public subsidy (some operational differences are discussed later). The Serpell Report (Serpell, 1983) concluded in 1983 that in order to make BR profitable, 84 per cent of its route miles would have to be closed. Hostile public reaction to such a prospect confirmed to ministers that moves to cut back BR's network before (or after) privatisation would be politically unacceptable and that at least some continuing financial support would be necessary to "sustain the... national network of services" at 1992 levels (Conservative Party, 1992: 35). As such, it was clear from the outset that it would be impossible – and, indeed, undesirable – for the state to reduce significantly its influence over certain parts of the industry despite a transfer of ownership (DoT, 1992a). Not only would the government's role continue through its financial contributions, but also by virtue of the fact that it could reasonably demand guaranteed levels of service in relation to subsidy where it was being paid. Some compromise of the neoliberal policy goals outlined in chapter two was always inevitable in the rail sell-off.

This situation notwithstanding, the promotion of actual, rather than surrogate, competition throughout most elements of the industry was a fundamental objective of the rail privatisation plans outlined in 1992. The Conservatives' election manifesto of that year noted:

> We believe the best way to produce profound and lasting improvements on the railways is to end BR's state monopoly... Companies have already said

42

that they want to introduce new railway services as soon as the monopoly is ended. We will give them that chance" (Conservative Party, 1992: 35).

New Opportunities for the Railways emphasised ministers' wish to reduce the role of the state in the railway industry in order to harness the "management skills, flair and entrepreneurial spirit" of the private sector (DoT, 1992a: i; Welsby and Nicholls, 1999). A complete reorganisation of the railway industry was advocated and the plans put forward in the White Paper – the so-called track authority model – essentially represented further experimentation with the method used to divest the electricity industry (Charlton *et al.*, 1997; Helm, 1996; Mountford, 1996). A company equivalent to the National Grid, Railtrack, was created and as well as introducing competition to the maintenance and 'support' aspects of BR's business, ministers also sought to liberalise passenger and freight train services.[1] The following five chapters analyse the BR sell-off in the context of competition and regulation established in chapter two. Chapters four to seven assess the policy's outcome in terms of liberalising the passenger rail market, but the remainder of this chapter is devoted to describing its development and establishing how the track authority model of rail privatisation came to be selected.

Debates within and around the Conservative Party concerning the privatisation and liberalisation of the railway industry were protracted, some even pre-dating the election of the first Thatcher administration in 1979. Evidence indicates that the DoT was attempting to sell parts of BR as early as 1980. Despite rail privatisation having been considered by the Conservatives for more than a decade before the publication of *New Opportunities for the Railways*, it would seem that neither the strategy outlined in that document, nor the decision to adopt it, was the result of a thorough or detailed policy analysis. This chapter argues that ministers had barely considered key implications of the track authority model before publishing the White Paper and suggests that, as a result, they were unclear as to whether some aspects of the proposals – especially those relating to the promotion of competition – would be capable of achieving what was expected of them. The purpose of this chapter is to investigate how and why this situation arose.

The study of rail privatisation policy development is not new and a number of academic accounts have examined the subject from various perspectives.[2] Gibb *et al.* (1996: 35) first advanced the argument that the process leading to BR's divestiture was extremely protracted. Zahariadis (1995, 1996) explained the timing of the BR sale through a conceptual model which drew upon the interaction of three policy 'streams': problems, solutions and politics. Both studies have made a useful contribution to the understanding of rail privatisation policy development, but the context of this book requires a new perspective in order to emphasise policy makers' evolving attitudes towards competition as plans to sell BR were developed. Moreover, the arguments advanced by Gibb *et al.* and Zahariadis rely heavily upon secondary data sources. Although this is not to contest the validity of the studies, their exclusion of primary data might have compromised the 'depth' of the empirical investigation undertaken in each. This chapter's original contribution to the understanding of rail privatisation policy development therefore relates both to content, with its focus on policy makers' attitudes towards market liberalisation, and to method, through its incorporation of primary interview/Parliamentary data to support its arguments.

3.2 Rail privatisation policy, 1979 – 1986

Debate within the Conservative Party regarding the privatisation and liberalisation of BR can be traced back to the late 1960s. The CRD's Committee on Nationalised Industries, which identified the need to begin a sustained programme of privatisation (see chapter two), considered divesting BR's core activities but concluded that denationalisation would be inappropriate because "there would be no takers at the price which would be acceptable to us" (CRD, 1968: 15). Instead, the Committee suggested that emphasis should be placed on securing better public sector management. Following the election of Thatcher as Party leader in 1975, support for the liberalisation of BR's market began to materialise among the Conservative Right. The Young Conservatives' (1976) *Key Policy Statement* called for the rail industry to be liberalised by allowing private operators onto the network to compete with BR, whilst the shadow transport spokesman, Norman Fowler, emphasised his support for market, rather than state, determination of transport provision (Fowler, 1977).

Considering Thatcher's cautious outlook on privatisation in the early 1980s, plans to attract private sector capital into the railway industry materialised remarkably quickly. This was probably because both the new

Transport Minister, Norman Fowler, and the British Railways Board (BRB) favoured private investment in BR's subsidiary industries (BRB, 1981; *Modern Railways*, 1980a, 1980b).[3] Proposals to achieve this were developed during 1980 and the result was the creation of a new holding company, British Rail Investments Ltd (BRIL), as a wholly owned subsidiary of the BRB. The assets of Sealink UK, British Transport Hotels, British Rail Hovercraft (Seaspeed) and British Rail Property Holdings were transferred to BRIL in order that private sector involvement could be administered separately from BR's core activities (*Modern Railways*, 1980c; 1981a).

The BRB saw its new subsidiary as a means of expanding the total level of investment in the existing businesses on top of government grants:

> For BR, the benefit of privatisation is seen as being two-fold: in addition to receiving the proceeds of sales, BR will also face reduced calls on the finance available within its investment ceiling as the investment requirements of the subsidiaries in the holding company will be met in part from the private sector (*Modern Railways*, 1980c: 386).

The Conservatives' primary motivation for establishing BRIL was soon revealed to be different from BR's. When ministers realised that revenue from asset sales could be used in order to 'massage' the PSBR (see chapter two), they prioritised the divestiture of BR's subsidiaries in order to reduce the overall level of its subsidy and raise money for the Exchequer (Jenkins, 1995). As noted by a respondent,

> ...the [government] got to work on all public assets and simply stripped them. A 1970s merchant banker couldn't have done better. 'Get rid of your hotels, get rid of your hovercraft, get rid of your ships, we don't want all these engineering works, we don't want any of this catering, get rid of it. But most of all get rid of your property. And give us the money.'

The 1981 Transport Act (House of Commons, 1981) provided for BR to dispose of its subsidiary businesses and these were sold throughout the 1980s (see Table 3.1).

Table 3.1   BR's subsidiary and peripheral business sales, 1981 – 1989 (excluding various property disposals)

Business Sold	Date of Sale
BR Hovercraft	October 1981
BR Hotels	1982-1984
Superbreak Mini Holidays	February 1983
Slateford Laundry	September 1983
Sealink UK	July 1984
British Transport Advertising	August 1987
Doncaster Wagon Works	October 1987
Horwich Foundry	August 1988
Travellers' Fare	December 1988
British Rail Engineering Ltd	April 1989
Golden Rail	May 1989

Source: *Hansard* (1995).

The sale of BR's subsidiaries in the early 1980s was consistent with the development of privatisation policy in other industrial sectors at the time, as all the divested companies were relatively small and already operated in competitive markets. But having established the concept of privatisation in the rail industry, it seems that the DoT was keen to press ahead with selling at least some of BR's core operations. A Monopolies and Mergers Commission (MMC) report on BR's Southern Region (SR) in 1980 had among other things concluded that more investment was needed in order to improve rail services in the area (MMC, 1980). Increased government expenditure was ruled out because this would clash with the policy of reducing BR's overall subsidy (and the PSBR), but Fowler did ask BR to investigate operational and managerial independence for the SR in order to seek clearer accountability for the operation of services (*Modern Railways*, 1981b). The Department's semantic subtlety, according to one respondent, concealed its real objective of finding a way to divest the SR, perhaps opening up an alternative investment source: "...Norman Fowler... did a study of the Southern Region. He got his officials to study privatising the SR as an experiment. 'Sell off the SR,' [he said]."

In addition to the SR, the Department examined proposals for the privatisation of rail operations in Scotland and Wales (Hope, 1983). The favoured approach at this stage was to auction franchises for vertically integrated, geographically discrete rail businesses broken from the rump of BR. In this sense, some provision had been made for competition *for* the rail market (as opposed to *in* it), although this was almost certainly by accident rather than by design. Early privatisation plans were crude and there is nothing to suggest that officials had submitted a blueprint capable of liberalising BR's core market; rather, the approach seems to have been to let the private sector formulate proposals of its own and present them to the Department (Abbott, 1984).

These early moves towards privatisation were not popular with the BRB and, in any case, were ultimately over-ridden by the Cabinet. Although numerous state-owned enterprises had been sold off by 1982, privatisation had not yet been extended to tackle the network industries and a BR sale was viewed by Fowler's colleagues as complicated and unworkable:

> It got absolutely nowhere because no-one believed in it. They didn't think it was going to happen, it was crazy, and so on... Norman pushed it quite hard, but... at the end of the day he just didn't have any clout.

The most influential objector to rail privatisation was Margaret Thatcher, who opposed the idea throughout the early 1980s (Jenkins, 1995). In addition to the fact that "she was not convinced that privatising a loss-making industry was feasible" – although she was shortly to sanction the sale of the National Bus Company (NBC) (see below and chapter seven) – Thatcher felt sure 'middle-England' held an inexplicable affection for its railways and that to tinker with BR's core activities would precipitate a political disaster. Whereas the then Prime Minister's cautious approach to privatisation was evaporating with regard to other industries, it remained acute in relation to the railways. A respondent said that when Nicholas Ridley, Secretary of State for Transport from 1983 to 1986, arranged a meeting with Thatcher specifically to obtain her support for rail privatisation,

> ...she told him never to mention the words again and that was it. She said 'railway privatisation will be the Waterloo of this government, I don't want to hear about it. Please never mention the railways to me again... Nick had a

very shrewd political sense and I remember him saying 'it's not worth a candle. As long as she's PM, there's no point in discussing railway privatisation.'

The divergence of opinion between the DoT and Downing Street resulted in the abandonment of attempts to divest train services. Although the rhetoric of privatisation was kept alive by the DoT – it recorded that it still supported the idea – the responsibility for encouraging private sector train operation was passed to BR (*Hansard*, 1983a, 1983b, 1984). In reality, however, with a majority of the BRB opposed to core activity privatisation, it is scarcely credible to suppose that the Board would pursue this option enthusiastically (perhaps the DoT pursued this strategy because it allowed a policy compromise whereby Fowler and his successors could maintain a position in favour of privatisation safe in the knowledge that it was unlikely to occur). By the mid 1980s, even the DoT appeared to have lost interest in selling BR. Notwithstanding claims from Conservative backbenchers that parts of BR were "positively crying out for privatisation" (*Hansard*, 1985: Cols 5-6), it stated that there were no plans to privatise any part of the rail network (*Hansard*, 1986). That official position did not change publicly until 1988.

3.3 External proposals

Despite the absence of a governmental commitment to rail privatisation, the DoT's initial enthusiasm aroused debate among interested observers regarding how BR might be sold. As in the case of BT, where divestiture plans had resulted in numerous analyses of potential methods of sale to promote competition (for example, Beesley, 1981; Kay and Silbertson, 1984; Veljanovski, 1989), suggestions regarding BR's future were advanced by academics (Beesley and Littlechild, 1983; Gylie, 1984; Starkie, 1984), think tanks (Adam Smith Institute (ASI), 1983; Gritten, 1988; Irvine, 1987, 1988) and Conservative backbenchers (*Hansard*, 1988a, 1988b). Some of the concepts and methods proposed influenced ministers' thoughts when they eventually came to privatise the railway industry.

Two suggestions were put forward in 1983, one by the ASI and the other by Beesley and Littlechild. Both elaborated upon the DoT's original concept of regional separation as they advocated selling vertically integrated, geographically discrete cost centres.   The ASI's (1983) *Omega Report* argued that the government should aim for a free market in public transport run by private enterprise and espoused charging road users in order to level the playing field between transport modes.   The report called for the restructuring of BR's management into cost centres to help identify financial and traffic records for lines which could then be auctioned, leasehold, to private bidders.   Hopelessly uneconomic and underused lines would be closed and disposed of, although where "politicians [were] insistent on keeping lines open" (ASI, 1983: 31) the report suggested a degree of competition for the market could be created by offering franchises. Competition in the market was largely overlooked, although restrictions to prevent one company buying up leases for adjacent lines were proposed in order to encourage competition between operators in 'border' areas.

Beesley and Littlechild (1983) emphasised the social, as well as the commercial, advantages rail privatisation could bring for consumers.   Unlike the ASI, Beesley and Littlechild took seriously the social and political problems which would have accompanied the withdrawal of services.   They suggested that once BR had been restructured (perhaps into the pre-1948 regions), it could be sold on the condition that successor companies committed themselves to a minimum programme of rail output.   Given that privatisation would, according to Beesley and Littlechild, make the successor companies much more efficient than BR, they could make better use of their equipment and a quite considerable passenger output could be insisted upon.   The model included the potential for new operators to introduce services in competition with the successor companies although, like the ASI, Beesley and Littlechild effectively dismissed the need for on-rail competition to develop.

Debate in 1984 shifted towards the possibility of vertically separating BR before privatisation in a manner similar to that suggested by Nigel Lawson for BT in 1982 (see section 2.4).   Vertical separation would involve splitting BR into two successor companies, one assuming responsibility for infrastructure and the other operations.   A key characteristic of this method is that it would expose BR's operations business as an *artificial* monopoly. Although the infrastructure company would retain its natural monopoly characteristics because of the prohibitive costs associated with building a competitor, there would, in theory, be no reason why any number of operators should be prevented from operating different services on track owned by a neutral agent ('on-rail' competition).[4]   Gylie (1984) advocated vertical separation primarily because he thought that by retaining the 'track authority' in the public sector, the government would be able to make strategic decisions regarding investment in surface transport infrastructure.

The first to advocate a significant liberalisation of BR's service market was Starkie (1984). Following Kay and Silberston (1984) he argued that, although privatisation alone would secure some consumer advantages, a divestiture which introduced competition between train operators would be more beneficial. Starkie (1984: 16) dismissed the effect of competitive pressures from other modes of transport because BR was "still not as efficient as it might be" despite their existence. Thus, "...the issue... [was] what form of privatisation [would] increase competitive forces within the railway industry [?]" (Starkie, 1984: 16). Starkie went on to suggest that although the government should retain control of the infrastructure, locomotives and rolling stock should be vested in a number of private sector companies who could compete over commercially attractive routes. In the case of socially necessary services, train operators could compete for a ring-fenced Public Service Obligation (PSO) grant to be awarded through a regime of competitive tendering. Starkie's model thus identified the potential for competition both in and for the market.

By the late 1980s, considerable emphasis was being placed by Conservative parliamentarians and think tanks upon the importance of liberalising the rail market. Two backbenchers, Keith Mans and Nicholas Bennett, suggested models through which on-rail competition could be achieved (*Hansard*, 1988a, 1988b). Both advocated a track authority with slight modifications to Starkie's suggestion. The ASI contributed further proposals with Kenneth Irvine's *The Right Lines* (1987) and *Track to the Future* (1988). Irvine's papers represented a shift of opinion for the ASI. Whereas *The Omega Report* had favoured a vertically integrated solution with minimal subsidy and limited competition, the ASI now championed a track authority supported by a grant to maximise competitive opportunities. Unlike Starkie, who had advocated a nationalised infrastructure company, Irvine contended that trains should be able to compete with each other on privately-owned track. With this exception, Irvine generally concurred with Starkie's ideas and developed them further in certain cases. For example, with reference to competitive tendering for loss-making services, Irvine borrowed from Beesley and Littlechild (1983) and suggested that, in return for compensating revenue losses, a franchise must include quality of service stipulations in order to guarantee an acceptable level of service for consumers.

Gritten (1988) returned the debate to vertical integration, although he placed a greater emphasis on the desirability of, and the prospects for, market liberalisation than either the ASI (1983) or Beesley and Littlechild (1983). Gritten argued that BR should be broken into a perhaps a dozen discrete operating areas and that such an approach would make commercial sense, provide efficiency and financial clarity. Competition might occur not only in border areas, but also within the regions themselves if companies were made to provide competitors with 'open access' to their tracks. Ring-fenced grants for loss-making services were again proposed, although Gritten made no mention of competitive tendering for these operations.

Methods of rail privatisation

The suggested methods of privatisation reviewed here fall into two categories. First, building upon the DoT's initial work, is the *regional* model. Beesley and Littlechild (1983), the ASI (1983) and Gritten (1988) supported breaking BR up into vertically integrated, geographically discrete operations with or without opportunities for competition. Second is the *track authority* model. Advanced initially by Gylie and developed by Starkie (1984), Irvine (1987, 1988) and backbench MPs (*Hansard*, 1988a, 1988b), this option involved the vertical separation of BR in order to allow either economies of scale from a state-owned combined track/highway company, or competition between different operators on the same tracks. Some competition for the market was also proposed.

In common with other academic thought regarding utility privatisation (see chapter two), none of the authors recommended that BR should be sold as one company. It is important to recognise, however, that the ASI (1983), Beesley and Littlechild (1983) and Gylie (1984) appear to have suggested disaggregating BR for reasons other than a desire to promote competition. This was most likely because the authors concerned regarded BR as one of many transport modes already in competition with one another; in other words, they disagreed with Starkie's (1984) view that BR constituted a monopoly.

A similar view prevailed in the railway industry and among pressure groups like Transport 2000 (1989), who argued that making rail operators compete with each other would distract their attention from the real issue which was competing with the private car. A logical extension of this might be that the loss-making nature of the rail industry would bring into question the sense of promoting internal competition on the grounds that the market may not be sufficiently robust to withstand it. Liberalising the market of a profitable company such as the CEGB may well have been a good idea, but evidence which emerged after the privatisation of the NBC in 1987 – widespread service instability, fare increases and the development of local and regional monopolies (see, for example, White, 1995; Wolmar, 1998) – certainly seemed to suggest that, in the case of a subsidised transport provider, it would be less appropriate. These issues are revisited later in the book. Only after Starkie (1984) had suggested that competition with other transport modes had little effect on BR's performance did others begin to assume that the company might in essence behave as a monopoly. Referring perhaps to ideological objections to monopolies (Friedman, 1962) and almost certainly to empirical experience of the disappointing performance after privatisation of BT and British Gas (see chapter two), the proposals began to advocate splitting BR up with a view to promoting competition.

Of course, the existence of numerous academic arguments regarding the need to liberalise the markets of network industries had not prevented the government from selling BT, BG and the water industry as regulated monopolies. So long as it was politically convenient to forego market liberalisation, there is no reason to suggest that the above models would have influenced ministers to any practical extent. However, as the next section explains, an announcement that BR would once again be considered for privatisation coincided with the publication of the electricity White Paper in 1988 (see chapter two). With ministers beginning to attach a higher priority to the promotion of competition during industry divestitures, there was now perhaps a more realistic expectation that BR might be restructured before it was privatised (see, for example, *The Economist*, 1991).

3.4 Rail privatisation and liberalisation: an idea whose time had come

It is argued by Gibb *et al.* (1996: 40) that rail privatisation was firmly established on the political agenda by the late 1980s: "[i]t was no longer a case of whether the government would decide to privatise, but of when and how the railways could be privatised." Paul Channon, Secretary of State for Transport from 1987 to 1989, was the first, in his words, to "fly a kite" regarding the sale of BR at the 1988 Conservative Party Conference (see also Webster, 1988).　Channon was publicly circumspect in that he committed himself only to investigating whether privatisation might be a viable option in the future, but personally he did not share Thatcher's view that the railways could not be sold:

> I became convinced that the government ought to grasp the nettle and do something about British Rail privatisation... It was something a Tory minister was bound to want to do, bound to want to look at, but I found it astonishing that it hadn't been looked at earlier in a big way... I was the first person to take a big step on it.

Why Thatcher dropped her earlier objections to a rail sell-off and allowed Channon to raise the issue so overtly remains unclear, even to Channon himself:

> I casually let it be known that I wanted to announce at the [1988] Party conference the fact that the government was going to privatise BR... I went to some meetings in September 1988 and asked permission to make this announcement at the Party conference. There were all sorts of wise people saying 'oh, you can't do that, it's much too dangerous, the ground hasn't been prepared' and all that and Mrs Thatcher was fairly lukewarm. She said I could say something if I would submit the exact form of words to her before the Party conference. So about a week before the Party conference, I wrote to her with the paragraphs that I wanted to use in my speech about rail privatisation. To my astonishment, within 48 hours I had them back with no comment.

Whatever Thatcher's reasoning, Channon announced shortly after the Conference that the DoT was considering potential models for rail privatisation (Webster, 1988).　In a speech at a Centre for Policy Studies (CPS) conference he listed them and outlined in general the pros and cons of each (see Table 3.2) (Channon, 1988).　Two of the sale options were lifted directly from the proposals outlined in section 4.3 above – the regional and track authority models – and three, 'BR plc,' sectorisation and a 'hybrid' approach, were new.

Table 3.2   Advantages and disadvantages of possible rail privatisation models identified by the DoT in 1988*

Model	Advantages	Disadvantages
Regional	Some competition, but largely indirect; Improved moral through local loyalty; Improved flexibility and efficiency	Potential difficulties with network benefits; Problems with through trains between regions; Possible loss of economies of scale; Business 'mix' within each region requires division of management attention
Track authority	Promotes competition	On-rail competition limited by railway practicalities, e.g. economics, capacity; Track authority still a monopoly and difficult to regulate; Track authority remote from rail users; Investment decisions difficult
BR plc	Continuity of style and structure; Minimal cost of privatisation	Not even limited competition; Size of BR has engendered 'diseconomies of complexity'; Lack of operational transparency
Sectoris-ation	Avoids dilution of commercial incentives by concentrating loss-making services together	Difficulties with track ownership
Hybrid	Better features of other models can be incorporated while their drawbacks can be avoided	

* The limited number and nature of points raised indicates that the proposals were still being considered at a general level.

Source: Channon (1988).

The BR plc option involved a direct transfer of BR from the public to the private sector in the same way that BT and BG had been sold. The sectorisation model was an extension of BR's existing management structure. Until 1982, BR had been organised largely on a regional basis, with each region managing its own planning, marketing and operation of services, as well as maintaining its own infrastructure. For commercial and accounting purposes BR was reorganised in 1982 into five business sectors, each designed to be relatively homogenous in the type of traffic it managed (the physical operation of trains was still undertaken by the regions at this stage). InterCity provided high speed services between major conurbations; London and South East served the commuter market in that area; Provincial operated the remaining, regional passenger services; and freight and parcels handled non-passenger trains. Although further reorganisation – to marry managerial and operational responsibility – would have been necessary before privatisation, it was these businesses which the sectorisation model would have sold to the private sector.[5] Finally, the form of the hybrid model had not been determined by 1988 and it was noted only that this "option would allow some of the better features of the other [proposals] to be incorporated, while avoiding some of the drawbacks" (Channon, 1988: 37).

Despite the emphasis placed on the potential for market liberalisation in some of the 1988 proposals (Redwood, 1988), Channon was not especially enthusiastic about the idea and was instead more concerned about effecting a straightforward sale (commenting about the approach finally adopted, he said: "my successors took all sorts of different decisions [but] I wouldn't have done it this way at all"). Reports had suggested that Channon was impressed by the sectorisation and 'BR plc' models (Leadbeater *et al.*, 1989; Brown, 1989). Not only would these methods obviate the need for a complex restructuring exercise, but they were also approved by BR's management. The BRB was of the opinion that if privatisation had to take place, it should do so by way of a unitary solution, but members were prepared to accept sectorisation as a possible alternative (a report by Coopers & Lybrand in 1989 would find in favour of the latter and the BRB endorsed its findings). In reality, Channon was not particularly swayed by the feelings of the BRB and instead favoured Gritten's (1988) regional approach, chiefly because he saw it as a potential vote-winner:

It would be in different regions again... That's the solution that I would have done – at least, when I left, that was the front runner. I was very keen to do that... I thought it would be nice, people would like to go back on the Great Western or whatever and that was certainly the chief runner at that stage.

Before Channon could examine his preferred choice more closely, he was replaced as Secretary of State for Transport by Cecil Parkinson. Parkinson's approach differed from Channon's in that his success at introducing competition into the electricity industry led him to sympathise with David Starkie's view that a degree of rail competition was needed, although in the absence of a sufficiently thorough analysis he did not necessarily favour Starkie's suggestion of how it should be secured.

Yet Parkinson found himself unable to advance the debate during his time as Secretary of State, as he discovered upon arrival at the DoT that Thatcher had again lost interest in selling BR after becoming alarmed at adverse public reaction to Channon's plans (Irvine, 1987). He sent Thatcher a draft copy of his speech for the 1989 Conservative Party Conference, which built upon Channon's announcement of the previous year, but "got a message back saying she'd be grateful if I'd leave the subject alone and not say anything." Press speculation began to suggest that the Conservatives were planning to shelve indefinitely their plans to sell BR (Stephens, 1989) and Parkinson felt it was necessary to emphasise that this was not the case:

> I got a message back saying she'd be grateful if I would leave the subject alone and not say anything. I actually went to see her in Blackpool and said 'look, if I don't say anything that will be seen as a retreat and... I don't think we should be seen to be backing off.' So we agreed a form of words like 'studies continue.'

Parkinson stated publicly after the conference that plans for selling BR "are not at the top of my list of priorities at the moment" (quoted in Stephens and Brown, 1989: 10), but he continued to pressure Thatcher into giving a firm commitment to privatise. He acknowledged that the government did not have a mandate to sell BR (a potential sale had not been mentioned in the 1987 election manifesto) but, drawing on his experience with electricity privatisation where "I had arrived at the beginning of a parliament with no plans" at all,

> I said that I would like to get it in the open so that we could start the discussions and we could develop our ideas. Then, by the time we came back after the next election, which was 1992... we could have [already] developed plans so we could crash straight into the business of getting on with it and reorganising [BR].

Thatcher finally changed her mind in the autumn of 1990, just prior to her being replaced against her wishes as Party leader, although once more it is uncertain why she changed her mind (a cynic might suggest she was leaving a hornets' nest for the successor administration as an act of revenge against certain individuals she accused of 'treachery'). Nevertheless, Parkinson was able to announce to Parliament that the government was now "determined to privatise British Rail" (*Hansard*, 1990, Col. 606).

In 1990, a decade after Norman Fowler had first suggested privatising BR's core activities, the Conservatives had finally announced a firm intention to sell the railways. The various disagreements and delays throughout the 1980s had, however, resulted in the DoT undertaking little detailed work on the subject. It had not yet been decided which of the five models advanced at the CPS conference would be employed to privatise BR – one former DoT official remembered that the period had been spent "looking at options and more options and saying, 'let's have a look at some options'" – and Thatcher (1993: 676) herself noted that such an exercise would pose "large questions which needed careful thought and economic analysis."

The working group

A working group comprising ministers and officials from the DoT, the Treasury and the Department of Trade and Industry was established in the autumn of 1990 to decide on a blueprint for the privatisation and liberalisation of BR. Parkinson left the DoT when Thatcher was ousted from Downing Street and, as a result, did not contribute in any meaningful way to the deliberations of the group. The latter was able to proceed without significant objections from Downing Street because the new Prime Minister, John Major, was an advocate of rail privatisation. Parkinson's replacement, Malcolm Rifkind, shared some of his predecessor's enthusiasm for market liberalisation, but concluded that Starkie's model of vertical separation would be unnecessarily complex.

Rifkind was particularly concerned that separating infrastructure from operations might place too high a proportion of train operators' costs at the whim of the track authority. He argued on this basis that vertical separation was not advisable and his initial thoughts were to modify the regional solution by keeping the InterCity business intact, possibly on an integrated basis. Not only would this allow a degree of continuity for passengers and rail managers, but it would also provide scope for some competition between origin/destination pairs served by both InterCity and a regional company. Rifkind's desire to liberalise BR's service market resulted in proposals for the swift introduction of on-rail competition and he wrote (with no impact) to the BRB asking it to consider admitting new entrants onto its network in advance of privatisation (Clarke, 2000). Rifkind's suggestions were designed to allow most operations to be undertaken by companies who owned and maintained at least some of their infrastructure.

In contrast, the Treasury and the DTI supported the track authority model. The bulk of the Treasury's enthusiasm for this option came about because of its apparent ability to promote competition. A small number of Treasury officials in particular were convinced by Starkie's argument that BR behaved like a monopoly, especially in major commuter areas such as London, and were fully persuaded by the case for vertical separation. It is important to note, however, that their enthusiasm for vertical separation was not the result of experience in the transport sector, but rather their involvement with the break up of the CEGB.

The sale of the CEGB had been a model neoliberal privatisation. Since restructuring, the electricity generating industry had seen genuine competition emerge and efficiency increase and the state had been able to significantly reduce its role in the industry's affairs (see chapter two). In comparing the performance of the electricity generators with that of BT and BG, the Treasury, like Parkinson, had come to believe that the fundamental requirement of privatisation policy was the promotion of genuine competition: greater efficiency and investment, improved levels of service and enhanced customer care would all *automatically* follow.

Whereas technical factors had prevented competition from being extended beyond the generating sector of the electricity industry, rail privatisation was seen as an opportunity to experiment further with vertical separation. Undeterred by the consideration that BR, unlike the CEGB, did not make a profit and that competition might be difficult to introduce into a loss-making industry, Treasury officials drew an analogy between the structure of the privatised electricity industry and the track authority model of rail privatisation. One senior civil servant remembers that:

> They [the Treasury] were convinced that the model was to try and strip things down to the natural monopoly... accept that was a monopoly and regulate it, but everywhere else bring in competition. So when they

approached BR, they said 'where is the natural monopoly in BR? Let's strip it down, let's isolate that, let's try and break the rest of it up into units which can be open for competition in a variety of ways'... And that's the model they were convinced of, as being right.

Treasury staff could even use the onset of a new recession (see chapter two) to their advantage. Whereas in the past the government had not broken up utilities on the grounds that monopolies fetched a higher sale price, evidence from the electricity privatisation now enabled officials to argue that competition created by vertical separation would increase rail operators' efficiency and thus lower the future subsidy bill.

In light of this disagreement between Departments, the working group's conclusions, outlined in a report in mid 1991, were a compromise. A hybrid solution was recommended, which suggested that there should be a separation of infrastructure and operations throughout most of the UK, but that the London commuter area should remain vertically integrated. Although Treasury officials thought that competition would be difficult to introduce in the South East if rail companies were vertically integrated, they accepted this compromise because they estimated that the amount of rail congestion around London would preclude most theoretical opportunities for competition there in any case. They also accepted that a degree of social and economic regulation, in addition to the imposition of minimum service levels (see section 3.1), would probably be needed to protect consumers in the absence of on-rail competition. The Treasury was not to know at this stage that its wish to create a network-wide track authority would subsequently be granted.

The conclusions of the working group were adopted in principle by Cabinet following the circulation of its report and the DoT and the Treasury were cleared to finalise policy details in the run-up to the 1992 general election (the DTI had stepped back from proceedings by this stage). Although a policy to secure a genuine move towards market liberalisation throughout most of the country had now been agreed, the practicalities and implications peculiar to the hybrid model had still to be analysed and legislation needed to be drafted. Key officials had hoped, like Parkinson in 1990, to undertake these tasks before the next general election, due no later than spring 1992, in order that the policy could be implemented quickly in the 1992-1997 Parliament. As the next section shows, however, a definitive policy decision was not taken as soon as many both within – and outside of – the government would have liked.

3.5 Adopting a model for rail privatisation

Although the conclusions of the working group were clear, Rifkind soon began to have second thoughts. The Secretary of State, as already noted, disliked the idea of a track authority and began to distance himself from the hybrid model (for which, of course, his Department was partly responsible). Rifkind attached a new importance to sectorisation, mainly because he now viewed it as the most straightforward way of retaining a vertically integrated InterCity business. As such, he devoted manpower to re-examining sectorisation and temporarily halted the development of the rail privatisation Bill. The ensuing delay intensely frustrated the Treasury because it had wanted to forge ahead with drafting legislation, but officials were able to use the extra time to subject their conception of a track authority to some further analysis and this was to prove beneficial because academics and transport economists had identified several operational shortcomings with the idea by this stage.

The advent of franchising

Although there was an apparent analogy between the separation of generation and distribution activities in the electricity industry and the creation of a track authority for the railways, it was in fact far from perfect (Adamson *et al.*, 1991). It has already been noted that BR, unlike the electricity industry, lost money. In terms of operations, however, perhaps the most obvious difference is that whilst electricity generated by competing companies can be supplied simultaneously to different customers using the same cables, it is clearly impossible to run two or more trains along a given stretch of track at the same time. Services between origin/destination pairs have to be run according to a series of dedicated train paths monitored by the track authority. According to one official, the Treasury had intended simply to auction available paths to whoever offered the highest bid or required the lowest subsidy:

They had a view... that, if they had the time, they would have devised a rather more sophisticated structure of allocating railway slots, which was effectively a system of auctioning... [but] with some minimum requirements for grossly anti-competitive behaviour like running a train fractionally in front of another train and all that kind of stuff.

In this way, not only would there be competition in the market, between train services, but also for the market, through the auctioning of paths.

It became evident that such a scheme would be inoperable, at least in the short term. The heterogeneous nature of rail services – trains serve different markets by running at different speeds and frequencies – means that they are vastly interdependent. Any company bidding for rights to run, for example, a half-hourly stopping service between London Euston and Birmingham New Street would generate certain train-path requirements over a route shared with other operators. Running this service would thus affect the availability of paths for other operators wishing to offer a different type of service on the same, or different, routes. Conflicts arising in this way were resolved by BR through co-ordination in the timetabling process, but in practical terms it would be extremely difficult to replicate this through market mechanisms (Nash, 1990; Nash and Preston, 1993). Bids from different companies for potential services over the whole network would inevitably clash and a first auction would become impossible. Unsuccessful tenderers would therefore need to reconsider their need for paths in the knowledge that some were already allocated to a competitor (Adamson *et al.*, 1991).

Moreover, even if paths could be efficiently allocated, day to day operational problems were identified in the form of *externalities* and the loss of *network benefits*. Externalities can be divided into two categories, 'train to train' and 'track to train' (Jones *et al.*, 1993). The former occur as delays to one service, perhaps owing to locomotive breakdown, affect the running of others, whereas the latter arise as trains are delayed by a failure of the infrastructure. Both often have a 'snowballing' effect because of the interdependency of rail services and their resolution presents a host of complex problems. As Foster (1992) notes, each late train requires a consequential decision: shall following trains be delayed? Whose train? Who should then compensate whom for lost traffic? It became evident that, even with a logical (yet elaborate) accounting scheme, such problems would probably not be soluble without considerable goodwill from the multitude of operators. The existence of such goodwill in a competitive industry could not be guaranteed.

Network benefits are advantages which accrue to passengers from the existence of a unified railway network (*House of Commons Papers*, 1993a). Tickets can be purchased from any one station on the network to any other; and tickets can be 'inter-available' – that is to say, passengers can purchase one ticket and use it on any train between an origin/destination pair. As Jones *et al.* (1993) point out, the fragmentation of rail operations can result in problems with co-ordinating the sale of 'through' tickets which involve numerous changes of operator and/or the cessation of ticket inter-availability. In cases of the latter, rail would lose its 'turn up and go' facility because passengers would have to buy operator-specific (or 'dedicated') tickets. A passenger wishing to travel from, say, Plymouth to Exeter St David's might purchase a ticket to use an infrequent Regional Railways train because it was cheaper, but in so doing would forfeit the right to travel by more frequent InterCity services.

Finally, arguments unconnected with trainpath auctioning were advanced in opposition to the track authority model. The DoT had noted that effecting a track-train split could result in the track authority abusing its monopoly; that the track authority would be remote from rail users and responsibility for service shortcomings would be difficult to pin down; and that investment would be difficult to attract and co-ordinate (Redwood, 1988; see also Helm and Thompson, 1991).[6] The combination of all the above factors led Adamson *et al.* (1991) to question whether the passenger train industry could be reorganised into a potentially competitive industry if it was vertically separated. Bradshaw (1991: 25) went further, suggesting that the track authority model offended "every professional principle of railway operation" and was "likely to result in an outcome which will be expensive, unsuitable and unsafe."

The Treasury was forced to concede that its plans for a system of train path auctioning would be unworkable given the limited time available to address these issues. It suggested passenger rail franchising as an alternative. Franchising had been employed by the Conservatives to privatise other industries, such as local authority services (see chapter two), and was perceived by ministers to be a generally successful method of privatisation (see also chapter seven). In the context of the railways it would mean combining groups of train paths, perhaps over a given area, to be offered to the private sector as one package. In this way, some competition for the market would be maintained by inviting tenders for subsidy relating to the whole package of routes and competition in the market would occur in border areas where operating territories overlapped. The Treasury argued in addition that open access operations should be permitted, where a market for them existed, subject to as yet undefined operating constraints arising from franchise commitments.

A senior official recalls that franchising was seen by the Treasury as a "much cruder model" than the "sophisticated auctioning of... slots," but recognised that it was a means of at least partially addressing the problems which arose under a regime of train-path auctioning. By combining the path requirements of numerous services, the potential for reducing the number of operators on the network – and thus the complexity of inter-operator dealings – would be considerable: trains could be co-ordinated in a central timetable before franchises were let (with a degree of flexibility retained for private operators to re-arrange service patterns in the future); the majority of train to train externalities could be 'internalised' because delays to any given service would principally affect other services run by the same operator; the resolution of track to train externalities would be simplified for the same reason; and attempts to secure network benefits would be somewhat more straightforward with a smaller number of operators working to a co-ordinated timetable. Once a framework to resolve these issues in the context of franchise operation had been established, it was suggested that open access services could be slotted in around existing services with relative ease.

Franchising did not provide a complete solution to the problems with train-path auctioning identified above – it only moderated them – and there was no guarantee that any remaining difficulties would be straightforward to resolve. Nevertheless, the Treasury had at least been working within the framework of the hybrid model advanced by the 1991 working group. In contrast, the DoT's position on rail privatisation, following Rifkind's decision to re-evaluate sectorisation, had fallen into disarray. An insider remembers Rifkind "agonising over whether InterCity should be vertically integrated or not," and that the remainder of 1991 was a "saga of... grief within the DoT." So long as the DoT failed to commit itself to a formal policy option, policy makers were unable to develop their ideas further and have legislation drafted.

With hindsight, it could be argued that decisive action by Downing Street at some point during this period would have helped restore a sense of direction to rail privatisation policy. What actually happened was precisely the opposite. Rather than instructing the DoT to accept the hybrid model on the basis that it had been formally adopted by the Cabinet, Major's Policy Unit began advancing solutions of its own based around the regional concept. Downing Street's action served only to confuse matters further and there was "tremendous faffing around... between the Department [of Transport], the Treasury and the cabinet secretariat who were trying to pull [rail privatisation policy] together – and not succeeding." At least three models were now being considered – hybrid, sectorisation and regional – with none, other than the track authority element of the hybrid model, having received much more than a cursory analysis.

Framing the policy

The Conservatives were obliged to call a general election by spring 1992, but at the beginning of that year there was still no consensus between Departments about rail privatisation. A White Paper on the subject had been promised for before the election but it was being delayed as ministers and officials continued to argue over the most appropriate industry structure (*Financial Times*, 1992a). As polling day neared, policy necessarily became considered in the context of an election campaign. One official pointed out that, "by the end of [1991] we'd lost a whole bloody year faffing around and number 10 suddenly said 'we've got to write an election manifesto.'" Thus:

> The deal was brokered not in the context of considered papers or great meetings; [it] was brokered by a guy, Jonathan Hill, in the policy unit at Number 10 essentially – almost literally – walking around Whitehall with the bit for the manifesto. That was the way the final deal was done.

It is perhaps an overstatement even to refer to the manifesto commitment as a 'deal'. The only firm policy decision which appears to have been taken in terms of industry structure by April 1992 was that of ruling out Rifkind's sectorisation model (Tomkins, 1992a). The manifesto (Conservative Party, 1992: 35-36) promised a track authority ("one part of BR will continue to be responsible for all track and infrastructure") and at the same time kept alive the possibility of regions ("our aim will be... to reflect regional and local identity... we want to... recapture the spirit of the old regional companies"). The wording could have referred to the hybrid solution, where BR would maintain control of operations in the Network SouthEast territory; the universal track authority solution; or a vertically integrated regional solution, where the infrastructure would be divided among several track authorities coinciding with the territories of train operators. As a respondent, who had been observing developments from outside government circles, correctly guessed,

> ...minister X wanted something in about competition, minister Y wanted something in about regions and so on. So they just cobbled something together which appeared, in manifesto terms, to satisfy all this lot. And they went with that.

When John MacGregor was appointed as Secretary of State for Transport following the Conservatives' election victory in 1992, there was, according to a former minister, "not quite a blank sheet of paper as our election commitment, but very close to it. Just a few outlines about how [rail privatisation] might work." Another respondent added that because of "Rifkind blowing [1991] out of the water and things being resolved in the context of drafting the manifesto, when they won the election we had nothing drafted at all. There was no base." MacGregor's job was to resolve the debate over industry structure and present a Bill before Parliament as soon as possible. Although ministers were quoted as saying privatisation would be gradual and might take up to 10 years (*Financial Times*, 1992b), the real intention was always to complete the sale before the next general election. As Roger Freeman, then Minister of State for Public Transport (effectively MacGregor's second-in-command), pointed out, "you either did it or you didn't – and if you did it, you had to complete it."

Along with officials and ministerial colleagues, MacGregor undertook a "huge amount of work" in May and June 1992 to frame final proposals outlining how BR would be privatised:

> He spent the first two months [after the election] making up his own mind as to whether the framework – almost the blank sheet of paper in the manifesto – was the right framework or whether we should go differently. Horizontal and vertical integration was one crucial aspect of that.

MacGregor was also assisted by Sir Christopher Foster, then a partner at Coopers & Lybrand, who had been appointed as a special advisor on rail privatisation. Foster was, like the Treasury, a proponent of the track authority model, although his enthusiasm for vertical separation was based on substantially different reasons than the Treasury's. Foster was not convinced by the case for on-rail competition, largely because he saw the potential for it to create instability in a loss-making industry, at least in the initial stages of privatisation (see chapter six). As he pointed out, "not too much should ever be expected of competition between trains on the same route" (Foster, 1994: 19). Foster instead saw opportunities for efficiency gains through the franchising process and the need to formalise by contract the relationships between the various components of the rail industry. He outlined his views in his subsequent publication, *The Economics of Rail Privatisation* (Foster, 1994).

Foster's arrival at the DoT was nevertheless to suit Treasury ministers and officials because it increased the likelihood of them realising their original aim of a network-wide track authority as opposed to the partial one included in the hybrid model. Following Rifkind's example of abandoning the hybrid in favour of his own preferences, the Treasury had by now decided to do likewise and seek a complete vertical separation. Just six weeks after the Conservatives' election victory, this is exactly what they got: although Foster recalls initial misgivings regarding this option on the part of some within the DoT, a policy outline advocating the creation of a network-wide track authority was "hammered out" and accepted by MacGregor.

A key point to note is that the decision to adopt the track authority model should not be regarded as the result of a particularly thorough or detailed policy analysis. Despite the protracted evolution of rail privatisation policy and the existence of numerous models advanced by academics, think tanks, politicians and civil servants, MacGregor did not have the time to choose the track authority model on the strength of a lengthy evaluation of the available options. In view of the time constraints which he faced, it seems that he was forced into accepting vertical separation as it was effectively his only choice. With Rifkind's sectorisation plans rejected and the DoT's half of the hybrid model still incomplete, the track authority had at least been subjected to an evaluation of sorts. If the railways were to be sold within the 1992-1997 Parliament, there would not have been time to analyse the remaining alternatives any further. Moreover, both the Treasury and Foster were able to contend – somewhat disingenuously – that a new European Directive, introduced in 1991 to require a split in accounting in member states' railway industries, now further supported their case for a network-wide track authority (see Knill and Lehmkuhl, 1998).[7] Freeman implies that he, along with many DoT officials, had resigned himself to the inevitability of vertical separation:

> Put it this way. MacGregor stood back and reviewed the options to familiarise himself with his brief at Transport. He just wanted to make sure that vertical separation would work. He may have said in public, 'we're doing another consultation', but in reality we all knew what the outcome would be.

Former BR chairman Sir Bob Reid identifies Foster's view as being the primary influence behind MacGregor's decision to adopt the track authority model. In 1995, Reid noted that the debate over how to privatise BR "was a dogmatic argument of three or four years ago. We lost [BR had, of course, supported a vertically integrated solution]. It means we now have a structure that is more complicated than necessary" (*The Guardian*, 1995: 6). Foster's support for vertical separation was no doubt high in MacGregor's mind when he took the decision to adopt it, but Reid's view overlooks the influence of the Treasury, whose desire to maximise competition had seen it campaigning for a track authority of one form or another since 1990. More significant, however, is the fact that although Foster did not support the enthusiastic and immediate pursuit of on-rail competition, *New Opportunities for the Railways* was to emphasise heavily its importance (see below) and this would suggest that MacGregor deferred to the preferences of the Treasury rather than those of his special advisor. MacGregor argues he knew early on that on-rail competition would not work but delayed announcing this for tactical reasons. Given the troubles which had beset rail privatisation policy formulation, this is perhaps understandable – as MacGregor's first priority was to resolve the policy debate, he couldn't risk any further delays which might have arisen if the Treasury had protested – but seems unlikely as there was a compelling *political* reason for him to avoid publicly endorsing the Treasury's proposals. As will be seen below and in subsequent chapters, the idea of on-rail competition – which by the time of the White Paper's publication was already being met with considerable hostility from commentators – would trouble MacGregor throughout much of his time as Secretary of State for Transport.

The Treasury, of course, favoured vertical separation as it was perceived to be the most effective means of liberalising BR's market.

Officials believed that on rail competition, a central plank of their strategy, would improve the efficiency and quality of services while decreasing their cost in the same way as in the electricity industry. Their assumption was that the model used to sell the CEGB could, with only a few minor changes, simply be transferred to the privatisation of BR. Yet relatively little consideration had been given to whether or not this approach was entirely suitable for privatising and liberalising the railway industry. Although both Starkie and the ASI had advocated competition through vertical separation before it was embraced by the Treasury, their analyses, in the context of exploring potential implementation strategies or even a broad range of likely outcomes, had been rather elementary – an editorial in *Modern Railways* (1988) described the thinking behind the ASI's arguments as being of less than A-level standard.

The Treasury's own evaluation was more rigorous – it acknowledged some of the more obvious shortcomings in the analogy between a track authority for BR and the National Grid for the electricity industry – but still provided MacGregor with only a framework, beyond which there was very minimal detail. Little had been worked out regarding: the calculation and allocation of track access charges; the formation and vesting of successor rail companies; the specifications and administration of franchises; the precise functions and responsibilities of the regulators; the likelihood of privatising the structure within one Parliament or the probable cost of the exercise. Most importantly in terms of this book, the opportunities for, and appropriateness of, service competition and the potential impact of market liberalisation upon the relationship between the railways and the state had not been closely examined.

Foster argues that there had been "substantial analysis of many points" in the short time before MacGregor made his decision and he identifies that ministers had taken time to satisfy themselves regarding basic concerns such as safety. Nevertheless, his comments should be taken in the context of the issues raised in this chapter. When *New Opportunities for the Railways* was published, it is probable that ministers could not be sure that many aspects of the track authority model would be capable of providing what was expected of it. MacGregor certainly could not be sure that the plans he had adopted would be capable of promoting actual, rather than surrogate, competition.

3.6 New opportunities for the railways

The White Paper

Having finally decided upon vertical separation, ministers were now faced
with the task of formulating policy detail and producing a workable industry
structure. This was essentially undertaken over a three year period between
1992 and 1995, beginning with the publication of *New Opportunities for the
Railways*. The document noted that ministers wished to see "a reliable,
efficient operation offering high quality services to users," and confirmed the
view that "the introduction of competition... and the ending of BR's
monopoly in the operation of services will be instrumental in achieving this"
(DoT, 1992a: 1). The government's wish to liberate private sector
management from state control in order to harness its "skills, flair and
entrepreneurial spirit" was also emphasised (DoT, 1992a: i; Welsby and
Nicholls, 1999). The White Paper set out the government's commitment to
establishing a track authority, Railtrack, and to splitting BR's passenger
services up into franchises which would be awarded by competitive
tendering. In addition, the document noted the intention to provide for open
access competition:

> Companies wishing to provide new railway services... will have a right of
> access to the railway network... [At present], there is no choice of operator
> for the rail passenger... liberalising access to the network will [provide] the
> opportunity for new operators to run services. This will give... rail operators
> the stimulus of competition to provide better service quality and value for
> money (DoT, 1992a: 13).

Responsibility for negotiating, awarding and monitoring franchises would be
transferred to a new Franchising Authority, whilst the rights of access for
both franchised and non-franchised operators would be overseen by a new
Rail Regulator.

Although it received some support (see, for example, *House of
Commons Papers*, 1992a) *New Opportunities for the Railways* attracted
numerous hostile commentaries, not least because the plans appeared ill-
considered and lacking in detail. Of course, a White Paper is not necessarily
the place in which a thorough exposition of a new government policy is
found, but *New Opportunities for the Railways* was seen by many as being

exceptionally vague. The then Chairman of the Transport Select Committee, Robert Adley MP, argued that a Green Paper should have preceded the White in order to allow a fuller debate of its detail and likely implications before legislation was published (*Hansard*, 1993a). MacGregor did not deny that "in working through some of the proposals, it is clear that much work remains to be done" (*Hansard*, 1992a: Col. 974). Crucial aspects of the work to which MacGregor referred were not, in fact, completed when the Railways Bill was presented to the House of Commons in early 1993 (Nash, 1993). As later chapters will show, certain issues had proved complicated to resolve and, because of the need to proceed with rail privatisation as soon as possible, it was decided not to wait until the plans were fully formulated before drafting legislation. The solution was to produce a Bill which contained numerous enabling powers and to continue policymaking during, and after, its passage through Parliament. As one respondent who was involved in drafting the legislation admitted, "the Bill was a mess, and it had lots of enabling powers rather than specific proposals... [because] the thing wasn't properly prepared."

During the Bill's second reading, Liberal Democrat MP Nick Harvey mocked its vague content when he pointed out that:

> The Bill comprises 132 clauses and 11 schedules and gives massive powers to the Secretary of State... It might have been preferable to have had a Bill of one clause which simply said 'the Secretary of State can do what he likes, how he likes when he likes and where he likes.' It would have had more or less the same effect (*Hansard*, 1993b: 190).

MacGregor, in contrast, argued that "the principles and the main structure of the Bill are entirely consistent with [those in] the White Paper" (*Hansard*, 1993b: 160). It is true that the offices of the Rail Regulator and Franchising Director were established, along with the concept of franchising and several technical details such as closure procedures. Beyond this, however, MacGregor's assertion is somewhat spurious. Although a deviation from the White Paper was *unlikely* because of the circumstances in which the policy had been decided, the Bill was not necessarily consistent with *New Opportunities for the Railways* in several crucial areas precisely because it was vague. To illustrate, no details were provided as to: the structure of the industry (the Bill noted merely that the Secretary of State could instruct the BRB to form a number of companies); the framework within which on-rail competition could develop (it was stated only that a facility owner might be instructed to allow more than one company access to its assets); or how it would be regulated (although some duties were assigned to the Regulator and the Franchising Director, the majority of their functions were to be prescribed by the Secretary of State at a future, unspecified, date) (House of Commons, 1993).

The new railway structure

The majority of these details were finally forthcoming in 1994 and were summarised in *Britain's Railways: A new Era* (DoT, 1994). Although the 'new' railway appears complex in comparison with its predecessor, BR, the structure is in fact quite logical when viewed in the context of the electricity industry privatisation (or, indeed, any industry which is characterised by a substantial vertical division of labour). A brief overview of the new structure is presented here and further details regarding the provision of passenger services are given as appropriate in chapters four to six.

As indicated in the White Paper, BR was divided into two basic elements: infrastructure and operations. Control of the rail infrastructure passed to Railtrack, which became responsible for the safety, maintenance and renewal of the railway network and now operates in seven zonal divisions.[8] Railtrack also co-ordinates train movements and, subject to the Regulator's approval, grants train operators access to the track. BR's operations business was divided into 91 separate companies which can be placed in six groups that reflect the nature of their activities (DoT, 1994; 1996a). These are:

- *Train Operating Companies (TOCs)* – 25 franchises to provide passenger rail services. The franchises were awarded to the private sector by competitive tender and, at the time of divestiture, the TOCs accounted for passenger services formerly operated by BR. In addition to the 25 TOCs, the Railways Act provided for the operation of non-franchised passenger services on an open access basis. These trains would run in addition to those operated by TOCs to stimulate further on-rail competition (see chapter six).
- *Freight* – seven companies to operate freight trains. Five (Rail Express Systems, Loadhaul, Mainline, Transrail and Railfreight Distribution) were sold to a business consortium led by Wisconsin Central

Transportation, now trading as English, Welsh and Scottish Railway (EWS). Red Star Parcels and Freightliner were sold to management buy-out teams (MBOs). Open access competition in the freight sector is also provided for the by the Railways Act.

- *Rolling Stock Companies (Roscos)* – three businesses, Porterbrook Leasing, Eversholt Leasing (now HSBC Rail) and Angel Train Contracts, established to lease rolling stock and locomotives to the TOCs. BR's railway vehicles were divided such that each Rosco owned a balanced portfolio at the time of divestiture.

- *British Rail Infrastructure Services (BRIS)* – 20 companies concerned with the maintenance of track and signalling established initially on a regional basis.

- *British Rail Maintenance Limited (BRML)* – seven businesses to undertake the heavy overhaul of rolling stock and locomotives.

- *Central* – 27 companies to provide general support services to the industry such as telecommunications, consultancy and research.

With the exception of TOCs, all businesses were sold outright to the private sector.[9] A full list of all the rail businesses established, along with their sale details, is provided in appendix one.

Companies within the new structure interact on a commercial, contractual basis and the whole system is essentially financed through the TOCs. TOCs' payment of track access charges, rolling stock leasing charges and other bills in turn enables Railtrack and the Roscos to let contracts for maintenance, renewal, support services and so on (see Figure 3.1). Subsidy is paid to TOCs to cover any shortfalls between their costs and revenue receipts – at the time of privatisation one TOC, Gatwick Express, paid a premium for the right to run its services on account of their profitability – and the amounts payable were determined by competitive tender during the franchising process. TOCs receive a declining level of support (or pay increasing premia) – thus increasing their risk of financial loss – because their bids were predicated on a substantial growth in business over the coming years (see chapter five). If a franchisee goes bankrupt, the state reassumes control of the affected TOC(s) and initiates a new round of tendering. Subsidy cannot be paid to open access operators, as their services must be run on a commercial basis.

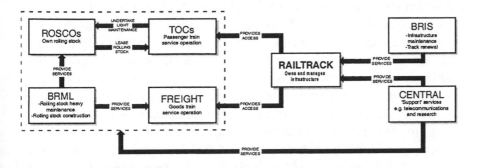

Figure 3.1   Company-group interactions in the new railway structure

Source: Charlton *et al.*, 1997.

Despite predictions that the government would save money through vertical integration (see section 3.4), the overall level of subsidy payable to the railway industry increased as a result of privatisation (Knowles, 1998). By splitting BR into 92 companies, the Conservatives vastly increased the transaction costs within the industry because each new business needed to trade at a profit. When the railway was still in public ownership, the net subsidy payable by the government was similar to that prior to reorganisation because the Treasury would administer and receive the profits made by all 92 companies (these have been estimated by White (1998) as amounting to around £880m per year). When these companies were privatised, however, their profits passed to the private sector while the level of subsidy remained static. White (1998) has calculated that, even when sales revenues from Railtrack, the Roscos and other rail businesses are accounted for, privatising BR could – although such a scenario is highly unlikely – have incurred a net *cost* to the state of as much as £2.2 billion 15 years after the sale. (Harris and Godward (1997) suggest this cost might be as high as £5 billion.) The potential for net gains depends on the declining subsidy payments to TOCs secured during the franchising process (see chapters five and seven).

The creation of a number of companies within each group provided the potential for competition not only among train operators but, excepting the infrastructure, throughout the whole industry. In theory, a TOC can choose between competing Roscos; Railtrack can choose between competing track maintenance companies and so on. Leaving passenger train operators aside (they are considered in chapters four to six), competition was initially slow to emerge throughout the industry. Partly this was because the Conservatives misjudged market conditions (for example, the relatively small rail freight business could not support seven discrete companies) and partly it was owing to the nature of contracts drawn up to formalise working arrangements between each of the individual businesses (Charlton *et al.*, 1997). Most firms were sold with fixed term contracts which guaranteed them a market for a finite period (thereby raising their sale value above a nominal level). For example, whereas in theory TOCs could choose between three competing Roscos to negotiate rolling stock deals, in practice most leasing contracts were designed to match the length of the first franchise period (OPRAF, 1996a); TOCs were bound by *de facto* monopolies as a result. The same was true of Railtrack's relationship with the BRIS units, although competition is now developing for infrastructure maintenance contracts (SBC Warburg, 1996; *Modern Railways*, 1998a).

Of course, many would argue that the imposition of fixed term contracts was a necessary stabilising measure in a newly restructured industry and that competition will emerge when current deals expire and are re-negotiated. This will to some extent be the case, although a marked trend of horizontal and vertical integration currently occurring within the industry could limit considerably the potential for market liberalisation in the future (see, for example, Charlton *et al.*, 1997; Curwen, 1997; Simonian, 1996).

The regulatory framework within which the industry operates was established in large part by the Regulator and the Franchising Director, following directions from the Secretary of State. At the simplest level, the Regulator is responsible for granting and monitoring licences to TOCs, approving access agreements between Railtrack and train operators, protecting consumers and promoting competition (Office of the Rail Regulator (ORR), 1996). Constitutionally, the Regulator is independent from the government, although he was required to take account of guidance from the Secretary of State until January 1st, 1996.

The Franchising Director was given the roles of transferring the TOCs from the public to the private sector as quickly as reasonably practicable, paying subsidies to (and, in some cases, collecting premiums from) TOCs and undertaking consumer protection measures which complement those of the Regulator (OPRAF, 1994; 1996a). Unlike the Regulator, the Franchising Director does not enjoy constitutional independence from the government, primarily because he administers subsidy on its behalf. As a result, he is obliged to follow Objectives, Instructions and Guidance given to him from time to time by the Secretary of State. Whereas the roles of the Regulator and Franchising Director in relation to this book are discussed in more detail later, fuller analyses of the interaction between all the various actors in the new railway can be found elsewhere in the literature (see, for example, Bradshaw, 1997a; Curwen, 1997; Charlton *et al.*, 1997; DoT, 1994; Freeman and Shaw, 2000; Harris and Godward, 1997; OPRAF, 1996a).

3.7 Conclusion

This chapter has reviewed the development of rail policy in the context of privatisation and market liberalisation established in chapter two. The track authority model of rail privatisation was employed to break what was perceived by some – including Conservative ministers and senior Treasury officials – as BR's monopoly and it essentially represented further experimentation with the method used to privatise the profitable electricity industry (Charlton *et al.*, 1997; Helm, 1996; Mountford, 1996) which had promoted actual, rather than surrogate, competition. A track authority, Railtrack, was created and the remainder of BR's operations were split into 91 separate companies in order to maximise competitive opportunities (Gibb *et al.*, 1998).

Yet the chapter has suggested that although a BR sell-off was considered by the Conservatives for more than a decade before the publication of *New Opportunities for the Railways*, neither the strategy outlined in that document nor the decision to adopt it should be regarded as the result of a thorough policy analysis. Despite the existence of a conceptual and empirical base from which to formulate rail privatisation policy options – models advanced by think tanks, academics, politicians and civil servants were complemented by the practical experience of other network industry divestitures – ministers were unable, before the 1992 general election, to decide upon a method of selling BR. There is a strong possibility that the model of rail privatisation chosen by MacGregor was his only viable policy option, in the sense that others had not been sufficiently developed, given the time constraints in which he was forced to work.

The plans announced in *New Opportunities for the Railways* were perceived by many commentators as being ill-prepared and lacking in practical detail. John MacGregor defended the logic of the government's proposals to Parliament and the Transport Select Committee, but the chairman of that Committee, Robert Adley, remained sceptical, noting that:

> The Secretary of State, the Minister of State and Department [of Transport] officials have appeared before this committee and... it seems to me that none of them, quite frankly, have a clue about how all this is going to be worked out (*House of Commons Papers*, 1992b: 52).

Key questions regarding many aspects of the track authority model had still to be resolved when the White Paper was published; of central importance to this book is the fact that the opportunities for, and even appropriateness of, competition between passenger operators and its potential impact upon the relationship between the railways and the state had not really been investigated. Notwithstanding the fact that some compromise of neoliberal policy goals would always be inevitable in rail privatisation because of the need for the state to provide subsidy and demand guaranteed service levels in return (see section 3.1), the White Paper argued that the promotion of a competitive, 'free' railway market was a key policy priority. Ministers could not, however, be sure that the plans contained in *New Opportunities for the Railways* would be capable of promoting actual, rather than surrogate, competition.

Against this background, the following chapters now examine the detailed development and the outcome of this aspect of rail privatisation policy. The discussion investigates competition *in* the market in chapter six, but begins in chapters four and five by assessing competition *for* the market through the franchising process.

Notes

1. This book is of course primarily concerned with passenger train services.
2. The two most comprehensive examples are mentioned here. Others are: Economic Research Centre, 1993; Harris and Godward, 1997; Jenkins, 1995; Shaw *et al.*, 1998; Truelove, 1991; Turton, 1992; Williams, 1992; Wolmar, 1996.
3. Because there were too many cabinet ministers for the government legally to pay their salaries, Norman Fowler initially served as Minister (not Minister of State) for

Transport outside the cabinet but attended its meetings. In January 1981, following the removal of Norman St John-Stevas and Angus Maude, Fowler was accommodated as Secretary of State for Transport.

4. In practice there can be numerous difficulties with introducing such an arrangement and they are discussed in section 3.5 and chapter six.

5. London and South East and Provincial were later renamed Network SouthEast and Regional Railways respectively and all the sectors were reorganised into fully vertically-integrated businesses under the Organising for Quality (OforQ) initiative in 1991 (see chapter four). The sectorisation model would most likely have involved a similar restructuring exercise to remove idiosyncrasies from the mid-1980s arrangement.

6. Further objections to the track authority concept were advanced by transport academics after the Treasury's deliberations had concluded. Among these – some of which are expanded upon later where relevant – were: the loss of cross-subsidisation opportunities for operators (Glaister and Travers, 1993); the incompatibility of franchising and open access operations (Charlton *et al.*, 1997); an increase in transaction costs between operators and the track authority (Else, 1996); the difficulties of co-ordinating maintenance work and investment between train operators and the track authority (Dodgson, 1994); the (in)appropriateness of establishing a heavily contractual industry structure (Foster, 1994); and problems with creating train operators with no day to day control over a chief aspect of their operations, i.e. their infrastructure (Shires *et al.*, 1994a).

7. EC 91/440 requires that member states' railways account for their infrastructure and operations businesses independently of one another. The idea is that trans-Europe freight and passenger movements will increase as one member state's rail operator could gain access to another's tracks following the simple calculation of a track access fee. Because the whole process is transparent, discriminating in favour of the incumbent operator becomes more difficult. However, it is important to emphasise that the directive only requires separate *accounting* – it does not require separate ownership of track and trains.

8. Railtrack does, however, lease most of its stations and light maintenance depots out to train operators. The company has retained direct management of only 14 stations throughout the network: London Charing Cross, London Euston, London King's Cross, London Liverpool Street, London Bridge, London Paddington, London Victoria, London Waterloo (excluding Waterloo International), Birmingham New Street, Edinburgh Waverly, Gatwick Airport, Glasgow Central, Leeds and Manchester Piccadilly. Railtrack was privatised by share issue in 1996.

9. The assets of European Passenger Services (which operated Eurostar) and Union Railways passed to central government prior to their divestiture. The two companies were combined as part of the Channel Tunnel Rail Link (CTRL) deal.

4 Competition for the Market: Creating the TOCs

4.1 Introduction

Since 1996, numerous authors have reviewed the franchising process in relation to both the level of competition it generated and the benefits (or otherwise) it bequeathed to rail users and taxpayers (Freeman and Shaw, 2000; Glover, 1997; Harris and Godward, 1997; Knowles, 1998; National Audit Office (NAO), 1996; Powell, 1997; White, 1998). Whilst there is limited consensus regarding the effects of franchising on the overall quality of privatised rail services, it is generally agreed that the process was successful in terms of generating competition for the passenger rail market. All 25 TOCs were transferred to the private sector by April 1997 and the number of shortlisted bidders in each franchise round ensured the generation of "relatively intense" competition (Preston, 1997: 15; White, 1998). The NAO (1996: 25) confirmed that OPRAF had attracted and maintained a "good level of competition" in the early bidding rounds and Knowles (1998) found that the franchising process became more competitive over time. Subsidy levels will be significantly lower than those claimed by BR at the time of letting and a number of market-driven quality of service enhancements were also secured as a result of the tendering process. It is not the purpose here to restate the conclusions of the above studies, but rather to develop an understanding, in the context of arguments already advanced in the book, of how franchising policy developed, why it became successful at generating competition and what impact it has had on the relationship between the rail industry and the state. This chapter and the following chapter address these issues.

Despite the intensity of competition ultimately generated for the passenger rail market, it was for a long time unclear whether the private sector would actually bid for the right to run TOCs. For a variety of reasons, some unquestionably the result of events discussed in chapter three, many potential bidders viewed rail privatisation as something of an uncertain proposition. Although some (notably Stagecoach and Virgin) had expressed an interest, others suggested that they were not persuaded of the government's case and would be unlikely to bid in competitive tendering rounds (*House of Commons Papers*, 1993a). Tomkins (1993) found that private sector interest in rail franchising was extremely low, with most TOCs attracting little or no corporate interest. Moreover, although the government argued that healthy competition would be assured by the presence of Management Employee Buy-Outs (MEBOs), a large majority – 91 per cent – of BR managers were opposed to the track authority method of privatisation and almost three-quarters indicated that they did not see MEBOs as a primary means of privatising TOCs (Smithers, 1993a). Financiers were also sceptical to the point that one, NatWest, refused to become involved with rail privatisation (Grantham, 1998) and Preston (1996) raised concerns about the risk of the entire franchising process being characterised by minimal competition and collusion among bidders.

Against this background, this chapter examines the development of passenger rail franchising policy. It argues that the nature of the franchising policy finally adopted was heavily influenced by the government's need to convince the private sector of the viability of passenger rail franchising. Focus shifted from the ideological to the practical because senior policy makers harboured doubts as to whether they would be able to create a market for passenger rail franchises (*House of Commons Papers*, 1996). Certainly, the degree of competition which ultimately developed among franchise bidders was considerably in excess of that which officials had expected. Chapter five reviews the extent to which the franchising market was ultimately contested and seeks to ascertain, from a bidder's perspective, the principal reasons why this was so. Both chapters are drawn together in a concluding discussion which considers the franchising process in terms of the extent to which it impacted upon the role of the state in the passenger railway industry.

4.2 Passenger rail franchising: an uncertain proposition

Several factors combined to make passenger rail franchising appear unattractive to potential bidders. First, as noted in chapter two, the British economy had slumped into recession by 1992 and the viability of the whole rail privatisation exercise was being undermined by the prevailing economic conditions. While the fortunes of many industries are tied up with the overall performance of the economy, this is especially true of the railways (Nash and Preston, 1993). In previous recessions, fewer jobs in the major conurbations had led to a decrease in the number of rail commuters and the demand for leisure travel had fallen as people changed their patterns of expenditure. Potential bidders were aware that the economic downturn of the early 1990s was having the same effect as the government was again being forced to increase BR's subsidy (Welsby and Nicholls, 1999). In 1989/90, the final 'boom' year of the late 1980s, the total government grant to BR had been £705 million, but by 1991/92 it had risen by over 40 per cent to £1035 million (Nash and Preston, 1993). Prospective franchisees were very much aware that subsidy following privatisation was unlikely to be so flexible, especially if it were determined by contract, and that they could be left in severe financial difficulties in a future recession.[1] Moreover, concern about the viability of rail privatisation was heightened following the collapse of two private-sector initiatives in the early 1990s. Charterail, a private sector freight company, fell into receivership and Stagecoach withdrew its Aberdeen-Edinburgh-London and Glasgow-London overnight services because of lack of demand (Dynes, 1992; White and Smithers, 1993).

Second, the rail privatisation plans were facing hostility from interested parties both within, and outside of, the railway industry and this had the effect of "talking the risks up and the value down." As already noted, most BR managers disliked the track authority model and rejected the idea of MEBOs as a principal vehicle of rail privatisation (Smithers, 1993a). Although many of these managers were subsequently to modify their opinions (as Table 5.2 will show, MEBO bids were submitted for most TOCs), their misgivings in 1993 did not serve to endorse the franchising proposition. The rail privatisation plans were also being criticised by journalists (NAO, 1998a), transport academics (Bradshaw, 1991; Dnes, 1993; Harman, 1993) and politicians of all major parties – including senior Conservative backbenchers (*Hansard*, 1993a) – but perhaps the most effective opposition campaign was being led by the Labour Party, which had committed itself to a "publicly owned, publicly accountable" railway (Labour Party, 1996).[2] Labour exploited the Conservatives' small majority and, although it was not absolutely certain that Major's government would lose the forthcoming general election, based the authority of their attacks on the probability of this happening. Opposition spokesmen made clear their contempt for rail privatisation (*Hansard*, 1992b) and promised that the operational environment for franchise holders would be considerably more demanding under a Labour administration than a Conservative one (Labour Party, 1996). As Michael Meacher, then Shadow Transport Secretary, told the Labour Party Conference:

> If there are any investors thinking of buying into our rail system, I have a message for you. The railways depended on public subsidy last year to the tune of £1.8 billion. There can be no guarantee from any government that such a subsidy will continue indefinitely at that level... If you want to buy a pig in a poke in all those circumstances, it's up to you. But don't come crying to me when it all ends in tears (quoted in Landale, 1995: 12).

Third, there was no international precedent for the proposed model of rail privatisation from which prospective bidders could judge the likely implications of acquiring a franchise. Although other examples of rail privatisation existed around the world, Britain's plans were unique in their complexity (Shires *et al.*, 1994b). Schemes in Japan, New Zealand and Argentina had all been undertaken on a vertically integrated basis and whilst the Swedish approach had created a track authority, the post-privatisation industry structure remained relatively simple in comparison with that proposed in *New Opportunities for the Railways*. Although franchising was a major component of the Swedish proposals, little emphasis had been placed on the need for open access competition and, under interrogation by the Transport Select Committee, DoT official Philip Wood confirmed that the British proposals were "uniquely different from anybody else's" (*House of Commons Papers*, 1992c: 28).

Finally, and not insignificantly, the effect of these factors was compounded by uncertainty surrounding the nature of the franchising proposition itself (Welsby, 1997). Because *New Opportunities for the Railways* had advanced little more than an industry framework, it was unclear at the outset as to precisely what the government was going to sell. MacGregor reported that the private sector had expressed some interest in taking on rail franchises and that they wanted "to go into a great deal of detail... about what a franchise will comprise and so on" (*House of Commons Papers*, 1992d: 5). Accordingly, a consultation document, *The Franchising of Passenger Rail Services*, was published in October 1992 to describe how the franchising process would work (DoT, 1992b) and prospective bidders were asked to respond to questions about the Secretary of State's proposals. The document provided basic information about franchise administration, noting that successful bidders would be expected to provide a level of service at least comparable with that of BR and that this would be subject to certain quality benchmarks (see chapter six). However, details of franchise specification were couched in very broad terms. No firm decisions had been taken on the size, length and depth of franchises and, in this sense, there was very little for prospective bidders to respond *to*. As Andrew MacKinlay of the Transport Select Committee pointed out:

> If you look at the franchising document, if I can use that term, I strain to find anything new in that, anything additionally revealing in substance to that which was in the White Paper... I cannot see any substance in terms of beef being put on the issue (*House of Commons Papers*, 1992d: 9).

The Committee's chairman, Robert Adley, agreed, noting that there was not "enough information for people to come forward with answers to the questions the Secretary of State is asking and on which the future of our railway depends" (*House of Commons Papers*, 1992b: 49).

A possible reason for the vagueness of *The Franchising of Passenger Rail Services* was that the policy making process was badly managed at first.[3] Although the formulation of rail privatisation policy had become, in the words of one respondent, "one of the biggest tasks of project management that's ever been seen in government anywhere at all," responsibility for organising the entire project was vested in policy analysts rather than project managers. The result was inefficiency, not just in relation to franchising, but in all aspects of policy development:

> [To begin,] they staffed it with very bright people who were used to doing policy analysis, but weren't used to managing a project process... [For example] just very simple things like if you've got advisors on a project like this, your advisors have to be absolutely comprehensive in their understanding of what's going on, who is meant to be doing what, when, all these kinds of things. [One policymaker's] view was you may or may not have them all in for a meeting, you may or may not tell them all what had happened. It just didn't work, it's as simple as that.

This situation was ultimately resolved by the appointment of an experienced privatisation project co-ordinator, but in the meantime MacGregor was forced to defend the contents of the consultation document before the Transport Select Committee. He did this by stressing the importance of retaining flexibility in the process in order to gear "the system to the needs of the marketplace rather than sitting in Marsham Street [the DoT's location] and deciding how you think it will run" (*House of Commons Papers*, 1992d: 10). He continued:

> We will have a variety of different shapes and sizes of franchises. A variety of depth of franchises. Some operators will mainly want to do a marketing operation, perhaps not even employ the drivers. Others will want to employ depots, maintenance depots, for the period of the franchise and may well want to get involved with stations.

MacGregor's enthusiasm for flexibility appeared to exceed that which had been intended in the consultation document. Despite its general paucity of detail, the document had implied that over-reliance on the wishes of the private sector might be impractical, especially if 'cherry picking' left the government with a disaggregated residue of unsaleable services. Accordingly, *The Franchising of Passenger Rail Services* had noted that franchisees would assume responsibility for managing all aspects of train operation and would be grouped in a way which made commercial and operational sense, had regard to markets being served and promoted competition. Notwithstanding these points, the majority feeling of the Transport Select Committee after MacGregor's appearance was that "the government do not really know what to do," and ministers admitted that there were still huge areas of detail which needed filling in before the private sector could be convinced that rail franchising was an attractive opportunity (*House of Commons Papers*, 1992d: 22; Tomkins and Smith, 1992).

4.3 Determining franchise specifications

Franchise size

As noted above, the main aims of *The Franchising of Passenger Rail Services* were to group services in a way that made operational and commercial sense, that had regard to markets being served and that promoted competition.   These last two aims reflected the agendas of Downing Street and the Treasury respectively.   Although the preference of John Major's Policy Unit for a regionally-based railway had lost out to the track authority model in summer 1992, "there were those, including the Prime Minister, who [remained] keen to develop regional identities in the railways," and this idea could be realised through exerting an influence over the franchise boundaries.   Meanwhile the Treasury, having been forced to abandon its idea of train-path auctioning (see chapter three), was keen to negotiate the next best thing by disaggregating BR into as many franchises as reasonably possible.   A large number of franchises would maximise competition *for* the market, by increasing the amount of competitive tenders, and *in* the market by boosting the amount of shared track miles (see chapter six).   According to Grantham (1998), for example, the Treasury advanced the idea of splitting BR's South Western Division into as many as eight different companies (it was eventually franchised as two).

Far more important to the DoT, however, was to effect a split which made operational and commercial sense.   Officials were aware that private sector confidence in rail privatisation was low and realised that further delays in policy development would jeopardise the likelihood of their creating a market for TOCs.   Protracted disputes might also have hampered the Conservatives' attempts to complete rail privatisation within one Parliament.   Accordingly, the DoT argued that, provided they were generally consistent with the policy outlined in *New Opportunities for the Railways*, solutions to arising complications should be determined by practicality:

> We were driven by the practical necessity of getting the franchising programme launched... It had never been done before anywhere else in the world and we were anxious to try and reduce uncertainties and risks wherever that was possible, but consistent with the policy... It [needed to be] a practical, sensible decision to make sure that we didn't waste any time.

The problem with both Downing Street and the Treasury's proposals was that they were driven by romanticism or ideology rather than practicality and, although each might have been feasible in the longer term, the DoT could not risk approaching its task from a Utopian standpoint. Officials in Marsham Street recognised the need to establish pilot franchises in order that potential bidders could gain some idea of how the TOCs would function and what the costs associated with running them would be (*Hansard*, 1993a; *House of Commons Papers*, 1993a). As such, accommodating the whims of others, particularly those of the Treasury, was,

> ...not at all, absolutely not at all [a factor]. We had an awful lot to do very quickly. We had to provide as good a track record as BR's accounting system would allow us to do for potential buyers.

Academics and transport consultants offered their suggestions regarding the optimum size for franchises. Most argued for splitting BR into a few, large operating businesses. Nash and Preston (1993) and Dodgson (1994) referred to evidence from the United States to show that dividing BR into 20 or more companies could result in at least some of them using rolling stock inefficiently. The Economic Research Centre (1993) reviewed literature which suggested the optimum size for a rail firm was around one third that of BR, especially where economies of density were being maximised.[4] Jones *et al.* (1993) also advocated large franchises because they would limit the transaction costs associated with train to train externalities (see chapter three).

Although these suggestions provided the DoT with further policy options, there were practical difficulties associated with creating larger franchises because this would have involved a significant – and therefore lengthy – restructuring of BR's passenger businesses and might even have virtually reconstituted BR's business sectors, an option ruled out by the election manifesto. Moreover, as Williams (1992) has pointed out, the significant turnovers which would have been associated with large franchises (up to £1 billion) might have discouraged many potential bidders. Increasingly it became obvious to observers (Nash and Preston, 1993, Tomkins, 1992b) that the shape of the franchises would be largely based on BR's existing profit centres.

After sectorisation in the mid 1980s (see chapter three), BR underwent a further restructuring exercise in 1992, Organising for Quality (O for Q). The O for Q initiative separated each of BR's business sectors into a series of individual profit centres, each with its own management reporting to the relevant sectoral Director. A total of 19 were created and these are listed in Table 4.1. The profit centre approach to franchising offered four key advantages as far as the DoT was concerned. First, and most obviously, BR had already designed its profit centres to make operational and commercial sense.   Second, track records for the new franchises would be *relatively* straightforward to assemble.   Third, the transition from sectorised to franchised management would be eased if a degree of continuity in senior personnel were maintained (Tomkins, 1992b; Grantham, 1998) and, finally, the profit centre approach appeared likely to generate interest among potential bidders as some (Stagecoach in particular) had indicated that they wanted to acquire rail operations in this form (*House of Commons Papers*, 1992e).   As a respondent pointed out:

> We knew how BR organised itself [in 1993] and that seemed a sensible number of TOCs both in terms of the speed in which you could generate interest and complete the franchising programme within the Department.   So we ruled out half a dozen [TOCs], we ruled out hundreds and the existing structure seemed to present a practical and sensible way forward.

Table 4.1   BR's profit centres

InterCity	Network SouthEast	Regional Railways
Great Western	South West	Central
West Coast	South East	North West
East Coast	South Central	North East
Midlands/Cross Country	Thames and Chiltern	South Wales and West
Gatwick and Anglia	Great Eastern	ScotRail
	North	
	Thameslink	
	West Anglia Great Northern	
	London, Tilbury, Southend	

Source: Tomkins (1992b).

MacGregor announced the first batch of franchises in February 1993 and a draft structure of 25 TOCs three months later (*Hansard*, 1993c; 1993d).   The franchises were indeed based around BR's profit centres, although some changes had been made to further localise the management of certain route groups following suggestions from potential bidders: in

InterCity, Midlands/Cross Country and Gatwick and Anglia were both separated; in Network SouthEast, Island Line was removed from the South Western Division and Thames and Chiltern were separated; and in Regional Railways, Merseyrail Electrics was split from North West and the Cardiff Valley Lines were separated from South Wales and West. Some of the 25 TOCs have now undergone name changes and these are listed in Table 4.2.

Figures 4.1 to 4.3 show, somewhat schematically owing to local complexities, the final disaggregation of BR. Although it came about primarily for practical reasons, the final franchising map did offer Downing Street some regionally based franchises (such as Anglia and ScotRail) and the Treasury a considerable amount of competition. One respondent argued that "after all, 25 was not an inconsiderable number" of auctions to hold. The potential for competition in the market was also substantial as 56.4 per cent of all rail journeys under the O for Q structure were undertaken by more than one company (ORR, 1994a). However, as chapter six will show, it turned out that the scope for this type of on-rail competition was largely theoretical as it was subsequently restricted by a number of regulatory and operational factors.

Franchise length

The Franchising of Passenger Rail Services (DoT, 1992b) noted that no decisions had been taken regarding franchise length by October 1992 and just as the Treasury and the DoT had been at odds over the size of franchises, so they also fought over their length. The Treasury was again anxious to maximise competition and therefore sought to minimise the interval between competitive tenders for each TOC. Treasury officials argued at first that franchises should be short, no longer than "three to five" years:

> We were saying 'no, this is competition for the market. We want franchises which are long enough for people to make change and benefit from it, but we want the prospect of re-tendering.'

Table 4.2   The 25 TOCs*

InterCity	Network SouthEast	Regional Railways
Great Western Trains (First Great Western)	South West Trains	Central Trains
InterCity West Coast (Virgin Trains)	South Eastern (Connex South Eastern)	North West Regional Railways (First North Western)
InterCity East Coast (GNER)	Network South Central (Connex South Central)	Regional Railways North East (Northern Spirit)
Midland Mainline	Thames Trains	South Wales and West (Wales & West)
CrossCountry (Virgin Trains)	Chiltern Railways	ScotRail
Gatwick Express	Great Eastern (First Great Eastern)	Cardiff Railway Company
Anglia	North London Railways (Silverlink) Thameslink West Anglia Great Northern LTS Rail (c2c) Island Line	Merseyrail Electrics

* Names outside brackets are those which TOCs were franchised under.

Source: OPRAF, 1998a.

The DoT, on the other hand, disagreed:

> I always felt that we would have to go for longer franchises than the Treasury were initially trying to argue for, because I didn't think it was practical otherwise, we wouldn't get the bidders... There was a great debate about that.

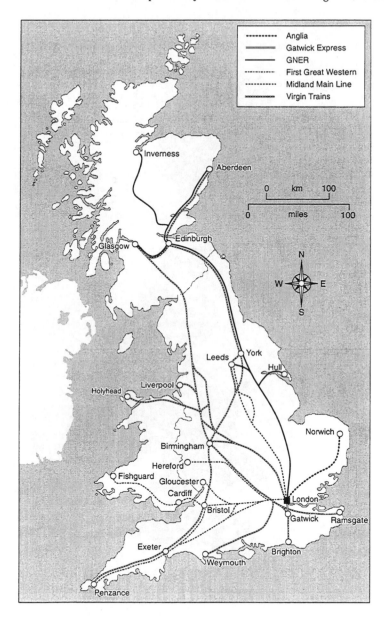

Figure 4.1   Route plans of the former InterCity TOCs

Source: Shaw *et al.*, 1998.

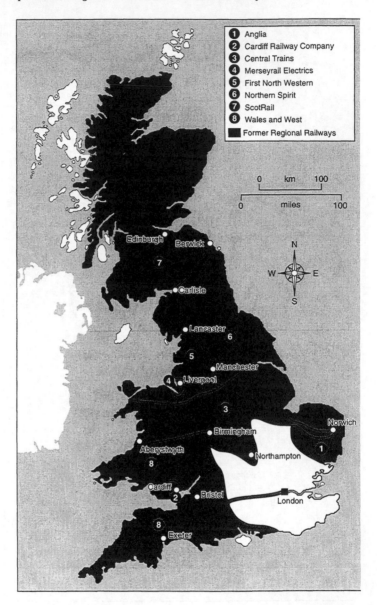

Figure 4.2   Operating territories of the former Regional Railways TOCs

Source: Shaw *et al.*, 1998.

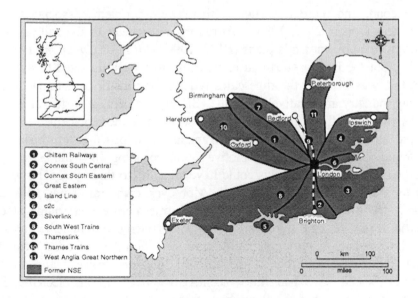

Figure 4.3   Operating territories of the former Network SouthEast TOCs

Source: Shaw *et al.*, 1998.

The DoT had once more recognised that, although the Treasury's stance might be appropriate in the longer term, it would not be practical in the initial franchising round. There were two main reasons why the franchise terms needed lengthening out to make them more attractive to potential bidders. First, there was the simple issue of branding. *The Franchising of Passenger Railway Services* had suggested that franchisees would be able to trade under their own brand image, but as the Bow Group, a right-wing think tank, pointed out, re-branding a railway takes a considerable amount of time. When Network SouthEast was relaunched in the late 1980s, for example, it took three years to fully establish its corporate identity (Campbell-Bannerman, 1993). It was argued as a result that short franchise contracts would negate any benefits which might be associated with establishing a new corporate identity.

Second, and more importantly, there were problems associated with investment (Jones *et al.*, 1993). Attracting investment to the railway was central to the government's plans (BBC, 1996; *House of Commons Papers*, 1993a), but the DoT argued that short franchises were unsuited to this. In part, this was because the timescales required for major investment in the railway industry are relatively lengthy. BR did not carry a surfeit of excess rolling stock and the introduction of new services or the replacement of life-expired stock would have required franchisees to procure refurbished or new-build carriages and locomotives. Depending on the size and specifications of the order, this could have taken up to three years, by which time the franchise might have expired. Moreover, many railway investments exhibit strong complementarities between infrastructure and rolling stock. Electric trains require third rail systems or overhead catenery, modern signalling systems require compatible train detection devices on or near the tracks and on rolling stock if they are to function properly and so on. Railtrack would have had little incentive to invest in an electrification scheme if it knew that the incumbent franchisee might be replaced by a diesel traction enthusiast before the project was complete.

The most significant investment-related problem from a franchisee's point of view was that of residual value risk. Railway assets are generally long-lived and highly specific. As such, investment in infrastructure under the franchisee's control (e.g. stations) is to all intents and purposes sunk and, although rolling stock can often be transferred to other areas of the network, there was no guarantee that an active second hand market would have developed by the time the first generation of franchises ran out. With the residual value of assets highly uncertain, a franchisee would have sought to amortise them during the course of its contract and Jones *et al.* (1993) argued that extremely high subsidies – or greatly inflated ticket prices – would have been required to encourage private sector bids in these circumstances. A solution to this problem in relation to infrastructure was devised to give the Franchising Director the authority to designate 'franchise assets' which an incoming franchisee must take on. With rolling stock, however, the answer was to establish a leasing market in order to ensure that residual value risk was assumed by a third party. Ministers had recognised in 1992 that, although some franchisees may wish to buy physical assets outright, leasing was likely to be the favoured option for most and the creation of rolling stock leasing companies (Roscos) was announced in mid-

1993 to accommodate this (DoT, 1992b, 1993a; *House of Commons Papers*, 1993c; see also Mountford, 1996; Prideaux, 2000).

In theory, the advent of Roscos lent weight to the Treasury's case for short operating contracts because franchisees, relieved of residual value risk, could replace rolling stock without making the capital investment themselves. Nevertheless, the DoT continued to press for longer franchises because it still felt that bidders would submit tenders only if they were offered a degree of temporal security. One respondent,

> certainly felt that franchises of 10 or more years would attract more interest... I had spent the summer of 1992 talking to potential bidders for the franchises. Of course, these conversations had nothing to draw upon in terms of experience anywhere else in the world or in the United Kingdom and I do recall the initial reaction of the companies I spoke to... was that they would look for a longer period than three to five years in order to recover any [non-rolling stock] investment that was made.

This was a view shared by the first Franchising Director, Roger Salmon, whose answer, according to a senior civil servant, "to just about everything was to lengthen out the franchise terms. If you had longer franchises, it looked a more enticing process and so on." The *Draft Objectives, Instructions and Guidance* to the Franchising Director (*House of Commons Papers*, 1993a) signalled a partial victory for the DoT in that the basic franchise term had been lengthened out to seven years; the Secretary of State's approval would have to be sought if a longer contract was proposed. The civil servant recalled that in private, however, the DoT's case had more or less prevailed in full, as "where there was a good case for reinvestment in rolling stock" the Treasury had conceded "OK, we can see the case for a longer contract" of up to 15 years.

Franchise depth

Despite the White Paper being seen, in one former minister's words, "as a clear victory for the track authority option, the opposite of vertical integration," some potential bidders – and, as already noted, the majority of BR managers (Smithers, 1993a) – disagreed with the concept of vertical separation and began to stress the importance of infrastructure ownership to any franchising prospect. Their concerns revolved around the degree to which, under the track authority model, a franchisee would be dependent on a monopoly (Railtrack), particularly with regard to cost control and managerial responsibility (*House of Commons Papers*, 1993a).   Sea Containers argued that Railtrack's ownership of the infrastructure would substantially reduce the prospects of being able to run a profitable TOC. Referring to a proposal he had advanced to operate the southern region of BR, James Sherwood, president of Sea Containers, suggested that:

> If we maintain the track and signalling ourselves... we could save £50 million a year over what British Rail is paying today. So if the idea is that British Rail [as Railtrack] are going to continue to run the track and the signalling, then there is no scope for us to achieve that £50 million of saving (*House of Commons Papers*, 1992e: 196).

Apprehension over the loss of managerial responsibility was heightened when Chris Green, then Director of InterCity, pointed out that vertical integration of his business under O for Q had enabled it to make good progress towards delivering a high quality service. Brian Scott, Director of InterCity's Great Western Region, added that, as an operator, he could not contemplate forfeiting control over infrastructure because, if he did, he would no longer be in charge of all the key components of his own business (see also Shires *et al.*, 1994b):

> As an experienced, professional railway business manager, I would not put my money into a train operating company... without having day to day command and control of operations, including signalling, track and signals maintenance [as it would be] an act of folly to buy into something with so little control of performance and, therefore, profit (*House of Commons Papers*, 1993a: lii).

Given the struggle preceding the selection of the track authority model, it was unlikely that ministers would have been prepared, in the words of a respondent, to "junk it," even in the face of such criticism. Policy makers could afford to let debates over the size and length of franchises be guided by the views of potential bidders because they were not likely to compromise the fundamental aims of vertical separation.   A significant number of competitive opportunities would still exist even if the Treasury's plans were rejected.   But vertical integration was anathema to the concept of a track authority and it might have been expected that any circumstances in which it would be permitted as an expedient would be minimal.   Somewhat surprisingly, however, a passage in *The Franchising of Passenger Rail Services* suggested that a franchisee might "take on a 'vertically integrated' franchise covering the operation of track and signalling as well as trains" (DoT, 1992a: 13). The *Railways Bill*, published in January 1993, also left the government's options open.[5] As one witness told the Transport Select Committee:

> The Bill... bears no relation to the White Paper because technically it allows the government to dispose of BR in any way it sees fit. There is no mention of Railtrack within the Bill... As far as I can see... they can split it up into a hundred million parts, vertically integrated, laterally separated or whatever (*House of Commons Papers*, 1993a: 708).

The decision to allow a degree of vertical integration was not originally adopted as a result of the arguments advanced by prospective franchisees – in fact, it pre-empted them – but was agreed on the basis that there were likely to be exceptional circumstances around the network where vertical separation was neither logical nor desirable. In particular, ministers were aware that Island Line, the Isle of Wight's single track, eight-mile Ryde to Shanklin route, was so isolated and subsidy-dependent that it was unlikely to attract open access operators and raise issues of anti-competitive practice. As policy developed, however, the DoT began to argue that vertical integration might have to be considered more favourably with regard to other self-contained TOCs such as LTS Rail.   Again, agreement from the Treasury was obtained:

> There was a theoretical possibility that in certain cases [a degree of vertical integration] might become necessary...   That indication that vertical integration would be possible in certain circumstances was just to make sure that if there were any major problems in getting the franchises away, then some modest compromise within the idea of a single, unified track authority was possible.

The "modest compromise" to which the respondent referred would have resulted in Railtrack retaining ownership of the infrastructure, but then leasing it to the TOC for a period coterminous with the length of its franchise. In the event, only Island Line was franchised in this manner as had originally been envisaged; all TOCs on the British mainland were vertically separated, although they were to lease stations and light maintenance depots from Railtrack (see chapter three).[6]

Basic franchise specifications

By mid-1993, almost a year after the publication of the White Paper, the Conservatives had finally decided upon the basic franchise specifications to complement the administration requirements it had outlined in *The Franchising of Passenger Railways*. There would be 25 TOCs, each franchised for a period of between seven and 15 years, and all but Island Line would be vertically separated.[7] Franchisees would also be expected to provide a level of service which, at a minimum, roughly reflected that of BR immediately prior to privatisation. In attempting to resolve policy matters quickly and to address the uncertainty surrounding the franchising proposition, the DoT – with the approval of Downing Street and, more importantly, the Treasury – pursued a pragmatic line to define the basic characteristics of the TOCs.

Yet a question remains as to how the DoT was able to convince the Treasury of the need to adopt its plans. As chapter three made clear, the period leading up to the publication of *New Opportunities for the Railways* was dominated by the Treasury. In securing pragmatic solutions to franchise-related problems, however, officials in the DoT effectively reversed the prevailing hierarchy in rail privatisation policy formulation. Whereas the DoT had previously been forced to accept the track authority model on the basis that it maximised competitive opportunities, so the Treasury became obliged to concede the impracticability of many of these opportunities as policy details were developed in 1993 and 1994. As a senior civil servant put it:

> You could sum up the whole process as follows: at the outset, [the Treasury] fought for – and won – the structure that was going to deliver the most competitive industry post-privatisation. [It] then spent the implementation years defining the exact *trade-off* between competition... and the practicalities of getting the businesses ready for sale... In lots of areas, [the Treasury] had to accept that greater competition would be introduced over time rather than immediately.

A combination of two factors seems to explain why the Treasury's position was weakened. First, as the above sections have shown, the DoT became aware from its discussions with prospective franchisees that implementing the Treasury's proposals would jeopardise its chances of creating a market for TOCs (see also chapter six). Failure to let franchises would not only defeat the object of passenger rail privatisation, but also limit the potential for future subsidy reductions. There was the further possibility that the flotation value of Railtrack and the Roscos – upon which the Conservatives were dependent for a variety of reasons including planned tax cuts (see Jenkins, 1995) – could be damaged.

In different circumstances, the Treasury might have dismissed the DoT's concerns by arguing that the would-be bidders were seeking to strengthen their bargaining position before entering into negotiations with the government, but the continuing poor performance of the economy served to undermine such a position. Since 1991, the Treasury had been struggling to contain public expenditure and was becoming vulnerable to charges that its ideas about rail privatisation would further extend the PSBR. Proponents of service competition had been protected from such charges because little was understood about the policy's likely implications. Following their experience with electricity privatisation, Treasury officials had argued strongly that vertical separation would benefit the taxpayer because of the myriad opportunities for competition, and thus cost reduction, it presented. Moreover, the contractual nature of the track authority model would ensure that subsidy would remain stable during future recessions (see section 4.2). Although these were compelling theoretical arguments, the reality of the higher transactional costs associated with the track authority model were by now starting to reveal themselves (see chapter three) and it became obvious that there would need to be a complete privatisation – and, crucially, strong competition for the market – if these were to be offset. As such, the Treasury was forced to concede that creating extremely short franchises and excessively disaggregating BR were no longer viable policy options. A former minister pointed out that:

> The Treasury's role in controlling public expenditure... became more dominant than competition and [rail] industry experts within the Treasury. Therefore, they were particularly susceptible to any arguments which protected the value of Railtrack for a public flotation and the ability to generate competition for franchises. So it was a question of the DoT saying

'this is what you're going to have to do, this will maximise our chance of getting the whole thing away with reasonable returns and results'. Then the Treasury was more amenable [to the DoT's position].

By accepting the DoT's re-orientation of the policy-making agenda away from ideology and towards practicality, the Treasury was forced to recognise the paradox that its own plans, which heavily emphasised market liberalisation, were likely to result in less competition than the DoT's, which did not.

Despite having won this battle, key officials in the DoT and OPRAF remained sceptical as to whether they would be able to create a market for TOCs. Although the basic franchise specifications had now been decided upon, a vast amount of policy detail needed filling in before the competitive tendering process could begin. TOCs' assets had to be assigned and incorporated, the contractual matrix through which the train operators would interact with other rail businesses needed to be assembled (see Grantham, 1998) and regulations governing the new industry had to be formulated.[8] The most significant regulation was the Passenger Service Requirement (PSR), the manifestation of the Conservatives' commitment to maintain the "current national network of services" (Conservative Party, 1992: 35).

PSRs detail the minimum amount of trains each TOC must run in return for its subsidy (quality of service regulations are discussed in chapter six). They do not function explicitly as timetables, but instead set parameters, based largely on BR's service levels of 1992, within which TOCs must construct their timetables. The PSR for South West Trains, for example, stipulates that at least a two-hourly service must run between London Waterloo and Exeter St David's on weekdays and Saturdays and that the last train to Exeter must leave at or after 18.30.

The number of services stipulated in PSRs is generally less than that operated by BR, but operators are free to run more should they deem them commercially viable. Although ministers expected that this would happen – and thus that 1992 service levels would remain constant or even increase (*House of Commons Papers*, 1993a) – their optimism was not shared by opponents of rail privatisation. Opposition spokesmen led a campaign to suggest that the policy would lead to service cuts and the pressure group Save Our Railways launched a court action in an attempt to increase the number of services included in PSRs (Grantham, 1998).[9] Notwithstanding courtroom distractions, the production of PSRs was novel and complex and some delay was perhaps inevitable because of the likelihood of errors. OPRAF admitted to producing an unworkable PSR for South West Trains where it experienced difficulties with train paths out of London Waterloo and similar problems were encountered with LTS Rail. As a result, the PSRs – and, indeed, other sales documentation – were not completed by the time bidders were invited to tender for TOCs, a fact which led Grantham (1998: 132) to suggest that the franchising process "was being conducted with a paucity of detail."

Sale prospects

Such was the perception of rail privatisation whilst the TOCs were being created that opposition frontbenchers genuinely believed franchising would be significantly short of completion by the 1997 general election (Grantham, 1998). The only factor which appeared to be working in the government's favour was the economy. The recession which had beset the early 1990s was over by 1995 and ministers were assured that business confidence was generally higher than it had been in the recent past. As one respondent (rather prosaically) pointed out, had the economy still been in a slump when competitive tendering began, the latter would have been "an absolute fucking disaster." The DoT had ascertained that there were around 20 or 30 companies interested in bidding for TOCs – despite MacGregor having earlier put the figure as high as 50 – but was unsure whether any would participate in the franchising process. Indeed, Tomkins (1993) had suggested that MacGregor was being disingenuous in that many of the companies included in his figure were organisations such as banks and venture capitalists who were unlikely to bid themselves. A respondent admitted: "no-one really knew. I could not put my hand on my heart and say 'they will bid.'" Key personnel in the Department still feared that, despite their efforts to minimise the commercial uncertainties associated with passenger rail franchising, potential bidders would still consider the proposition too risky:

> We were saying to people, 'come buy these train companies. All you've got to do is, today – when there isn't a private sector train running on the network; when the company that we're asking you to buy has been run for the last 50 years as a sort of business sector part of BR and a vertically integrated business sector at that; where difficult decisions are forced up the

line [of companies within the new structure] and so on and so forth; all the problems of buying a subsidiary where there's no track record of the company operating – all you need to do is tell us how much money you're going to need over the next seven years to run that franchise. No break clauses saying 'if you think you've got it wrong in two years' time come back for more.' Tell us now how much money you need in 2002. So that's a really difficult proposition for franchisees to bid on... We weren't sure who the hell we were going to sell these franchises to.

Some within OPRAF were of a similar opinion:

The reality with OPRAF, and in particular OPRAF under Salmon, was that they badly lacked confidence for a long time that they were going to actually sell these things. Salmon's great worry was that no-one was going to come forward and bid for these things.

Roger Salmon himself subsequently admitted that, as late as May 1995, there had still been "very considerable uncertainty that we should ever sell any franchises. There was a widespread view that they were unsaleable" (*House of Commons Papers*, 1996: 13).

This situation might have been considerably different had the Conservatives been able to agree upon a suitable model for rail privatisation immediately following the circulation of the ministerial working group report in January 1991 (see chapter three). A significant amount of preparation could have been undertaken before the 1992 general election – legislation could have been drafted, analysis regarding the break-up of BR could have been undertaken – and operational records for the new companies could have been built up from at least 1993 onwards. Ministers would have been able to present and defend their plans with a better knowledge of how they were intended to work and with a reasonable expectation of what the policy's outcomes were likely to be. Notwithstanding any 'negotiating in public' on the part of prospective bidders, the success of passenger rail franchising would probably have been much more assured. As it was, despite the efforts of the DoT to make franchising a more enticing prospect, policy makers could not be sure that the process would even create a market for TOCs, let alone generate real competition for it. As one respondent summed up, "it was a bold act [for us] to proceed without knowing precisely who would come to the table and negotiate." Policy makers were understandably relieved, therefore, when bidders quickly began *queueing* to get to the table.

Notes

1.   Conversely, if the economy were to pick up after the franchises had been let, the government would have been burdened with a disproportionately high subsidy bill.

2.   This phrase is somewhat misleading. Labour did not expect rail privatisation to be completed by the time of the 1997 general election (Grantham, 1998) and, as such, resolved to keep what had not been sold in public ownership. It was not the case that an incoming Labour government would have repurchased companies where this involved significant capital expenditure: "Some people have argued that Labour could have halted the privatisation by simply seeking to repurchase parts of the rail network that have been sold off so cheaply. This is untrue. In the case of Railtrack, a promise to repurchase at anything less than the market price would be illegal under European law. A promise to repurchase at market price would... require considerable public resources, meaning that the taxpayer would be hit twice. It would also ensure that there would be insufficient resources left for investment. The challenge for an incoming Labour government is to deliver the improved railway network that we need whilst guaranteeing value and accountability for taxpayers' money" (Labour Party, 1996: 20).

3.   This argument is included with some reservation because only one respondent raised it (although he was directly involved with proceedings at the time). Nevertheless, it does offer a credible explanation for the fact that the advances in policy detail from *New Opportunities for the Railways* to *The Franchising of Passenger Rail Services* were slight with regard to franchise specifications.

4.   Economies of scale with respect to density increase as a rail operator makes more intensive use of its fixed assets. Economies of density are also related to size: for a given fixed cost (the infrastructure), a rail operator will have lower unit costs (the services) the greater its output (although there are limits to this – see, for example, Dodgson, 1989).

5.   Chapter three noted that the Bill was essentially a piece of enabling legislation which gave ministers the licence to create whatever they wished out of the BR monolith (see also Shaw *et al.*, 1998).

6.   As will become apparent later in the book, MacGregor's adoption of almost complete vertical separation did not discourage those who had opposed the idea from bidding for franchises. Brian Scott, for example, won the Great Western franchise as part of a MEBO in 1996 and then sold it to FirstGroup – at a personal profit of almost £3.8 million – in 1998 (*Railway Gazette International*, 1998).

7.   Reflecting its unique circumstances, Island Line was franchised for only five years.

8.   In addition, some broader policy issues were still to be resolved. As noted in chapter three, it was not envisaged in *New Opportunities for the Railways* that franchisees would have an exclusive right to operate services over any given stretch of track, but that other operators would be able to run competing trains on an open access basis. On-rail competition forms the basis for chapter six and is discussed more fully therein. Nevertheless, it is appropriate to note here that many potential bidders found the prospect of open access incompatible with franchising because it would pose a serious threat to the viability of their businesses. This issue was not finally resolved until December 1994 and, at the very least, reinforced the conviction of some

potential franchisees that the Conservatives did not fully understand the implications of their own policy (*House of Commons Papers*, 1993a).

9.   Save Our Railways argued that some of the PSRs suggested by OPRAF – in particular those for Gatwick Express, LTS Rail and InterCity East Coast – were unlawful because they would not, as stipulated in the Franchising Director's *Objectives, Instructions and Guidance*, protect an amount of services similar to that operated by BR immediately prior to franchising. In response, the Secretary of State for Transport simply rewrote his guidance to the Franchising Director, thus re-legalising the offending PSRs. As events have transpired, many service frequencies around the network have increased, although some TOCs are now beginning to cut back services, particularly in rural areas (see chapter seven).

5 Competition for the Market: Franchising the TOCs

5.1 The franchising process

The Franchising Director explained the franchising proposition to the media in December 1994 and outlined the bidding process through which companies would apply to acquire TOCs. The process would consist of five key stages (NAO, 1996). Interested parties would first be asked to pre-qualify, in order that OPRAF could check whether they had the financial backing and management competency to operate a franchise. Second, Invitations to Tender (ITTs) would be issued to those who had pre-qualified, inviting indicative bids. Third, a shortlist would be produced on the strength of the indicative bids and, fourth, a Preferred Bidder would be announced after final bids from shortlisted companies had been received. Finally, provided that contractual negotiations were successfully completed, the franchise would be awarded to the preferred bidder and private sector operation would commence. Although the bidding process may have seemed cumbersome, it was so designed in order to discourage all except *bona fide* bidders from submitting tenders. OPRAF were satisfied that, in general, the system achieved its aim in this regard (Grantham, 1998).

Financial and trade interest in the Franchising Director's announcement was such that OPRAF considered it unnecessary to take out more than minimal paid advertising (NAO, 1996). 246 potential bidders received pre-qualification documents for the first three franchises to be let, South West Trains, Great Western Trains and LTS Rail.[1] 36 organisations returned the documents to OPRAF by March 1995 and only six failed to progress to the ITT stage. 16 final bids were received from nine companies for the first three franchises (NAO, 1996). At first glance, it may seem that such a low 'interest to bid' ratio (246 originally interested parties resulted in 16 bids giving a ratio of around 15:1) demonstrated a lack of private sector interest in rail franchising and that the bidding process was unlikely to attract more than minimal competition. This view is justified in part by

103

previous experience as Kennedy (1995) had found that during the privatisation of the London bus companies, bidders behaved cautiously where uncertainty surrounding a sale was high. However, a respondent with considerable experience of competitive tendering pointed out that, "such ratios are not uncommon in business for ITTs," and academic analysis undertaken prior to the tendering process showed that shortlists of only three to five bidders per TOC – which OPRAF managed to secure – would lead to "relatively intense" competition (Preston, 1997: 15). In the event, the levels of subsidy negotiated by OPRAF for the first three TOCs were less than those claimed by BR in 1995/96 and the NAO (1996: 25 and 30) subsequently concluded that OPRAF had generated and sustained "a good level of competition" to secure "value for money" for the taxpayer.[2]

The exact meaning of the expression 'value for money' in rail privatisation terms had been a source of some contention since the announcement of franchising in *New Opportunities for the Railways* (DoT, 1992a). As stated in chapter four, all franchises were to be let subject to basic administrative requirements such as PSRs and some quality of service regulations. Assuming all bids met these stipulations, value for money could still be defined in a number of ways. Was it simply to mean the cheapest, 'no frills' tender? Did it refer to major quality enhancements over and above those required by the regulations carried out on an efficient basis? Or did it imply some kind of compromise between these two extremes? In cases where substantial investment was needed – for example, where rolling stock was life-expired – the government recognised that the likely outcome of attempts simply to minimise subsidy would be a deterioration in the provision of rail services.[3] Ministers argued that this would be undesirable and, under interrogation by the Transport Select Committee (*House of Commons Papers*, 1993a), insisted that it was not their intention to make rail privatisation primarily a means of securing financial advantages for the Treasury (although it will be recalled that the Conservatives were rather depending upon revenue they would obtain from the flotation of Railtrack and the Roscos). On the other hand, ministers did not wish for subsidy levels to impact excessively on the PSBR and a compromise approach to defining value for money became inevitable. Some differences of opinion existed between policy makers, especially those in OPRAF and the Treasury, over how this compromise would be reached. OPRAF appears to have been unable to decide whether it should err on the side of subsidy minimisation or quality maximisation, but it was finally accepted that value for money would have to be determined individually for each franchise. According to a respondent:

> Salmon was constantly hankering for the view that value for money either meant cheapest or meant lots of new kit. He kind of veered between the two at various times. The Treasury was saying 'no, value for money is a more holistic concept than that and it depends on what one's asking for in the way of minimum service levels, it depends on whether there's a good case for reinvestment or not'. Once they'd decided what the proposition enshrined in the particular franchise contract was, then at that point they wanted it let on the best financial terms they could. But in determining what the investment proposition was, as it were, it had many more dimensions to it than 'my Christ, how can we flog this to minimise the subsidy bill?'

Some TOCs, especially those which had received major investment from BR (examples are Thames Trains, Chiltern Railways and GNER), could be let 'as seen', whilst those at the opposite end of the scale (examples are LTS Rail and InterCity West Coast) might carry certain investment requirements or 'recommendations'. OPRAF asked bidders to attach the highest priority to minimising subsidy according to each individual franchising proposition and to include further quality of service enhancements only where they were self-financing or separately priced, in the form of 'non-compliant' bids (NAO, 1996).[4] In an attempt to ensure that bidders included at least some original service innovations, it was also made clear that in cases where two or more bids had identified similar subsidy requirements, detailed attention would be paid to their qualitative aspects.

Competition for the passenger rail market

Chapter four noted that competition for the passenger rail market and its impacts upon subsidy and investment levels have already been documented by numerous authors and, as such, they will only be reviewed here in brief. Table 5.1 shows the award and commencement dates, length and winner of each franchise. Shortlisted bidders for all franchises are shown in Table 5.2. The number of shortlisted bidders for each franchise is not in itself a good indicator of the degree of competition which took place at any one time in the bidding process because the shortlists remained roughly the same size regardless of the number and aggressiveness of indicative bids. The competitive pressure to minimise subsidy requirements during the franchising process is very apparent from Table 5.3. The total subsidy payable to the TOCs decreases from £1.7bn in 1997/98, the first full year of private sector operation, to £806m in 2002/03, the last full year before the majority of franchises end. Subsidies continue to fall – or premiums continue to rise – for those TOCs whose franchises extend up to 15 years in length. Whereas only one TOC, Gatwick Express, was making premium payments to the Franchising Director in 1997/98, four of the 11 former Network SouthEast TOCs and five of the former InterCity TOCs will be doing so by the final year of their franchises and a further TOC from each group will be receiving no subsidy (Knowles, 1998).

Although the NAO (1996: 25) concluded that "a good level of competition" had been generated by OPRAF for the first three franchises, bids became very much more competitive immediately afterwards. Respondents who won TOCs shortly after South West Trains, First Great Western and LTS Rail had been let, noted:

> We put in quite an aggressive bid... We did a lot of work on it and we came to a view that was supported but looked quite aggressive compared to South West Trains. SWT, in retrospect, was easy and if we'd have won we'd all be millionaires by now... But potentially we could be seen as one of those ground-breakers.

> People applied very aggressive ratios to the costs and revenues... In the final lot of franchises... we lost by some substantial margin. We never really changed our risk profile throughout the whole process. We applied the same risk, slightly up or down depending on whether we liked the franchise or not, but essentially the same. We were very successful in the first half of the process, [but] in the final rounds we weren't very close at all to the winning subsidy.

Table 5.1   Franchise award/commencement dates, holder and length

Train Operating Company	Franchise awarded / commenced	Franchise holder	Franchise length (yr/mo)
South West Trains	Dec 19, 1995 / Feb 4, 1996	Stagecoach Holdings	7
First Great Western	Dec 20, 1995 / Feb 4, 1996	Great Western Holdings	10
c2c	May 9, 1996 / May 26, 1996	Prism Rail	15
GNER	Mar 29, 1996 / Apr 28, 1996	Sea Containers	7
Gatwick Express	Apr 3, 1996 / Apr 28, 1996	National Express Group	15
Midland Mainline	Apr 22, 1996 / Apr 28, 1996	National Express Group	10
Connex South Central	Apr 12, 1996 / May 26, 1996	CGEA	7
Chiltern Railways	Jun 26, 1996 / Jul 21, 1996	M40 Trains	7
Connex South Eastern	Aug 21, 1996 / Oct 13, 1996	CGEA	15
Wales & West	Sep 17, 1996 / Oct 13, 1996	Prism Rail	7/6
Cardiff Railway Company	Sep 17, 1996 / Oct 13, 1996	Prism Rail	7/6
Thames Trains	Sep 19, 1996 / Oct 13, 1996	Victory Railways	7/6
Island Line	Sep 20, 1996 / Oct 13, 1996	Stagecoach Holdings	5
Virgin CrossCountry	Nov 29, 1996 / Jan 5, 1997	Virgin Rail Group	15
First Great Eastern	Dec 4, 1996 / Jan 5, 1997	First Group	7/3
Anglia Railways	Dec 6, 1996 / Jan 5, 1997	GB Rail	7/3
West Anglia Great Northern	Dec 6, 1996 / Jan 5, 1997	Prism Rail	7/3
Merseyrail Electrics	Dec 20, 1996 / Jan 19, 1997	MTL Trust Holdings	7/2
First North Western	Feb 5, 1997 / Mar 2, 1997	Great Western Holdings	7/1
Silverlink	Feb 7, 1997 / Mar 2, 1997	National Express Group	7/6
Northern Spirit	Feb 10, 1997 / Mar 2, 1997	MTL Trust Holdings	7/1
Thameslink	Feb 11, 1997 / Mar 2, 1997	Go-Ahead/VIA	7/1
Central Trains	Feb 17, 1997 / Mar 2, 1997	National Express Group	7/1
Virgin West Coast	Feb 19, 1997 / Mar 9, 1997	Virgin Rail Group	15
ScotRail	Feb 25, 1997 / April 1, 1997	National Express Group	7

Source: Knowles, 1998; OPRAF, 1998a.

	Nat Exp	Stage.	Prism	First Group	MTL	Go-Ahead	CGEA	Sea Con	Virgin	GB Rail	Govia	Halc.	Cowie	Resurgence	GW Hol	M40	MBO
South West Tr.	N	Y					(N)[1]	N									(N)[1]
First Gt West.	N	N	Y	(Y)[2]			N	N		N				N	(Y)[2]		(Y)[2]
c2c		N															N[3]
GNER	N	N	N				(N)[4]	Y	N	N							(N)[4]
Gatwick Exp.	Y		N														N
Midland Main.	N				N												
Connex SC		(N)[5]					Y										(N)[5]
Chiltern Rlys		N					N									(Y)[6]	(Y)[6]
Connex SE		N		(N)[7]			Y										N
Wales and W.		N	Y		N					N							N
Cardiff Railway			Y									N			N		
Thames Trains			N			(Y)[8]										N	(Y)[8]
Island Line		Y[9]	N														
Virgin XC		N					(N)[10]		Y					N			(N)[10]
First Gt East.	N		N	Y		Y			N	Y							
Anglia Rlys	N		Y	N		N				N							
WAGN			N	(N)[11]													(N)[11]
Merseyrail		N			Y										Y		
First Nth. West.		N															
Silverlink	Y	N															
Northern Spt							N				(N)[12]			N	N		(N)[12]
Thameslink		N			Y						Y[13]		(N)[14]				(N)[14]
Central Trains	Y	N		(N)[15]			N	N	N	N	N						(N)[15]
Virgin WC		N						N	Y								
ScotRail	Y		N					N									N

Key: Y = successful bidder (Ys or Ns in parenthesis indicate shared or otherwise allied bids); N = unsuccessful bidder.

Notes

1. MBO bid was in conjunction with CGEA.
2. Great Western Holdings was a MEBO in conjunction with FirstGroup and 3i.
3. MBO bid originally successful then revoked.
4. MBO bid in conjunction with CGEA.
5. MBO bid in conjunction with Stagecoach.
6. M40 Trains was an MBO in conjunction with Laing plc.
7. MBO bid in conjunction with FirstGroup.
8. MBO bid in conjunction with Go-Ahead.
9. No shortlist published.
10. MBO bid in conjunction with CGEA.
11. MBO bid in conjunction with FirstGroup.
12. MBO bid in conjunction with GoVia (see below).
13. GoVia is a partnership between Go-Ahead (65%) and VIA GTI (35%).
14. MBO bid in conjunction with Cowie.
15. MBO bid in conjunction with FirstGroup.

Table 5.2   Shortlisted bidders in the franchising process

Source: Cormack and Pigott, 1997.

Train Operating Company	1995/96	1996/97	1997/98	1998/99	1999/2000	2000/01	2001/02	2002/03	2003/04	2004/05	2005/06	2006/07	2007/08	2008/09	2009/10	2010/11	2011/12
Anglia Railways		8.8	36.2	26.9	22.8	16.5	13.4	8.8	6.5								
Cardiff Railway Co.		10.2	20.6	18.7	17.6	16.3	15.5	14.7	14								
Central Trains		11.5	187.5	173.4	153.7	145.8	140.9	136.6	132.6								
Chiltern Railways		11.6	14.3	12.9	10.2	6.9	4.8	3.4	0.4								
Connex South Central		75.8	76	56.2	48.5	44.8	39.6	37.1	34.6								
Connex South Eastern		57.7	114.6	87.4	63.2	50.7	41.7	33.7	28.5	24.5	19.8	16.8	11.8	8.1	3.3	-1.3	-1.6
Virgin CrossCountry		30.6	115.9	95.5	80	72	66	49.2	38.4	21.5	13.4	6.9	3	0.8	0	-5	-10
Gatwick Express		-4.1	-6.2	-8.1	-10.1	-11	-11.8	-12.4	-13.7	-15.1	-16.7	-17.3	-18.8	-20.5	-22.1	-23.9	-1.9
First Great Eastern		5.6	28.6	14.4	8.4	2.8	-0.3	-5.2	-9.8								
GNER		61.4	55	37.4	17	6.4	2	0.1	0								
First Great Western	9.4	61.8	58.9	55.5	49.4	42.8	35.1	28.2	18.2	8.7	-2.7						
Island Line		0.9	1.9	1.9	1.9	1.8	0.9										
c2c		25.4	27.6	25.8	24.1	22.6	21.2	19.9	18.7	17.6	16.5	15.5	14.5	13.6	12.8	12	1.8
Merseyrail Electrics		7.5	7.4	6.7	6.1	5.8	5.5	5.7	5.4								
Midland Mainline		16.1	8.2	2.5	0.9	-0.5	-2.6	-4.5	-6.4	-8.4	-10.5	-0.9					
First North Western		12.5	100.3	92.4	84.3	77.4	74.1	71.3	69								
Northern Spirit		12.3	224.5	197.1	175.8	164.3	156.3	150.5	145.6								
ScotRail			280.1	264.8	250.5	234.9	220.4	209.3	202.5								
Silverlink		4.2	49.3	36.5	30.6	27.3	23.8	20.6	17.4	16.3							
South West Trains	9.3	63.2	62.6	62.7	57.5	52.2	46.7	36.9									
Thameslink		1.3	2.5	-6.9	-16.7	-23.2	-24	-27.9	-29.4								
Thames Trains		18.7	33.5	25.6	17.5	14	7.8	3.9	0								
Wales & West		38.3	73.5	64.2	59.3	53.1	49.1	45.5	40.5								
West Anglia Gt Nth		14	54.5	35.9	26.2	13.5	4.4	-15	-26.3								
Virgin West Coast		5.8	76.6	70.4	58	55.5	54	-4	-54.5	-57.7	-74.4	-130.9	-156.7	-173.3	-201.8	-209.1	-227.8
TOTAL			1704	1450	1237	1093	984	806									

Table 5.3   TOCs' subsidy profiles, 1995/96 – 2011/12*

* Positive figures represent subsidies payable by OPRAF, negative figures represent premiums payable to OPRAF. Figures in the extreme left columns may be part-year only, depending upon the commencement date of franchises. Figures are in 1998 money terms.

Source: OPRAF, 1998.

The annual financial improvements needed by TOCs to compensate for declining subsidies or increasing premium payments are shown in Figure 5.1. Although there is by no means a neat time/subsidy correlation, the important point to note is the significant increase in the financial improvements required before and after the first three franchises were let. GNER, the first InterCity-type operator to be franchised after First Great Western, needs to improve its financial performance by more than twice that of the latter. Other than Gatwick Express, no other former Inter-City franchise can afford to improve its performance less than GNER. Similarly, Connex South Central must improve its finances by more than three times the figure required of South West Trains and twice that of LTS Rail. Only Connex South Eastern has a less demanding financial task among the former Network SouthEast TOCs. A Regional Railways-style operator was not let in the first batch of franchises, but the minimum financial improvement required by a TOC in this group is 8.3 per cent per year, over six times that of South West Trains and over four times those of First Great Western and LTS Rail. All of the other companies in this group must improve their revenues by the same, or a higher, amount in order to remain profitable.

The ambitious targets set by private sector operators mean that both substantial increases in revenue and cost-cutting are required in order for the TOCs to remain financially viable. For some TOCs, the overall financial improvement required exceeds their ticket revenue at the beginning of the franchise (Knowles, 1998) and such improvements must be achieved by better marketing and/or provision of services and more stringent revenue protection. InterCity-type TOCs are in a good position to expand their businesses because they serve heavily used corridors between major destinations. Former Network SouthEast TOCs have an even greater growth potential because of their large amounts of spare off-peak capacity. Continuing economic growth in the city will also increase their revenue bases. Equally, however, the Network SouthEast-type TOCs could also be the hardest hit in a future recession precisely because of their dependence on commuter business (Knight, 1998).

Train Operating Company

Annual Financial Improvements (%)

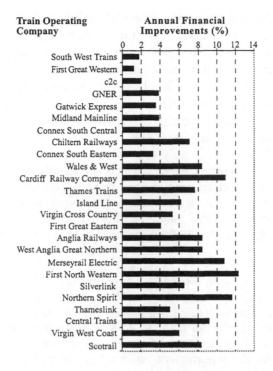

Figure 5.1   Annual financial improvements required by TOCs in order of letting

Source: Glover, 1997.

Former Regional Railways TOCs are arguably the least well-placed to grow their passenger revenues significantly, despite the fact that they generally need the highest annual financial improvements. Not only are they heavily reliant upon peak-time commuting in their urban markets, but many serve rural or semi-rural areas with infrequent trains and limited growth potential (see Thornton, 1999a, regarding rural operators). All TOCs will be vulnerable to future economic downturns (see chapter four) and have only limited scope to reduce operating costs because a large proportion of them are fixed by track access or rolling stock leasing charges.[5]

The medium- and long-term financial viability of TOCs may impact significantly upon the outcome of future bidding rounds. If franchisees begin to lose money, subsidies for at least the next franchise period will have to rise significantly in order to ensure continued private sector interest in the passenger rail industry. Whilst all respondents believed that many TOCs would flourish, some were of the opinion that competition for the market in 1996/97 had been so aggressive that a number of TOCs would be unable to achieve their financial targets:

> We suspect other bidders might [have been] slightly optimistic about how they'll restructure their companies – and that's bad enough – but then we look at some of the revenue assumptions underpinning some of these subsidy reductions and we think some of [them] are very aggressive indeed. Something's got to give... we think others may have some difficulties towards the end.

> Everyone that I know in the industry says [that one TOC will be] impossible. Normally some people say 'oh yeah, this one isn't too bad, or 'you never know'. It's a standard commuter franchise, with a few rural lines. There's no magic to it and they're not going to do anything with the train service that's spectacular. And yet they've... well, we tried to do some rough sums on it and it's spectacular, the improvement they must get. Maybe they will. I hope they do... But if they achieve that, we'll have so much money flowing out of the coffers it'll be ridiculous. We'll all be heroes. So far, there's no indication that's going to happen.

In addition to securing subsidy minimisation, competition for the passenger rail market also manifested itself in terms of quality enhancements (Knowles, 1998). At first, although OPRAF had indicated that it would consider original bid enhancements where two or more tenders were similarly priced, at least three companies submitted non-compliant tenders which sought to provide a greatly improved quality of service in exchange for a high level of subsidy. One respondent, who submitted such a tender for South West Trains, offered to resign from his post as a bidding consultant because he was "miles out" in terms of subsidy from the winning bid. A feeling of disillusionment grew among some bidders, with respondents lamenting OPRAF's apparent uninterest in non-compliant bids:

> [We thought we] could offer to improve the service in some way, presumably there might be some trade off in terms of the level of subsidy the government

would be prepared to put in. I never saw any evidence of that taking place. It was 'who will give me the lowest subsidy or greatest level of premium for taking this franchise off our hands?' ...It certainly took us a painful lesson or two to realise that was the case... We were surprised to realise that all that quality stuff was just put to one side. 'Very nice, thankyou, but irrelevant.'

But the fact that some bidders held these opinions did not serve to undermine the importance of qualitative elements in the franchising process, especially in later bids. In a climate of intensifying competition, the difference between the subsidy profiles of different bidders was reducing considerably. Respondents perceived that low subsidy requirements in themselves became insufficient to guarantee winning franchises and, as a result, the inclusion of – or at least a willingness to negotiate – a host of "goodies" in compliant bids became *de rigueur*:

They [bidders] knew that we [OPRAF] were explicit about the numbers, but we also said that we would look hard at the qualitative aspects of the deal. If we felt, in the round, that one bid might be slightly more expensive, but provided substantially better outputs, we may have chosen that. The bidders could not just have put in bids which were very low and offered nothing because they thought – and they would have been right – that we may have preferred another bid which provided more.

To many bidders, including 'goodies' in tenders made business, as well as bidding, sense. Respondents took the view that certain improvement initiatives, including those which required major investment, were business-case driven in the sense that by 'speculating to accumulate' they would be able to improve their revenue predictions and thus secure a further reduction in the subsidy profile. More conservative bidders, who would only consider investment proposals if the franchise terms were extended beyond those which OPRAF was prepared to let, were now effectively eliminated from the process. An OPRAF official commented:

Someone would say, 'I know you're offering a seven year franchise, but I'd like a 10 year one'. I'd say, 'great, wonderful, when we're offering one we'll give you a call. In the meantime, we'll deal with all the other people who are trying to buy what we're trying to sell.'

Table 5.4 outlines the key service quality enhancements which were secured by the Franchising Director during the competitive tendering process. All 25 franchisees made commitments to maintain service levels above those specified in the PSRs and/or provide more demanding improvements such as station or rolling stock upgrades. 22 franchises improved their targets for punctuality and/or reliability and extra train services were secured in 18 TOCs (Knowles, 1998).

Notwithstanding the subsidy reductions and quality of service enhancements which resulted from the franchising process, some observers maintained that the Franchising Director did little more than secure a 'cheap' railway and that the government overlooked an ideal opportunity to insist upon myriad service improvements not included under current franchising contracts (see chapter seven). At this stage, however, it is sufficient to note that the intensity and outcomes of the competition generated by the franchising process significantly exceeded anything many policy makers had expected given the uncertainty which surrounded rail privatisation before competitive tendering began.

5.2 Explaining competition for the market

OPRAF's judgement and the advantage of uncertainty

Speaking in front of the Committee of Public Accounts in October 1996, Roger Salmon suggested that "a good level of competition" (NAO, 1996: 25) had been generated for the first three TOCs for two reasons, both of which were related to OPRAF's handling of the franchising process. Salmon postulated, first, that his decision to prevent BR from tendering in the early stages of the process and, second, that OPRAF's helping bidders better understand the market, were instrumental in encouraging private sector interest in South West Trains, First Great Western and LTS Rail (*House of Commons Papers*, 1996). Whilst to a degree Salmon's arguments appear self-serving, evidence suggests that OPRAF's actions were indeed important to the success of the franchising process because they helped facilitate a market by removing at least some of the uncertainty which surrounded events at the time.

Train Operating Company	Rolling stock investment	Stations upgrade	New services	Improved passenger's charter
South West Trains	No	Yes	Bus links	Yes
First Great Western	Refurbished	No	Bus links	Yes
c2c	Fleet replacement	Yes	Bus links, off peak	Yes
GNER	Refurbished	No	Bus links	Yes
Gatwick Express	New	Yes	Off peak	Yes
Midland Mainline	New and refurbished	Yes	Extra and faster	Yes
Connex South Central	No	Yes	Off peak and faster	Yes
Chiltern Railways	New	Yes	Extra and faster	Yes
Connex South Eastern	Fleet replacement	Yes	Extra and bus links	Yes
Wales and West	Refurbished	Yes	New routes	Yes
Cardiff Railway Company	No	Yes	New routes and bus link	Yes
Thames Trains	No	Yes	Extra and faster	Yes
Island Line	No	Yes	No	Yes
Virgin CrossCountry	Fleet replacement	Yes	Extra, faster and bus link	Yes
First Great Eastern	Refurbished	Yes	Extra and bus link	Yes
Anglia Railways	New and refurbished	Yes	Extra, faster and bus/air link	Yes
West Anglia Great Northern	Refurbished	Yes	Extra, faster and bus links	Yes
Merseyrail Electrics	No	Yes	No	No
First North Western	Yes	Yes	Extra and new	Yes
Silverlink	New and/or refurbished	Yes	Extra, new and bus link	Yes
Northern Spirit	Yes	Yes	Extra and faster	Yes
Thameslink	Refurbished	Yes	Extra	Yes
Central Trains	No	Yes	New, extra, bus link, park and ride	Yes
Virgin West Coast	Fleet replacement	Yes	Extra, faster and electrification	No
ScotRail	Yes	Yes	Extra	Yes

Table 5.4   Quality of service enhancements secured during the franchising process (in order of letting)

Source: Knowles, 1998.

Although wishing to encourage privately-backed MEBO bids (Freeman, 1993), ministers consistently argued that the BRB should not be allowed to bid for the right to run TOCs (*The Times*, 1993). The government's position was understandable in the sense that the key aim of the 1993 Railways Act was to transfer the industry into the private sector. Letting BR bid for TOCs would have been like allowing the Post Office to buy BT. But the government's position had also been influenced by important practical considerations. First, allowing the BRB to submit tenders would probably have discouraged MEBO bids. Would-be franchisees in BR's employment were already facing the dilemma of separating their responsibilities to the BRB from those to their bid partners and allowing the Board to join the franchise competition would have created extreme conflicts of interest:

> It was difficult enough as it was, having duties to BR and to the State in general as they were paying your salary. You know, you'd accumulated all this knowledge [of how to run a railway] and then suddenly you are supposed to give all that knowledge to OPRAF and their agents so that [they] can get the best price for the franchise. If you also had your bosses, essentially, competing against you, then the conflicts become even more impossible.

Second, the prospect of tenders being submitted by the BRB would almost certainly have discouraged externals from bidding because they viewed BR as having an unfair commercial advantage.[6] Not only might the BRB have cross-subsidised its bids from other sections of its business (Wintour, 1993), but it was also perceived as having an infinite financial backer in the government. As a result, the Board may not have been forced to make commercial assessments of risk and return and the possibility of its submitting extraordinarily low bids could have distorted the entire franchising process. One respondent, a MEBO-turned-external bidder, argued in addition that the BRB's competitive position might have been strengthened by over-optimistic revenue projections made as a result of its approach to running the nationalised railway:

> I mean, they always set impossible targets for the management which were regularly missed. If they'd actually believed those targets, then it would have been impossible to compete against them.

Despite these arguments, the Transport Select Committee remained concerned that excluding the BRB from the franchising process could result in railway expertise being lost from the industry and recommended that it be allowed to participate (*House of Commons Papers*, 1993a). The House of Lords agreed and, in summer 1993, peers including former transport minister Lord Peyton passed an amendment which required that the Board be allowed to submit bids (Wintour, 1993). Reluctantly, after the Railways Bill had 'ping-ponged' between the elected and unelected chambers, the government conceded that the BRB would be allowed to bid for TOCs, but that tenders would be invited subject to the discretion of the Franchising Director (House of Commons, 1993; *The Times*, 1993).[7] Salmon announced in December 1994 that, in the interests of securing sufficient competition for the TOCs, he would 'provisionally' exclude the BRB from the initial franchising rounds (it was later confirmed that BR would not be allowed to bid in the first 13 rounds) (Smithers, 1994). His decision appears to have been an important factor in determining whether or not some bidders involved themselves in the early franchise competitions. A respondent noted that:

> We clearly welcomed the fact that BR weren't able to bid because we felt BR would have a clear inside track. To put a bid together did require very significant effort, time resources and costs... If we felt we were bidding on an uneven playing field, then we would very seriously have reconsidered our position and I suspect, but of course this didn't happen so I don't know, but I suspect we may well have sat back a little bit to see what happened before we decided to go in or not. In other words, to see if BR were picking up five out of the first six, if you like. So we welcomed the scenario where BR weren't able to bid.

The BRB subsequently decided that it would not take part in any of the franchising rounds, even those it could legally have entered, after it became apparent that sufficient private sector interest had been generated in the process (Prynn, 1996a).

Salmon's second assertion was that competition had been generated for the first three franchises because of OPRAF's commitment to helping bidders understand the market for which they were bidding. It has already been noted that passenger rail franchising was being conducted "with a paucity of detail" (Grantham, 1998: 132) and, in a confidential report to MacGregor's successor, Brian Mawhinney, in September 1995, the Franchising Director pointed out that early submissions to OPRAF had been "of variable quality which reflected bidders' immature understanding of the businesses concerned" (Salmon, quoted in Harper, 1995: 18).

OPRAF responded to this problem pro-actively. In addition to providing a suite of basic information sources for bidders – long form reports from accountants, 'data rooms' which detailed virtually all aspects of TOCs' operational environments and sales documentation – the Franchising Director made himself available to all interested parties and sent his staff to 'troubleshoot' at corporate/MEBO board meetings. OPRAF's own systems were still very much in flux at this stage in the franchising process, but respondents acknowledged that OPRAF had made every effort to provide them with information as and when it became available.

The provision of information to external bidders was a particularly important part of the task of maintaining a level playing field between MEBOs and those from outside the industry. One respondent, a member of a MEBO team, suggested that internal bidders had an inherent advantage over their competitors because of their 'inside' knowledge of the rail industry. Significantly, a number of BR's middle-managers, including those who subsequently assembled MEBO bids, were involved in the process of establishing TOCs and liaised with the consultants writing long-form reports. One respondent remembered, "long nights sat in Samuel Montagu's offices drafting ITTs which became a bit of a bench mark for the future." To combat potential problems in this area, OPRAF enforced disclosure regulations to ensure that TOC managers passed on all relevant business information to external bidders. Respondents generally viewed these regulations as effective although some, including those from MEBOs, acknowledged that there was a 'grey area' which incumbent managers exploited to secrete ideas and business propositions they had formulated as a result of their familiarity with the industry:

> Perhaps we had an inside track, sort of 'here's an idea of what we'll do, what do you think?' before it went to Sea Containers and so on... We knew stuff and said 'well we're not going to talk about that unless we're asked'... But we had a bright idea and, you know, we'll put that one in the bottom drawer, save that one. The other management teams were doing the same, clearly, it was obvious.

That said, it is important not to overstate the significance of this 'inside' information. MEBOs had no more access to financial performance data than external bidders because track records had only recently become available. Externals bidding for more than one TOC also accumulated the benefit of repeated exposure to the franchising process, something MEBO teams would clearly lack (although Table 5.2 shows that some MEBOs were supported by experienced corporate bidders). Furthermore, it is likely that any inherent advantage to MEBOs in terms of information was cancelled out by difficulties they experienced in raising bid-capital.[8] Because banks in the UK were suspicious of rail privatisation, some MEBOs were forced to seek funding from foreign institutions or venture capitalists whose high rates of interest impacted significantly on the cost – and hence the competitiveness – of their bids. Moreover, many venture capitalists were conservative with regard to the rail industry's future growth prospects and refused to back MEBOs if their bids were predicated on optimistic revenue predictions:

> Whereas many of us [MEBO bidders] believed that franchises ought to be capable of generating growth of five per cent a year compound, the financial institutions wouldn't accept that on the history of BR's performance in previous years. So the maximum which would have got in the plan was three per cent compound.

Corporate bidders, on the other hand, could take advantage of an established credit history, initiate a stock market flotation or even finance a bid from their own balance sheet to raise capital:

> Those with a healthy balance sheet who were prepared to provide finance for a franchise bid won the franchises because the venture capitalists on which the management teams depended wouldn't match that optimism for revenue growth... We bid for [a TOC], for example. There was no way that in our bid there was a suggestion that subsidy could be removed altogether in the way that [the eventual winner] had done.

Although most external bidders were generally satisfied that OPRAF had sought to eliminate information asymmetries between themselves and MEBOs, it is clearly possible that their views were coloured at least in part by the above considerations.

By excluding BR from the initial franchising rounds and helping bidders understand the market in which they were to become involved, OPRAF removed some of the doubts about rail privatisation harboured by the private sector. Yet even taken together, these two factors do not adequately explain why competition was generated for the South West Trains, First Great Western and LTS Rail franchises. Aside from the fact that OPRAF could only pass on information to bidders when it became available (and in some cases this was late into the tendering process), the

Franchising Director could do little about the general level of uncertainty being sustained by media and political opposition to rail privatisation and there was still no international precedent upon which bidders could draw to gain a better understanding of how the track authority model would work in practice. Two additional factors were found to augment Salmon's account of why bidders became involved in the initial franchising rounds.

First, there were bidders who had always supported the rail privatisation process, or who at least viewed it as an ideal means of adding further transport-related businesses to their portfolios, regardless of the uncertainty surrounding it. One bidder's interest stemmed from the fact that privatisation would give him, as an 'enthusiast', the opportunity to run a railway, but others were more convinced that the proposals made commercial sense, especially in the medium to long-term. Such bidders presumed that, given the increasing political, economic and environmental concerns about traffic congestion and pollution (see, for example, Banister, 1998; Banister and Button, 1993; Goodwin *et al.*, 1991; Hughes, 1993; Preston, 1980; Royal Commission on Environmental Pollution, 1994; Whitelegg, 1993), rail was highly likely to be a growth industry in the future. Moreover, it was felt that any political risk associated with rail privatisation had been overstated because the Labour Party, if it was to form the next government, would be unlikely to renationalise the railways (see chapter four). Indeed, one respondent noted that, perhaps ironically, the prospects for a privately-owned railway were brighter under Labour than the Conservatives because the former was "more likely to be anti-car and that has to help train operators from a commercial point of view."

Second, at least two bidders realised that they could use the general level of uncertainty surrounding the proposition to their advantage in the early bidding rounds. These respondents reasoned that many of their potential competitors were likely to distance themselves from the franchising process initially in order to gauge the outcome before committing themselves. Thus, although cautious bidders would ensure that they did not waste resources should franchising prove a failure, their entrepreneurial counterparts would be more likely secure a TOC at good value in the face of limited competition. Drawing upon their experience from earlier bus privatisations where this pattern had prevailed (see also Knowles, 1989; Wolmar, 1998), the bidders noted:

> With 25 franchises I suppose [being conservative at first] is a strategy you could justify, you don't need to be one of the first three. Our counter to that is our experience... has generally been that you get the best value at the

beginning of a privatisation, you get the best value for the relatively unfancied franchises. If you have an auction process where there's 10 or 15 bidding, you tend to get more overpricing... than you would with [only] two or three.

There are advantages in the information not being very clear at the outset because people are inherently cautious and risk averse, whereas I suppose we're a bit more entrepreneurial so these things can work to our advantage. Contrast that with what's going on now [outside of rail privatisation]. If we tender for an airport, we might find that we were info. memo. number 87... That points to like 100 interested parties. From our point of view, that's not a very good privatisation structure because we're not going to get value for our shareholders. [But] if there's only two or three serious bidders [we will].

To their further advantage, early bidders were rewarded upon committing themselves to the process with the realisation that the limited information available to them in the early stages of the franchising process was not necessarily a handicap when it came to assembling a tender. Although "track records would have been nice," the bidders became aware that other details could easily be estimated, especially at the non-binding, indicative bid stage of the process. For example, although the finalised PSRs were not available when ITTs were issued, it could be presumed that their contents would be similar to the draft documents which bidders had seen:

I think it's always very easy [for people] to get diverted by relatively minute levels of information... The PSR did follow on by a few weeks, but anyone understanding the franchise and the terms of it knew within a minute proportion what level of service would be required. It really was, you know, whether the first departure in the morning had to be before 8.00 or 8.15, it was that sort of detail. So to be honest, I don't think that should have affected anyone's overall appraisal of the business.

Bidders who declined to submit tenders for any of the first three franchises realised in retrospect their mistake. One respondent claimed (rather bitterly) that the initial bidders "got a better deal than they should have," although he did acknowledge that "there is an argument [which says] they deserved it because they were the first people to bid."

A 'ridiculous pandemonium'

The speed at which competition intensified after the first three TOCs had been let surprised some bidders who had expected others (and, in some cases, themselves) to remain cautious throughout much of the process:

> We had expected [that] after these people had sat on the fence the first time that they would still be very cautious because of the uncertainty, the general election looming, all this sort of doom and gloom. This was a privatisation too far, all that business. [But] I don't think that happened. People did have the confidence to come in and come in big... We thought some of the outsiders might have been scared off as a lot of the banks were.

Salmon again suggested that his handling of the franchising process was at least in part responsible for the unexpected bullishness of the market (*House of Commons Papers*, 1996). Respondents acknowledged that they were confident in the system established by the Franchising Director and had no reservations about re-entering later rounds following unsuccessful bids. Using its experience from the initial franchising rounds, OPRAF had been able to standardise almost all procedures and sales documentation and the business of letting franchises was streamlined considerably as a result. In addition, OPRAF quickly established a reputation for integrity among bidders. Respondents commended OPRAF regarding the transparency with which franchising was conducted, some noting that previous franchising rounds in which they had been involved, especially those in the bus industry, had been characterised by,

> ...suspicions and doubts, people with chips on their shoulder, people being aggrieved because they hadn't been rewarded in the way they thought they would and so on.

OPRAF sought to avoid this by publishing the terms of winning bids to provide a benchmark against which unsuccessful bidders could review their submissions. Moreover, the Franchising Director was concerned to ensure that his staff were beyond indiscretion. Only one respondent suspected unprofessionalism on the part of OPRAF (although no evidence could be found to confirm this) and the Franchising Director's diligence was appreciated by bidders:

I never felt that OPRAF people would give injudicious or indiscreet comments to people which was terribly tempting for them if you're letting one of these things [a franchise]. 'Just push it up a bit more...' You never got a sense of them doing that which gave people some confidence.

My cousin worked for OPRAF... He was absolutely obsessive about not being anywhere near me for two years! He had nothing to do with my bid. Even when they had senior management meetings and mentioned [this particular TOC], he would excuse himself. It became one of the OPRAF jokes, but it's actually a great tribute to him and to OPRAF's integrity that they take these issues so seriously.

Although OPRAF's continuing management of the franchising process provided a foundation upon which the market for TOCs could be established, easily the most significant reason for the increase in competition seems to have been a straightforward and very sudden change in market sentiment. Salmon recognised this:

In each case the level of subsidy was ultimately set by competition and after people saw the first franchises sold, saw the reception of those sales on the stock market, saw that serious companies were interested saw the comment of the press, they became keener to bid and put in keener bids to me (*House of Commons Papers*, 1996: 14).

The pessimism with which the private sector had previously viewed passenger rail privatisation transformed quickly into virtually unfettered optimism. Respondents had seen that the contractual minefield of passenger rail franchising could be negotiated and that TOCs could pass into private hands with relatively few problems. Most importantly, however, they had seen that money could be made from rail privatisation. The successful bidders, particularly Stagecoach, had taken over TOCs at a level of subsidy which, when combined with forecasts of even minimal revenue growth, would ensure "a very handsome profit" (*The Times*, 1995: 28). Stagecoach had made few commitments to invest in South West Trains and the bus operator's reputation as an aggressive cost-cutter, notwithstanding the limited opportunities for reducing costs within franchises, led city analysts to predict profits of up to £12 million per year by 1998 (as chapter seven shows, South West Trains actually exceeded this expectation) (*The Times*, 1995).

The subsequent behaviour of Stagecoach was instrumental in alerting potential bidders to the benefits of rail franchising. At a presentation to the

City after securing the South West Trains franchise, Stagecoach, according to a senior OPRAF official, "did a very good job of informing their shareholders of the deal they had done." Derek Scott, then Stagecoach's Financial Director, told Grantham (1998: 144) that:

> As soon as we made a presentation to the City in December 1995 the genie was out of the box. [They said] 'these guys have bought a £280m turnover business, they say they'll average a nine percent margin in seven years and they've bought it for a pound.

In a volatile market unnerved by a sudden tumble on Wall Street (Pangalos, 1995), Stagecoach's share price rose by 17 per cent in the week after it had acquired South West Trains and by a further seven per cent the following week. The *Financial Times* (1996) was later to comment that a key reason FirstBus's shares were performing poorly in relation to Stagecoach's was because the former had failed to obtain a controlling interest in any rail businesses (FirstBus did have a 24.5 per cent stake in Great Western Holdings).

Stagecoach's bravado, along with what was perceived as an aggressive bid from Connex Rail for the South Central franchise soon afterwards, "had the effect of galvanising the market and suddenly lots of other bidders realised this was a market they wanted to be in." Although some bidders applied a consistent rate of return to their tenders throughout the process, others, especially those who had lost out in previous rounds, became much more aggressive as they attempted to win a franchise. A 'must have' culture developed as bidders and investors grew increasingly confident of rail privatisation's financial allure:

> The bus companies got on the bandwagon when they saw how well Stagecoach shares were doing, and National Express, and they thought 'we must have a franchise!' FirstBus got Great Eastern, MTL got North East and so on. So, good luck!

> Clearly other players came in, either desperate to win something because they had not yet won anything or to build a portfolio and time was running out.

> It's so easy to forget the circumstances. The early franchises had been quite a problem one way or another. They'd taken a hell of a long time to get away and the notion was around for a very long time that by the time of the general election it would be impossible to have let all these franchises. So I think people were... saying, 'oh yes, that's what's happening here and four have

gone now [but] there's another 20 left'. Suddenly they discover that actually there are only another 10 left and half of those they didn't like the look of. So they really needed to win X, Y and Z.

As franchising progressed, one city analyst remarked that the competitive tendering process had become "a ridiculous pandemonium" (Nelson, 1997: 32). A respondent who dealt with all the bidders suggested that this was so because ambition increasingly blinded their judgement. Later tenders in particular, he argued, were characterised by hopeless short-termism in the sense that many bidders seemed to ignore potential future problems – such as the traditional link between the economy and railway performance or the potential impact of on-rail competition – in order to lower their subsidy requirements as far as possible. Thaler (1988), on the other hand, has contended that aggressive bidding of this kind results from corporate arrogance. The 'hubris hypothesis' (Thaler, 1988) predicts that companies will attempt to buck the market on the misplaced assumption that they can estimate the true value of a franchise better than the market. This is irrational in the sense that all bidders have access to the same information and the theory suggests that the winning bid will overestimate the true value of the franchise in question and saddle its originator with an unprofitable or loss-making business – the 'winner's curse' (Kennedy, 1995). It has already been noted that respondents believed some of their competitors to have been afflicted.[9] The intensification of competition for the market generally resulted in those bidders who applied consistent rates of return to all their tenders failing to secure any TOCs in the later franchising rounds. One of these was Stagecoach. Despite bidding for virtually all the TOCs, the company won only one, the eight-mile Island Line, after its initial success with South West Trains.

5.3 Competition for the market reviewed: the changing role of the state

Chapters four and five have reviewed the development and initial outcome of passenger rail franchising policy. They have shown that, partly as a result of the circumstances in which the track authority model was adopted, the private sector viewed rail privatisation as something of an uncertain proposition before the TOCs were put on the market in 1995. As a result, the development of franchising policy was heavily influenced by the Conservatives' need to convince potential bidders that acquiring TOCs would make commercial sense. Although the Treasury initially sought to maximise competitive opportunities in the new railway structure, it relented after the DoT realised that such a policy could jeopardise the viability of the franchising process. Even though their position had prevailed, however, senior policy makers within the DoT and OPRAF remained sceptical as to whether meaningful competition for TOCs would actually materialise.

In the event, private sector interest in passenger rail franchising was remarkably buoyant. OPRAF's administrative competence, which removed at least some of the doubts surrounding rail privatisation and thus helped facilitate a market for TOCs, was at least partly responsible for this. More important, however, was the willingness of certain companies to take part in the initial franchising rounds and the sudden change in market sentiment that followed. A limited number of enthusiastic and entrepreneurial bidders were initially able to take advantage of the "doom and gloom" which surrounded rail privatisation to secure South West Trains, First Great Western and LTS Rail on favourable terms in the absence of fierce competition from rivals. Bidders not involved in these franchising rounds quickly became aware that the contractual minefield of acquiring a TOC could be successfully negotiated and, more importantly, that money might be made from rail privatisation.

Before attention is turned to assessing rail privatisation in terms of its generating competition in the market, it is necessary in the context of this book to consider the impact of the franchising process upon the relationship between the railway industry and the state. The level of private sector interest in passenger rail franchising has altered this association in three key areas. First, because all 25 TOCs were let – the franchising equivalent of asset transfer – the state was able to shift much of the responsibility for the provision of rail services to private companies. Franchisees now have (albeit temporary) control over the assets of the TOCs. It is true that the state has retained the right to stipulate minimum output standards in the form of PSRs but, as noted in chapter three, this was inevitable in rail privatisation given the loss-making nature of most rail services. The outcome of rail privatisation was always going to be different from that of other network industries in this sense because the government clearly has a right to demand certain levels of service in respect of the financial support it provides to train operators (quality of service stipulations are discussed in chapter six).

The level of financial support is the second area in which franchising has redefined the state's involvement with the rail industry. As a result of intense competition for TOCs, the subsidy required by franchisees will fall considerably below that which was required by BR at the time of letting. Whereas state support for TOCs was £2.1 billion in 1996/97, it should decline to £806 million by 2002/03, the last full year before the majority of franchisees expire (OPRAF, 1998; White, 1998).   Given that the track authority model increased the overall level of subsidy required by the rail industry before privatisation (see chapter three), the figures should be interpreted with some caution.   Even after sales revenues from Railtrack, the Roscos and other rail businesses are accounted for, the net costs of rail privatisation to the state *could* still be as high as £2.2 billion after 15 years (White, 1998).   Net gains to the state, if there are to be any, depend upon the declining subsidy payments to TOCs which resulted from competition generated by the franchising process.

The degree of competition generated for the market should result in subsidy falling considerably in comparison with that which was paid to BR at the point of privatisation (although it will remain above the amount received by BR prior to restructuring until at least 2001/02 (OPRAF, 1998)).   White (1998) has calculated that, provided OPRAF support payments adhere to current forecasts, the savings which accrue will present a net gain to the state of some £240m by 2002/03. This will increase over time if overall subsidy payments reduce still further.   Thus, the level of state involvement with the railway industry *in terms of financial support* will diminish from that which existed before privatisation in this scenario. As noted in sections 5.1 and 5.2, some respondents suggested that the aggressive bids tendered by some franchisees are not sustainable and that some TOCs, particularly those from the former Network SouthEast and Regional Railways business sectors let towards the end of the franchising process, could soon face financial difficulties.   Should these TOCs go bankrupt, their franchises would (under current legislation) be re-let. Notwithstanding the hubris hypothesis, it is almost certain that the outcome would be financially less favourable to the state because potential bidders would be less likely to over-price a TOC given the increased private sector experience in operating rail businesses.   Such subsidy rises could eliminate any net gains to the state or even, in the unlikely event that they were particularly significant, *increase* the amount of state involvement in the railways beyond that in 1996/97.   Whilst it is certain that government contributions would be higher than at present had competition for the TOCs been less aggressive, the franchising process has not, as yet, diminished the financial role of the state in the passenger rail industry.   These issues are considered in more detail in chapter seven.

Finally, franchising competition produced an unexpected role for the market in terms of investment planning within the rail industry. Section 5.1 noted that the 'value for money' criterion on which franchises were let determined that the state would identify where significant investment (for example, replacement rolling stock) around the network was required and that the market, through competitive tendering, would determine the cost of that investment to the Treasury. However, as franchising progressed and as competition between bidders became more intense, market forces began to both identify and pay for investment opportunities in the privatised railway to the extent that all 25 franchises were let on terms more favourable to rail users than the government had initially envisaged. Bidders improved – or at least signalled to OPRAF a willingness to improve – the qualitative aspects of their bids because they perceived that aggressive subsidy reduction would not in itself be sufficient to secure a TOC. The nature and amount of improvements secured in this way represents a degree of market, rather than state, determination of post-privatisation investment requirements. Although the state did not reduce its role in rail investment planning in an absolute sense, the degree of competition for franchises resulted in the market increasing its relative involvement in this area.

Notes

1. The LTS Rail franchise was revoked after it had been awarded to the MBO team because of financial irregularities. OPRAF re-opened negotiations with the other shortlisted bidders and the TOC was subsequently re-let in May 1996 on slightly more competitive terms than were contained in the original contract. See Grantham (1998) and Wolmar (2000) for a review of events.
2. The average annual claim for South West Trains was £49m (£54.7m in the first year declining to £40.9m in the last), compared to £63.5 million paid to BR in 1995/96 (OPRAF, 1996a). For Great Western the average claim was £40.1m (£53.2m in the first years and £38.2 in the last) compared to £47.3m paid to BR in 1995/96 (OPRAF, 1996b). After LTS had been re-tendered, its average claim was £18.1m (£27.6m in the first year and £12m in the last) compared to £31m paid to BR in 1995/96 (NAO, 1996; OPRAF, 1998a).
3. Life-expired rolling stock is more likely to present maintenance problems (as is currently the case on, for example, the Gospel Oak to Barking Line (*Rail*, 1999a)) which impact upon a TOC's ability to maintain a prescribed minimum level of service.
4. A bid was compliant if it conformed to the requirements or recommendations stipulated by OPRAF. Non-compliant bids might suggest longer franchise terms or offer higher levels of investment, usually at a higher level of subsidy. As will be shown, OPRAF received many non-compliant bids at the beginning of the process, particularly from bidders who misunderstood its definition of value for money.

5. Track access and rolling stock leasing costs are in large part fixed and amount to over 70 per cent of a TOC's total costs (*Modern Railways*, 1995).

6. Ford (1995) took issue with this point at a press conference in late 1995 during the following exchange between himself and Roger Salmon when he found out that BR would be unable to bid: "'Why not?' I asked. 'Because private companies might be put off if they had to compete with BR' said Mr Salmon. 'Oh, come on, everyone knows that BR is "deeply inefficient" (Major J.) and "inadequate" (Major J. again) and the dynamic thrusting private sector companies will run rings around it.'"

7. Realising that the Secretary of State would in all likelihood instruct the Franchising Director behind closed doors to block BR bids, opponents of this compromise noted that the government had missed the point of the Lords' objections. Labour MPs had also foreseen that this tactic was a con (Wintour, 1993).

8. A key characteristic of franchising is of course that it removes the need for bidders to inject a significant amount of capital into a business. However, in order to ensure that a franchisee could not simply walk away from a TOC if its business plans were going awry, the Franchising Director demanded that each successful bidder pay capitalisation and a performance bond. Capitalisation covers the high level of fares paid to TOCs in advance (especially annual season tickets) and performance bonds, which amounted to 15 per cent of a TOC's turnover (First Great Western's was around £14m, for example), are only refundable once a franchise term has been completed (see OPRAF, 1996a).

9. Perhaps predictably, no bidder admitted to having been afflicted *themselves*.

6 Competition in the Market

6.1 Introduction

The purpose of this chapter is to examine the extent to which competition had materialised *in* the passenger rail market by early 1998.[1] The chapter seeks to identify the opportunities for on-rail competition which existed at that time, to assess whether these were being exploited and to discuss their impact upon the relationship between the passenger rail industry and the state. It will be remembered that the promotion of on-rail competition was a primary objective of the track authority model of rail privatisation outlined in *New Opportunities for the Railways*:

> The Government proposes to provide a right of access to the rail network for the private sector operators of passenger services... [Because of this] new operators will be allowed to provide services giving customers a choice stimulating improved services and value (DoT, 1992a: 4).

Section 6.2 of this chapter reviews debates surrounding the appropriateness of on-rail competition and begins by demonstrating that many potential opportunities for competition between passenger operators exist within the new industry structure. As noted in chapter four, however, the plans advanced in the White Paper provoked concerns from observers regarding the compatibility of on-rail competition with the franchising process (*House of Commons Papers*, 1993a; Gibb *et al.*, 1998). Although it was immediately clear to many that the pursuit of on-rail competition might jeopardise the entire rail privatisation exercise, it seems that, for various reasons, the government was initially reluctant to compromise its commitment to this form of market liberalisation. Indeed, it did not formally do so until early 1993, when it announced that some competition would have to be 'moderated' (DoT, 1993b).

The principal argument of this chapter is developed in sections 6.3 and 6.4. The policies ultimately adopted by the Conservatives to moderate competition between TOCs are examined and each is assessed in detail according to the extent to which the passenger rail market had been liberalised by early 1998. It is suggested that, although certain types of competition were permitted and were clearly taking place, most significant competitive opportunities were being restricted by regulation and/or operational factors such as network capacity and rolling stock availability. As a result, much of the passenger rail market was still characterised by monopoly and the industry was based on a comprehensive array of regulatory mechanisms designed to promote a form of surrogate competition comparable to that which governs the utilities discussed in chapter two.

6.2 On-rail competition and the formulation of competition policy

Opportunities for competition

After encountering significant difficulties in adopting the track authority model, ministers' priority following the publication of *New Opportunities for the Railways* was to make it work. The promotion of competition between train operators was an important policy objective in the context of the White Paper. The Treasury in particular, having sacrificed its original plan of train-path auctioning, was keen to ensure that the passenger railway market was liberalised as far as possible (see chapters three and four). In Parliament and in front of the Transport Select Committee, MacGregor and his Minister of State, Roger Freeman, delivered a number of speeches in support of the proposals. MacGregor claimed "it is important... that we carry forward our thinking" because publicly owned transportation systems "could not hold a candle to the market and competition as the best ways of determining what the travelling public... want" (*Hansard*, 1992b: Cols 1161-1162). The track authority option would be "a great deal better than what we have at the moment, a monolithic system with no competition in it" (*House of Commons Papers*, 1992d: 21) and, Freeman noted, open access competition would "start in April 1994," following the reorganisation of BR (*Hansard*, 1993e: Cols 411-412w).

The industry structure envisaged in *New Opportunities for the Railways* provided for at least three different types of on-rail competition – competitive new entry, competition along shared route miles and competition along duplicated routes – and these could occur both between TOCs and non-franchised operators and between TOCs themselves. In addition, the potential for some indirect competition – by emulation – also existed. Each of these types of competition can be characterised by price, where operators would seek to undercut each others' fares, or by quality of service, where an operator might seek to offer a quicker, more convenient or more comfortable journey than its competitors. A combination of both these elements would also be possible (and highly likely).

Competitive new entry rests upon the theory of contestable markets (Baumol, 1982). The theory maintains that incumbents will be incentivised to produce efficiently because of the threat of new market entry from potential competitors. The open access regime allows for the initiation of new services either to compete with those already provided by incumbent TOCs, or to link destination pairs currently unconnected by direct trains on a scheduled or charter basis (Swift, 1997a). These services can be provided in either of two ways: a TOC can expand its operations into the 'patch' of a counterpart, or a non-franchised company can enter the market specifically to provide them (DoT, 1994). Regardless of who works non-franchised services, they are not eligible for subsidy and must be run on a commercial basis. Thus, if a TOC initiates new services of this kind, it must do so *in addition to* the conditions of its original franchise. On the other hand, a non-franchised operator is not constrained by a PSR and, as such, may choose to operate only one service a day on one route if this is considered to be the most profitable option.

Competition on the passenger railway network is not solely dependent upon opportunities for new entry. Despite considerations of market liberalisation being absent when the franchise boundaries were decided (see chapter four), there is considerable overlap in the operating territories of some TOCs and competition along shared route miles can occur where two or more TOCs operate along the same stretch of track (ORR, 1994b). The potential for this type of competition was already considerable before privatisation because, as noted in chapter four, more than half of all rail journeys (56.4 per cent) could be made with more than one of BR's profit centres (ORR, 1994a). Basing the creation of the TOCs on these profit centres maintained this situation and good examples of shared routes are London to Gatwick Airport (Connex South Central, Gatwick Express and Thameslink), London Euston to Birmingham (Virgin Trains and Silverlink) and Penzance to Exeter (Virgin Trains, Great Western and Wales and West).

Likewise, competition along duplicated routes can also occur without competitive new entry. This kind of competition arises when each route is worked by a different TOC (ORR, 1994a) and can exist in two scenarios. The first is between the origin/destination points of the duplicated routes and examples are London to Glasgow (Virgin Trains via Preston, and Great North Eastern Railway (GNER) via York) and London to Exeter (Great Western via Westbury and South West Trains via Salisbury – see Figure 6.1). The second scenario is between stations *along* duplicated routes and their origin/destination points (hereinafter competition 'along route corridors'). As a respondent pointed out,

> If you look at the geography of railway lines emanating out of London, up as far as Milton Keynes, Northampton, Bedford, Huntingdon and Peterborough, then there's not more than 10 miles quite often [between] these particular services. If you live in one of the villages [between these lines] you can go either way.

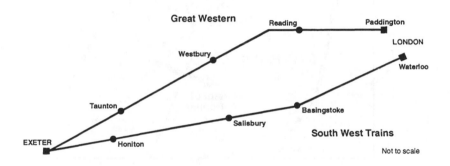

Figure 6.1   Duplicated routes between London and Exeter

To illustrate, a customer living in Dunstable can either 'turn left out of his drive' to use a Silverlink service from Leighton Buzzard to London, or 'turn right out of his drive' to use a Thameslink service from Luton to London (see Figure 6.2). In this example, the TOCs might focus their efforts on shifting an imaginary line which exists between their two routes; Silverlink would want to move the line as far to the right as possible, thus capturing Thameslink's customers, whilst Thameslink would seek to do precisely the opposite. Although this kind of competition can result in additional revenue generation, it was indicated that it is not always as significant as it might seem because of the *relatively* small populations situated between the larger towns served by the train. Moreover, because of the distance people in these 'hinterland' areas must travel to reach a station, they are significantly less likely to consider using the train for non-commuter journeys (Lowndes, 1997).

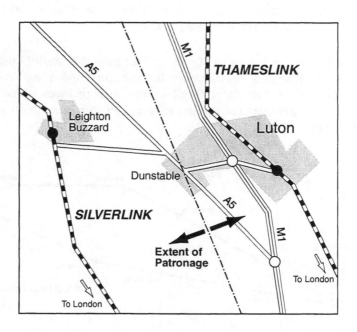

Figure 6.2   Competition along a route corridor

Finally, competition by emulation does not require franchises to be in direct competition with each other (although they can be). This kind of competition, also known as 'yardstick' competition (Foster, 1992) and 'comparative' competition (Williams, 1992), rests on the assumption that companies are keen to be – and be perceived by others as being – leaders in their field. The concept is not new in the railway industry. As noted by Waghorn (1905: 26), in 1876 the Midland Railway Company "adopted the practice of conveying third class passengers by all trains... [and] whether other companies approved or not, they were all compelled... to place themselves on an equality with the Midland Company." An example of how competition by emulation could occur between TOCs was given by a respondent:

> If Richard Branson and James Sherwood are together at a function and Branson's sounding off about how much money he's spending on tilting trains and how wonderful his staff are, you can bet your bottom dollar Sherwood doesn't want to be put in the shade by Branson... There's going to be the pride, the competition of standards. So a report in the FT that says 'the standard of service on GNER's restaurant car is much better than on Virgin Trains" will count for a lot.

As noted in chapter two, competition by emulation was initially regarded as a potentially useful regulatory tool when the water industry was privatised because it was thought capable of providing yardsticks from which comparative performance could be judged. Although it was discovered that comparisons were difficult because of the greatly varying characteristics of each water company – considerable differences existed in costs and other measures of efficiency or service quality (Foster, 1992) – ministers remained keen to promote competition by emulation because it was seen as a means of complementing on-track competition to stimulate additional innovation among TOCs:

> We believed that by allowing many different private sector companies to run the railways – 25 franchises – different ideas about innovation, about service delivery, about pricing, about marketing, about management, about the type of rolling stock, would emerge. And you'd have not one idea, a monolithic idea, British Rail's idea, but you'd have many ideas about how to compete.

The scope for competition by emulation has been formally recognised by the industry and those around it through such events as the Railway Innovation Awards, which honour innovations made by TOCs regardless of whether they compete directly with each other (*Modern Railways*, 1998b).

Constraints on competition

Although these different types of competition were theoretically possible within the reorganised passenger railway industry, policy makers had, by the summer of 1992, paid comparatively little attention to devising means through which they could be administered. Complex issues such as compensation regimes and ticket interavailability were still to be resolved and, perhaps most importantly, the extent to which competition could be introduced into a loss-making industry needed thoroughly evaluating. Because ministers wanted to privatise BR in one parliament (see chapter three), it was especially important that these aspects – along with all others – of rail privatisation policy were completed quickly and efficiently. But as already noted in chapter four, when work began on formulating policy details, progress was initially hampered by a degree of confusion among key actors. Competition policy was not exempt from this and published evidence hints at a degree of misunderstanding between ministers and officials. Ministers' statements to the Transport Select Committee regarding market liberalisation in autumn 1992 were at variance with those of senior civil servants (see, for example, *House of Commons Papers*, 1992c, 1992d) and it is unlikely this was deliberate because, in the words of a civil servant, "there was obviously no overt dichotomy between officials and ministers because that has to be unthinkable." Perhaps as a direct consequence of the above, the Conservatives were initially reluctant to compromise their commitment to on-rail competition despite concerns raised in relation to its appropriateness in the passenger rail industry (*House of Commons Papers*, 1992c; 1992e; 1992f).

Regarding competitive new entry, commentators suggested that the concept of open access competition could be incompatible with the franchising process to such an extent that it might jeopardise the entire rail privatisation exercise. Although in 1992 no decisions had been taken regarding the specifications of individual franchises (DoT, 1992b), it was regarded as probable – and of course turned out to be the case – that most TOCs would be allocated a varied portfolio of routes, some highly lucrative, others less so. A franchisee would therefore need to earn enough profit on its remunerative lines, given its level of subsidy, to ensure an adequate financial return on its whole operation. Meanwhile, open access operators running on lucrative trainpaths would not have the same obligation to maintain uneconomic services and would thus be able to undercut incumbent franchisees. The prospect of revenue dilution on high-earning routes would drastically reduce or even eliminate a franchisee's profitability and, without being able to plan their businesses to any reasonable degree of certainty, potential franchisees would either require extremely high subsidies or refrain from bidding altogether (Foster, 1994; Gibb *et al.*, 1998).

The Transport Select Committee acquired evidence from potential franchisees indicating that open access would create difficulties for franchise bidders in predicting costs and revenues from service operation (*House of Commons Papers*, 1993a). Sea Containers Ltd noted that "it is not clear to us why anyone should bother with a franchise if the [potentially more lucrative] alternative of open access is available" (*House of Commons Papers*, 1992e: 194).

Despite these concerns, the DoT's document *The Franchising of Passenger Rail Services*, published in October of 1992, noted that although franchisees would have an exclusive claim on grant awarded in respect of their contract, they could "not [expect] an exclusive right to run all the services on any particular route" (DoT, 1992b: 15). Primarily at the behest of the Treasury, suggestions which challenged the logic of this assertion were countered (*House of Commons Papers*, 1992d), the views of the BRB were overlooked (see below) and ministers' attitude was increasingly viewed as dogmatic. The government's failure to publicly rule out open access competition added to the general level of uncertainty surrounding passenger rail franchising (see chapter four) and questions were asked as to whether ministers were pursuing ideology at the expense of improving railway services (*House of Commons Papers*, 1992g). James Sherwood, a prospective franchisee, felt "the problem [was] that no-one [had] looked yet at the private sector and said 'how is he going to make a profit from this business?'" (*House of Commons Papers*, 1992e: 196).

As late as November 1992, Freeman insisted that the Transport Committee was "mistaken to suggest that the government has concluded that franchising and open access are incompatible" (*House of Commons Papers*, 1992a: 304), but his position changed soon afterwards. Presumably capitalising on the DoT's increasing influence over rail privatisation policy development (see chapter four), Freeman recognised that a continuing emphasis on open access competition could endanger the completion of rail privatisation. He indicated in December 1992 that the government was now ready to allow some operators exclusivity in order to expedite the franchising process (Tomkins, 1992c) and it was officially announced the following month that open access competition "just wasn't [going to be] practicable." MacGregor accepted that "the prospect of unlimited competition was a major deterrent to prospective franchise holders" (Smithers, 1993b: 3) and *Gaining Access to the Railway Network: the Government's Proposals*, published by the DoT in February 1993, stated accordingly that the government now acknowledged there was a:

...potential tension between liberalising access for private sector operators and successfully franchising British Rail's existing passenger services. This means that to the extent that it is necessary to ensure the success of the first generation of franchises, on-track competition between operators of passenger services may have to be moderated for a limited and specified period (DoT, 1993b: 7).

Whatever form competition policy was to take, its outcome was likely to involve a significant reduction in the potential for competitive new entry into the passenger rail market.

Coinciding with the debate about competitive new entry, questions were also being raised regarding the potential role and scope of price competition along shared and separate route miles. Chapter three identified how these kinds of competition – which, of course, could arise in the absence of open access operators – might create difficulties regarding the establishment of (for example) inter-operator compensation regimes and the maintenance of network benefits. Although the concept of franchising had partially addressed these problems by reducing the number of operators using the network, potentially serious difficulties remained. In particular, concerns revolved around the assertion that competition along shared and separate route miles would erode ticket interavailability (see chapter three), which was widely believed to account for a significant proportion of the rail industry's business (Curwen, 1997; *House of Commons Papers*, 1992e, 1993a).

New Opportunities for the Railways (DoT, 1992a: 19-20) had noted that although the Conservatives were concerned to ensure that "customers continue to enjoy the advantages they get from a national rail system... in the arrangements made for... ticketing," it would be "for the train operators to make arrangements to accept each other's tickets." During its investigations into the future of the railways, the Transport Select Committee found consistent hostility towards this position (*House of Commons Papers*, 1993a). As BRB chairman John Welsby pointed out, it was unlikely that voluntary interavailability would feature in a liberalised regime because where more than one operator ran services between an origin/destination pair they would have no incentive to accept each other's tickets:

> ... as a private sector operator... the last thing I may actually wish to have is your tickets on my train or vice versa. [I] would advise the Secretary of State

very strongly... that in the interests of the customer there has got to be interavailability of tickets (*House of Commons Papers*, 1993a: lxxx).

Welsby's view was corroborated by evidence from the deregulated bus industry, where only 25 per cent of operators accepted each other's tickets, and the experience of Stagecoach, the only company to have recent experience of running a private passenger train service. Stagecoach argued that the government should compel private operators to accept each others' tickets. Its overnight services had been disadvantaged by a lack of interavailability and the company argued that, if necessary, TOCs should have a revenue allocation system forced upon them (*House of Commons Papers*, 1992e).[2]

As with their stance on competitive new entry, ministers at first appeared sceptical of measures which would curtail the prospects for market liberalisation in the new railway industry but eventually conceded that the regulatory authorities should at least have the power to insist on interavailability. The *Draft Objectives for the Franchising Director* (quoted in *House of Commons Papers*, 1993a: para 16) noted that the policy of the government was that ticket interavailability should be considered where "the benefits clearly outweigh the benefits of competition or service diversity." Thus, with competitive new entry already to be restricted, an interavailability requirement would, depending on its scope, remove some or all of the remaining potential for price competition between private train operators on the passenger network.

Looking back on this period of the rail privatisation exercise, a senior policy maker admitted that,

...at some points in the early stages we were being theoretical and what was becoming very evident [elsewhere], that we were heading for competition for the market rather than in the market, didn't dawn on us.[3]

Thus the period between July 1992 and January 1993 had largely been wasted in terms of developing railway competition policy and when the need to restrict market liberalisation was finally accepted, ministers did not know how it would be done. Whilst giving evidence to the Transport Select Committee, MacGregor suggested that restricting competition might be the remit of the Franchising Director or the Rail Regulator, but no details were provided as to how or when regulation might be forthcoming (*House of*

Commons Papers, 1993a). After firing a number of questions regarding details which caused MacGregor to stumble, Committee member Andrew MacKinlay suggested to the Secretary of State that "you do not know, do you sir?" (*House of Commons Papers*, 1993a: 744).   MacGregor acknowledged that the issue needed further consideration: "I think it is important to stress that... there is still, at this stage, quite a lot of detailed information... to be filled out" (*House of Commons Papers*, 1993a: 728).[4]

This task of 'filling out' was ultimately devolved to the ORR and OPRAF and each developed regulatory regimes which, between them, sought to 'moderate' on-rail competition (Gibb *et al.*, 1998). Competitive new entry would be restricted by the Regulator's policy of 'Controlled Competition In Contestable Markets' (more commonly known as 'Moderation of Competition', or MoC) (ORR, 1994c) and price competition along shared route miles would be limited by the Franchising Director's 'Compulsory Interavailability' (CI) requirement (OPRAF, 1996a). Perhaps in an attempt to secure at least some market liberalisation, no administrative restrictions were placed on competition along duplicated routes or competition by emulation; however, what had become very clear by early 1993 was that the outcome of rail privatisation policy, at least in terms of on-track competition, would be substantially different to that which had been envisaged in *New Opportunities for the Railways*. Indeed, in February 1993 the Labour Party's transport spokesman, John Prescott, scoffed:

> If the proposals will not lead to competition in the provision of services... instead of the public monopoly about which the government are so concerned, we shall have what the Secretary of State called 'exclusive service' – in other words, a private monopoly. We shall be replacing a public monopoly with a private one (*Hansard*, 1993b: 176-177).

The following sections of this chapter examine MoC and CI and assess each in detail according to the extent to which the passenger rail market had been liberalised by early 1998.

6.3 The scope for competition in the passenger rail market

Moderation of Competition and competitive new entry

MoC was implemented by the ORR following a period of consultation with interested parties. The Regulator's paper, *Competition for railway passenger services: a consultation document* (ORR, 1994b), stressed the need for policy both to moderate open access competition in the short term and to retain a degree of flexibility in the longer term should market liberalisation become appropriate in the future. The paper suggested four policy options, three of which, 'negotiated charges', 'equalised access charges' and 'access deficit charges' were financial mechanisms based upon different means of charging operators for access to the rail network (see appendix two). The mechanistic approaches were ultimately regarded as unsuitable by the ORR either (a) because they were not capable of moderating competition at all and therefore did not address the problem at hand, and/or (b) because they created barriers to entry, some artificial, which would have been difficult to surmount in the future (ORR, 1994b; 1994c). MoC was the fourth option suggested. In contrast to the mechanistic approaches, MoC was predominantly administrative in nature and was perceived as being the most likely to achieve the ORR's stated policy goals of providing sufficient immediate moderation of competition and long-term flexibility.

MoC would achieve these goals by operating in two stages. Stage one accorded TOCs "effective exclusivity" (OPRAF, 1996a: 65) until late 1999, whilst stage two imposes fewer restrictions to competitive open access entry and will run until at least 2002 (ORR, 1998a). Possible outcomes and implications of stage two are considered in chapter seven. Stage one of MoC worked by defining TOCs' markets as a series of 'point-to-point flows' and by protecting these flows from competitive open access entry subject to certain restrictions (ORR, 1994c). Point-to-point flows comprise services operated by a TOC between any two destinations on its network. For example, a Great Western service from Plymouth to London Paddington will serve a number of point to point flows – Plymouth to Exeter St David's, Exeter St David's to Taunton, Taunton to London Paddington and so on – not just Plymouth to London Paddington. For stage one of MoC, TOCs identified all point to point flows within their network and nominated those on which they required protection. The Regulator protected nominated flows by controlling Railtrack's ability to sell access rights to other operators.

Stage one of MoC thus restricted competitive new entry by making virtually all of the passenger rail market incontestable – crudely, the regulations meant that incumbents were allowed to operate trains whereas potential new entrants were not. In practice, the policy was largely effective, resulting in only "very limited opportunities for train operators to introduce new services" (ORR, 1998a: 1) although this, as the Regulator points out, "is not surprising [as it is] the natural consequence of granting effective exclusivity" to TOCs in stage one of MoC (ORR, 1998a: i). The "very limited opportunities" to which the Regulator referred arose where TOCs joined existing access rights together to create a new direct service between an origin/destination pair already served by another operator (ORR, 1997a). MoC did not envisage this scenario would arise and it was regarded as something of a 'grey area' by TOCs until Wales and West Passenger Trains sought regulatory approval to combine two of its paths between Manchester and Penzance (Batchelor, 1997). A respondent pointed out that, in Wales and West's judgement,

> ...it was absolutely necessary for the industry to establish how the rules of this particular game were going to be played. And it had better be done early, because they've got a seven and a half year franchise and every day ticks away and it's getting very costly for them not to have taken action that day... Therefore it was desperately important that they understood [whether] there was a market which was not being fulfilled.

The affected operator, Virgin Trains, initially suggested that the proposal would breach the principles of MoC because it was "purely a poaching exercise." The Regulator ruled in Wales and West's favour, but Virgin, rather than pursuing its initial grievance, accepted the Regulator's decision:

> It was quite interesting what Virgin's final reaction to that was, [because] although they had initially opposed it, when the Regulator announced his decision they welcomed it because CrossCountry, with its rather complex access rights, may have considerable opportunities to do the same sort of thing.

Following the Regulator's decision, respondents confirmed that other TOCs began examining opportunities for combining access rights to introduce competitive new services. In particular, this was the case where

TOCs had a number of 'dormant' access rights which, although included in the franchising process, were not being used when contracts were let:

> One of the nice things about the... franchises we have got is that there were actually track access agreements in place that weren't being exercised... It is easy for us to reactivate those access agreements at no extra cost, and [combine them with others] without fear of anyone else calling foul and saying 'oh you can't do it because you're poaching... our business.

However, the number of potentially lucrative dormant access rights is relatively low and, by early 1998, this kind of competition was not in evidence elsewhere around the network.

Whereas MoC prevented most competitive new entry, it did not forbid the initiation of what are termed 'non-competitive' open access services (ORR, 1994c). As such, there were two types of flow which TOCs generally could not nominate for protection – non-material flows and flows where the TOC did not serve both the origin and destination points. A flow was non-material if it represented less than 0.2 per cent of a TOC's total farebox revenue. New entry on such flows was obviously unlikely but, if it were to take place, could not significantly affect the incumbent's total income and was therefore deemed uncompetitive. Where TOCs did not serve both the origin and destination points of a flow – for example, Virgin Trains did not serve Aberystwyth to London – they could not nominate that flow because such action might have prevented an open access operator (say, Central Trains) from developing a new, direct service along it. A new 'niche' service such as this would have benefited passengers in mid-Wales and competed with Virgin in the sense that it would provide an alternative for those customers travelling from mid-Wales to London, who would otherwise have had to change onto a Virgin Trains service at Wolverhampton. Central's service would not, however, have run in direct competition with Virgin's operations beyond Wolverhampton because it would not have been able to pick up passengers on Virgin's protected flows to London.

An interesting quirk of MoC stage one was that it seemed to stimulate a degree of competition among operators for the right to provide potentially lucrative niche services – in other words, competition for non-competitive new entry. This kind of competition was particularly evident during the franchising process, with a number of bids including plans for niche service provision (notable examples are North Western Trains' Rochdale, Blackpool and Newton-le-Willows to London trains and Connex South Central's Rugby to Gatwick Airport services). Post-franchising opportunities for non-competitive entry still existed in 1998 (such as Central Trains' operations into Manchester airport) and one respondent suggested that there remained some degree of competition between TOCs to identify them:

> I don't think there's any doubt that if we didn't go to [a destination], somebody else would... It's obviously important to get in on these routes which we think have got an opportunity as soon as possible.

Other TOCs shared this view, with one noting that "there's enough niches neglected... [which] need to be filled."

Compulsory Interavailability and competition along shared route miles

Although stage one of MoC protected TOCs from the threat of competitive new entry, it did nothing to address competition along shared route miles which could have resulted had TOCs introduced an unrestricted range of dedicated tickets at the expense of interavailable ones. As noted in section 6.2, the policy of Compulsory Interavailability (CI) was formulated by the Franchising Director to deal with this issue and still remains in force. CI ensures the continued interavailability of virtually all ticket types on all but one flow on the network. As will become evident, some price competition is permitted by CI, although relatively little had actually materialised by early 1998. CI works in two stages. First, it identifies a 'lead operator' for each interavailable flow served by more than one TOC (as with MoC, CI defines point to point journeys as flows). The lead operator is usually the TOC with the greatest commercial interest over any given flow. Second, the lead operator is required to create fares for the flow, which other TOCs (secondary operators) running trains along it must honour. In this way, a customer can buy one ticket and use it to travel on "the trains of different passenger operators which run in parallel on the same flow" (OPRAF, 1996a: 185). Revenue is 'pooled' and divided among operators by Operational Research Computer Allocation of Tickets to Services (ORCATS), a computerised allocation system, according to passenger miles travelled (see below).

The Franchising Director considers that "the benefits of inter-availability will be outweighed by the potential benefits of price competition" (OPRAF, 1996a: 186) only on the London to Gatwick Airport line and competition on this stretch of railway has developed quickly. Although it is by no means cut-throat, differential pricing is evident and all three companies have engaged in ambitious advertising campaigns to promote their rival services.[5] As one respondent pointed out:

> You [can] go to Victoria station now and see how much [another operator] is investing in competing with us down what is considered to be a lucrative piece of railway. You'll see if you walk around the station there's a lot of effort being concentrated on what's perceived to be a lucrative corridor.

Elsewhere, CI ensures the interavailability of most tickets. Lead operators are permitted to offer dedicated fares for only four ticket types: first class, temporary, special and certain kinds of advance purchase. Each of these fares can be sold for use solely on a lead operator's services and, as such, the associated revenue bypasses the ORCATS system and goes directly to the relevant TOC. Secondary operators are given more freedom. In addition to the above, they are in fact allowed to set dedicated fares for all of their other ticket types. These fares co-exist with their interavailable counterparts to provide opportunities for price competition notwithstanding the CI regulations. Revenue generated in this way also avoids ORCATS. Although all these opportunities for price competition might appear significant, it is shown below that, predominantly for operational reasons, they were often somewhat limited in practice.

First class facilities along shared route miles were usually provided by 'long distance' operators – especially former InterCity TOCs – and it was generally the case that only one operator offered this standard of accommodation over flows to which CI applied. There were, of course, exceptions – for example, first class was provided between Penzance and Bristol by Great Western and Virgin Trains; between London Paddington and Reading/Worcester by Great Western and Thames Trains; and between London King's Cross and Peterborough by GNER and West Anglia Great Northern (WAGN) (Railtrack, 1998). In addition, Thameslink offered dedicated first class travel cards and a season ticket (Thameslink, 1997), but other instances of competition for the first class market between operators were rare despite the apparent logic of discounting tickets to fill currently under-used capacity.

Temporary fares were used by TOCs predominantly to facilitate short-term promotions such as such as Midland Main Line's 'Chatsworth Day Out' offer (Midland Main Line, 1997a). In order to qualify for exemption from CI, temporary fares created by TOCs must not exceed 12 weeks' (17 weeks if the TOC is not a lead operator) duration (OPRAF, 1996a). Although they resulted in pockets of price competition between TOCs, the effects of temporary fares were transient and, therefore, limited in nature. Indeed, this type of fare was designed specifically to prevent initiating operators from gaining a sustainable competitive advantage over other TOCs (OPRAF, 1996a).

Special fares are an obscure collection of ticket types bunched together at the time of privatisation because, according to an OPRAF official, "they could not be included in the compulsory interavailability regulations in any other way." Special fares are unique in the way that they are retailed; predominantly, they are created for localised user groups in order to account for discounts negotiated with TOCs (OPRAF, 1996a). An example would be the Bournemouth Rail Travel Association, where members can purchase discounted tickets for travel with South West Trains from Bournemouth station. Although the potential for this kind of competition existed at stations served by more than one operator, a respondent confirmed that no special fares had been created by any operator since privatisation.

Dedicated, advance purchase fares provide more scope for competition than those mentioned above and generally fall into two categories, season tickets and 'Apex'-style tickets. Season tickets, as the name implies, entitle the holder to use services over a given flow or flows for a specified period of time, usually between one week and one year from the date of purchase. The tickets are primarily sold to commuters in and around the major conurbations, although they are also available on other routes. Price competition for the season ticket market was certainly evident and perhaps the most widely known example was WAGN's Peterborough to London ticket (WAGN, 1997). In early 1998, an interavailable annual season ticket from Peterborough to King's Cross cost £4,600, whereas WAGN's dedicated alternative was priced at £3,556.

The scope for further price competition for season tickets along shared route miles was restricted to the relatively small number of major commuter stations served by more than one operator.[6] In addition, considerations of train loading were critical. Dedicated season tickets could work well from distant or semi-distant commuter nodes such as Peterborough because the amount of customers carried by each train during rush hours was 'manageable' from a TOC's point of view – in other words, it was possible to check customers' tickets after they had boarded the train. In contrast, trains serving more centrally located commuter stations – particularly in the south east – frequently ran in excess of their load factor requirements (OPRAF, 1998b) and revenue protection would have been fraught with difficulty.[7] As noted by a respondent,

> In a suburban railway like this, you can't do that [sell dedicated tickets]. I mean, we carry 80,000 people into London every morning and take them home again at night. You just can't tag people like that. I think in the long term we might have smart cards and all sorts of things and you might be able to have real person-specific journeys... But at the moment you can't do that.

Apex-style tickets are principally aimed at the leisure market and offer a discounted rate of travel for customers making journeys of around 100 miles or more provided certain conditions are met (this usually involves specifying dates and times of travel: see, for example, ATOC, 1998; Central Trains, 1997; GNER, 1997; Midland Main Line, 1997b; Virgin Rail Group, 1997). As with season tickets, it was possible to identify some instances of Apex competition between operators along shared route miles (see Bradshaw, 1997a).[8] Indeed, one respondent pointed out that Apex-style fares were a useful means of poaching business from another TOC:

> If people are travelling by rail anyway then they're fair game. They're easier to attract than a new person who has their company BMW. If somebody's already travelling by rail, I'd like them to travel with us... Being brutally honest... it's fun to grow your market where another operator has to pay.

There is no doubt that the range and number of Apex-style tickets had increased considerably since privatisation.[9] Nevertheless, there was little prospect of an explosion in Apex competition between operators. Apex fares are usually available only over longer distances, because requiring passengers to book days in advance for short journeys (say, Plymouth to Newton Abbot) is wholly impractical in operational terms. Thus, the journeys to which Apex tickets could sensibly be applied were frequently, though by no means exclusively, offered by only one operator. For example, Virgin's Value Fares (Virgin Rail Group, 1997) related to discounted tickets between London and many destinations along the West Coast Main Line

(WCML) such as Stafford, Crewe, Preston and Carlisle and direct travel between London and any of these destinations was only possible with Virgin Trains. When reviewing the extent of Apex-style competition, one respondent pointed out that:

> It's actually quite difficult [for a lead operator to compete on price] given the almost-total operation of interavailability... You could probably quote a hundred examples of it around the network, but a hundred examples in relation to the millions of flows that exist isn't enormous.

Finally, TOCs are permitted to offer dedicated fares for all their ticket types which pertain to flows on which they are a secondary operator. This was regarded by a prominent industry regulator as the primary opportunity for price competition and was "generally considered to be more significant than 'special' or 'Apex' tickets." However, aside from the fact that secondary operators' dedicated tickets do not represent true competition – they are something of a one-sided bargain as the lead operator cannot respond – there were still two operational factors which prevented some operators from competing along their secondary flows. First, irregular service patterns were a problem. Although many flows existed where secondary TOCs offered a frequent alternative to the lead operator's services (such as Silverlink's London Euston to Birmingham New Street trains), there were also instances where the opposite was the case (for example the North Wales Line). Some secondary operators could not address this issue because of the limited availability of rolling stock and trainpaths, especially during busy periods:

> Nobody that I know of has any peak rolling stock capacity spare. Not everybody's peak coincides with everybody else's peak, although there is a certain commonality. But I think you'll find that, with a trivial number of exceptions, everybody's rolling stock is fully utilised in the peak.

> There are some constraints in terms of... track capacity. Full stop. There are only so many trains you can run safely down one line... There will be some places where the simple constraints of capacity will mean competition has some limits.

Second, the bureaucracy involved in establishing dedicated fares on heavily loss-making lines – initiating TOCs have to create new flows and recalculate ORCATS revenue allocations over pre-existing ones (see note 12 below) –

outweighed the economic advantages secondary operators felt would have accrued and some TOCs were dissuaded from the exercise for this reason. As such, only seven operators had introduced dedicated, walk-on fares by early 1998 (see Table 6.1).

Table 6.1   Availability of dedicated, walk-on fares from secondary operators

Operator	Route
First Great Eastern	Ipswich to all Great Eastern Stations and London Liverpool Street
First North Western	Manchester and Blackpool to London Euston
Midland Mainline	Bedford to London first class
ScotRail	Sleepers to London
Silverlink	Birmingham New Street to Silverlink stations and London Euston
Thameslink	Bedford and stations to Luton first class travelcard.
WAGN	Peterborough to London King's Cross and other selected WAGN stations (including travelcard)

Competition for interavailable revenue

In addition to the opportunities for price competition, it was also possible to identify a kind of quality of service competition promoted by CI which is related to the ORCATS mechanism used to allocate interavailable revenue between TOCs. For each interavailable fare, ORCATS shares the total amount of revenue among the relevant TOCs according to the number of passenger miles travelled on each of their services in respect of that fare. ORCATS calculates passenger miles by taking into account factors such as timetabling and speed of journey and by making assumptions about passenger behaviour based on historical survey evidence (KPMG, 1996).

A simple example illustrates this concept. Two operators, 'A' and 'B', run services throughout the day between two sizeable towns. Operator A's trains are non-stop, depart on the hour and complete the journey in 30 minutes. Operator B's trains, on the other hand, call at all intermediate stations, depart at 10 minutes past the hour and have a journey time of 45 minutes. In this example, ORCATS will assume that, because passengers generally prefer a superior service, more people will use operator A's trains – perhaps eight out of every 10 – and the revenue will be divided between the two TOCs accordingly. ORCATS' principal shortcoming is that it cannot provide an entirely accurate record of passenger movements because its calculations are based on assumptions derived from one historical survey rather than continuous flowcounts: it is perfectly possible for the relative loading of operators' trains to change whilst the ORCATS allocations remain static.[10] Operators were aware of this situation but, according to respondents, generally accepted the ORCATS allocations in lieu of a more technologically advanced alternative:

> It's not an exact science, there's a few hundred thousand pounds slopping around in the system – which all sounds very unprofessional – but, if you're not careful, you end up having to sell [dedicated] tickets which restrict people's freedom.

Competition for interavailable revenue occurred when TOCs introduced additional services, or re-timetabled existing services, between an origin and destination pair because such action caused a reapportionment of ORCATS revenue between operators. There were difficulties in identifying genuine examples of this kind of competition – for example, re-timetabling might have been imposed on an operator by external forces such as long-term engineering or the actions of another TOC on a different route – but in general it could be categorised as either *generative service provision* or *ORCATS raiding.*[11]

A generative service is regarded as one which materially improves the overall level of service for passengers (ORR, 1998a). Referring back to the above example, a generative service might result if operator A introduced a new, fast train between the two towns at 07.30 to provide a half-hourly, instead of an hourly, service during the morning peak. The generative service would (in theory) reap a double 'reward' for operator A: first, the apportionment of existing interavailable revenue would shift marginally in its favour because ORCATS would assume that some people who took the 07.10 stopper would now take the 07.30 fast; second, the overall improvement in journey opportunities should encourage more commuters to take the train and increase the interavailable revenue pool for that flow. Thus, operator A should receive a larger proportion of income from an expanded revenue pool.

On the other hand, ORCATS raiding is a mischievous and cynical tactic rarely motivated by a desire to improve the level of service. Although ORCATS raiding had been outlawed by industry regulations, operators could still attempt it by manipulating their train times to increase the share of interavailable revenue beyond that to which they were actually entitled. An ORCATS raid would occur if operator B retimed its 07.10 stopping train to form a new, fast service to depart five minutes before operator A's 07:00 train. Because operator B's new train would reach its destination ahead of operator A's, ORCATS would now assume that most people would patronise the new service as opposed to the pre-existing one. In reality, of course, this may not necessarily be the case – perhaps a connecting bus did not arrive until 06.56 – but the result may be that the 06.55 would run nearly-empty and earn operator B a disproportionately large share of the interavailable revenue at operator A's expense. Such an abstractive technique would not generally increase rail business because it would lead to unnecessary service bunching at the expense of a more practical regular interval timetable (Jones *et al.*, 1993; ORR, 1998a).

It was clear in early 1998 that both generative service provision and ORCATS raiding took place, but attempting to gauge the extent of each was problematic because their precise definitions were open to subjective interpretation. As a respondent explained, the distinction between a generative, new service and an ORCATS raid is easily blurred:

> The economics of railways fundamentally are such that [even] a good, creative new service [which] generates some new business is going to abstract [from another incumbent]. It's probably going to abstract more than it generates. So when is a good, innovative service not an ORCATS raid? ...You have to make judgements.

In order to allow a degree of analytical consistency, respondents were asked to consider competition for interavailable revenue in terms of the ORR's (1997a: 18) position on the subject. This states that "where the demand of passengers to travel between two points is evenly spread over a given period," generative new rail services will ensure that "the overall pattern of rail services should be similarly spread over that period." Essentially, then, generative services were defined narrowly as those which promoted a regular interval timetable, whereas ORCATS raids were those which resulted in unnecessary service bunching.[12]

It was not expected that respondents would necessarily admit to ORCATS raiding themselves, but it was anticipated that they would accuse others of the practice where they felt it was taking place. Following the above definition, respondents suggested that some ORCATS raiding was evident in the period immediately following privatisation (see also *Rail Privatisation News*, 1997). It was pointed out that, in some ways, this was unsurprising:

> With the almost total operation of interavailability... [the new structure] encourages people to play the system which is in place – by that I mean the ORCATS system... A lot of opportunities [for competition] may well... be very related to what ORCATS will reward them [operators] with.

In some cases, opportunities to ORCATS raid were 'inherited' by the TOCs as a consequence of the franchising process and one respondent admitted that they provided a welcome source of additional revenue:

> We have inherited a situation at [one terminus]. We run three trains a day out of [there]. I think it's fair to say that we don't really carry many people on those services, but it gives us a slice of the large revenue that is available... For our 21 carriages in each direction we get a very large slice of revenue, thank you very much, which doesn't in any way equate to the number of people that we actually carry.

However, although ORCATS was initially seen to offer TOCs financial advantages, it was suggested that raids were reducing in number. Not only was this a function of the regulations, but also it was because ORCATS raids were increasingly found to be poor business practice as their effects would probably be short-term and possibly even counter productive:

> We are talking about a network and, to some extent, if you go and raid somebody else's business, sooner or later somebody's going to turn round and do it to you.

> I just think it's a no-brainer, you know. I'll do it this time and then 15 other guys will do it to me. It's just nonsense. I'm not interested in wasting... the limited amount of resources and energy that my business has got in robbing another company.

Numerous respondents believed that the decrease in ORCATS raids was symptomatic of a wider trend of industry maturity developing amongst TOCs, whereby the corporate culture had begun to embrace the virtues of long-term planning rather than short term gain. In particular,

> ...there's a natural, well I would suggest natural, human behavioural thing which says 'having restructured an industry which has created separate entities who are all needing to be the best, [and] to have a vision about how they can be the best, inevitably there's a natural emotive pressure on TOCs to do better than other TOCs.' To some extent, that will cause some reaction in terms of 'let's attack another TOC and see how we can take their business away.' I think there'll be an element of that. [However], there's a re-maturing process that the industry is going through. It's probably going through it faster than many people would have perhaps dared to think possible.... That maturing process... that's coming about quite quickly.

Thus, whereas "one or two companies started taking the odd swipe at each other... there's comparatively little of that [now]." The issue of industry maturity and its potential effect on competition is considered in more detail in chapter seven.

Instances of competition for interavailable revenue were, therefore, increasingly being based around attempts to provide generative new services rather than to execute ORCATS raids. One respondent, who had seen his own revenue decline over a flow following the extension of a service by another TOC, argued that this was very much the case. He pointed out that the other operator's services produced an enhanced timetable following a major investment programme:

> We'd seen a very large reduction, it was around £400,000... It was quite easy to see the swathe of cash that had been removed... Now, one could say 'is that an ORCATS raid?' But it's a consequence of investing... and I can't cry about new [investment] on the railway.

Although generative service provision was growing in popularity, it had not developed as widely as some, particularly those in the ORR, wanted to see. An ORR official lamented that there was still "limited case law" regarding competition for interavailable revenue.[13]

Unregulated competitive opportunites

No regulatory measures were deployed against competition along duplicated route miles or competition by emulation. Aside from the fact that it is practically impossible to legislate against the latter, the most likely reason for leaving these kinds of competition unregulated was because it allowed the government to claim that they had successfully liberalised at least some of the passenger railway market. As a respondent pointed out, this ensured "a couple of bits of it, sort of feather in the cap... [so they could say] 'look, we told you so.'"

The potential for competition along duplicated route miles was, in theory at least, substantial. Despite the network rationalisation which has taken place over the previous 50 years (BRB, 1962; Henshaw, 1991), it was possible to identify more than 80 instances on the passenger railway where competition between origin/destination pairs could have taken place (see appendix three). In practice, however, the opportunities for such competition were considerably more limited than this figure might suggest and this was the case for three main reasons. First, some significant potential for competition was passed up when the geography of TOCs was being determined. As noted in chapter five, delays in policy formulation at ministerial level left officials with little time to design the franchise map and TOCs were based upon BR's profit centres as the latter provided the quickest and easiest division of passenger services. At least 40 duplicated lines were allocated to one company when they could technically have been split between two (see appendix three). A notable example was London to Cambridge where the two routes, one from Liverpool Street and the other from King's Cross, were both served by WAGN.

Second, some franchises operating along duplicated routes were sold to the same owner (Knowles, 1998). Several examples of this were evident, especially in the Connex SouthCentral/Connex South Eastern operating areas. One respondent pointed out that, even though the potential existed for him to introduce a new, competitive service, there would be little point because his colleagues elsewhere in the group were already planning something similar: "we would see any plans to go to [a destination] as being better dealt with by [our sister company] rather than ourselves." Third, many of the remaining duplicated routes either served relatively insignificant markets and/or offered journeys which were not realistically comparable and were therefore neglected as candidates for competitive marketing by TOCs for these reasons. An example is Liverpool to Chester, operated by

Merseyrail Electrics and First North Western. The Merseyrail Electrics service departed every half hour throughout the day and took 38 minutes, whereas First North Western Trains left every hour or two hours (depending on the time of day), did not run before 8am and after 7.30pm and took almost twice as long. A respondent rubbished the possibility of competition existing or being likely to exist on this route.

Thus there were in practice only a small number of meaningful examples of competition along duplicated route miles scattered around the network (see also Adamson *et al.*, 1991), in particular: London to Birmingham, London to Bristol, London to Leeds, London to Exeter, London to Southend and London to Glasgow. Price and quality of service competition was evident on all these corridors, especially between London and Birmingham where in excess of 100 fares were being offered for the journey (BBC, 1996). Perhaps more significant on a network-wide basis were opportunities for competition along route corridors. This kind of competition was found to be possible in numerous places, but respondents indicated that it was taken most seriously by TOCs along six commuter corridors between London and the Home Counties (South West Trains and Thames Trains, Thames Trains and Chiltern Railways, Chiltern Railways and Silverlink, Silverlink and Thameslink, Thameslink and WAGN and Great Eastern and LTS Rail). It was argued that these instances were "not to be underestimated as real, *de facto* competition," and one company had amended its timetables to take account of "the fact that [another operator] is there... [In part] it's to improve our competitive position *vis á vis* the other operator." It should be remembered, however, that *relatively* few people live in the towns and villages between lines and there is limited scope for competition for non-commuter traffic (see section 6.2).

The final area where competition between operators was possible in the new railway industry was competition by emulation. Although dismissed as meaningless by some commentators (see, for example, *The Economist*, 1991), there was evidence to suggest that competitive opportunities opening up in this area were taken seriously by TOCs and did influence managerial decisions to a considerable extent:

> There certainly will be – and you can see it now – quite a lot of competition by emulation... There's a lot of watching over the fence going on in the industry and everyone's keen to make use of other people's good ideas.

Competition by emulation did not seem to greatly influence the pricing policies of most TOCs. It was not the case, for example, that GNER would be particularly concerned that their average fare per passenger mile was slightly different to Great Western's. There was some indication that each operator was keen to be perceived as well-managed, both financially and operationally, but the principal effect of competition by emulation was to provide a yardstick by which TOCs can measure their service standards relative to those of other operators:

> We're keen to be seen as innovators within the industry and your measures of that are other TOCs. So we're very much in competition to be seen delivering a better service... than any of the other operators. Competition by emulation, that's where it is at the moment. We're in competition in terms of column inches and city profile.

> We see competition regarding service as very straightforward. We aim to provide the best customer service that anybody will be able to experience on a railway train in this country. Now on that basis... the competition, if there is such a thing in that field, has got a lot to live up to.

Innovations in excess of those secured during the franchising process (see chapter five) had been initiated by TOCs eager to be perceived as market leaders in service quality. Examples from around the network were: continuing improvements to dedicated phone enquiry/booking services, complimentary refreshments for all passengers, a 'family carriage' provided for parents with young children, improved train cleanliness and revised catering arrangements.

Of particular importance to TOCs, especially former InterCity operators, were the opinions of business travellers. Business people were regarded as the most widely travelled type of customer and therefore the most likely to compare the relative service standards of each operator. As a respondent pointed out:

> On this railway, you are talking about your customers being at the top end of the market. They are people who get around. I should imagine if you surveyed our customers and said 'when did you go on this line or that other line?' that it wouldn't be very long ago and that they would be perfectly ready to make comparisons between us and [the others]. They know what's out there.

Innovations aimed at business travellers since privatisation include first class lounges, inclusive first class tickets (car parking, journey, food/drink and onward travel for one price), dedicated business coaches in standard class, frequent travellers' clubs and negotiated discounts with car rental companies.

The extent of on-rail competition

The previous four sections assessed MoC and CI in terms of the extent to which the passenger railway had been liberalised by early 1998. It was suggested that: competitive new entry was possible where TOCs joined existing access rights together or introduced 'non-competitive' new services; competition along shared route miles could take place between London and Gatwick Airport; lead operators could offer dedicated first class, temporary, special and dedicated advance purchase fares, whilst other operators could sell TOC-specific tickets of all types; a kind of service competition was possible along shared route miles as a result of the ORCATS revenue allocation system; and competition could also occur unregulated along duplicated route miles and by emulation.

There was therefore scope for competition in the new railway structure in early 1998 which TOCs were beginning to explore. But such market liberalisation must be viewed in relation to both that which would have been possible in the absence of MoC and CI and the various operational restrictions which prevented competition from developing where the regulations allowed it. MoC made virtually all of the passenger railway market incontestable by placing incumbents and potential new entrants asymmetrically. Without it, many more lines would have been subject to the threat of competitive new entry.[14] As things stood in early 1998, there were only "very limited opportunities for train operators to introduce new services" anywhere on the passenger railway network (ORR, 1998a: 1). CI limited price competition for the majority of fares on all but the London to Gatwick Airport line. In its absence, such competition would also have been feasible along other shared route miles. Instead, lead operators were permitted to compete using only four ticket types and, as this chapter has shown, various factors frequently limited the opportunities for market liberalisation even in these circumstances. To an extent, the same was true for secondary operators despite their freedom to compete with all ticket types. Although the ORCATS allocation system associated with CI did encourage a kind of service competition for interavailable revenue, this was generally marginal and was not always developed with the interest of passengers in mind.

The experience of the secondary operators with regard to price competition suggests that capacity constraints and the limited availability of spare rolling stock would always have restricted the amount of competitive new entry and competition along shared route miles it was possible to achieve around the network in the period immediately following privatisation. This does not, however, alter the fact that opportunities for these kinds of competition were primarily restricted by regulatory, rather than operational, factors in early 1998.

Opportunities for competition along duplicated route miles, a potentially significant form of market liberalisation, had failed to materialise on all but a handful of corridors. Despite being unregulated, various factors – such as a failure to allocate duplicated route miles among adjacent, potentially competing TOCs – had curtailed its development. Only competition by emulation, unrestricted by regulatory and operational factors, was acknowledged by a wide range of TOCs as a competitive force around the industry as a whole. However, the presence of this indirect form of competition, combined with the limited examples of direct competition noted above, were not sufficient to move the Regulator from his view that:

> The new railway structure is built on different forms of monopoly in the supply of railway services... The supply of passenger train services is based on 25 territorial franchises with full protection from competition... [G]enerally, passengers... have limited choice in respect of the particular train services they wish to use (Swift, 1997b: 8).

Although a key aim of *New Opportunities for the Railways* was to meaningfully liberalise the passenger rail market, ministers were ultimately forced to adopt regulatory measures which prevented the competition they had originally wanted to promote (Charlton *et al.*, 1997). Against this background, one respondent suggested that restructuring the railway industry to promote direct, on-rail competition was a "complete and utter waste of time." Although this view may be challenged as circumstances change in the future (see chapter seven), in early 1998 there was a strong sense in which 25 regional monopolies had, with relatively few exceptions, replaced BR's national one (Shaw *et al.*, 1998).

6.4 Surrogate competition and the continuing role of the state

The creation of a new generation of privatised monopolies has obvious regulatory implications. As already discussed in the book, there was always likely to be a degree of regulation in the privatised passenger railway industry. Minimum service levels, in the form of PSRs, were necessary to ensure that operators ran an acceptable number of trains in respect of subsidy being paid. In addition, further safeguards were perhaps inevitable in the London area because the prospects for on-rail competition developing along its congested lines were recognised as slim. These regulations were most likely to apply to TOCs by way of fares control and through quality of service requirements. *New Opportunities for the Railways* (DoT, 1992a) made it clear that the government would stipulate 'broad' regulatory objectives and that the Franchising Director would translate these into specific minimum standards by which private train operators would be contractually bound. Beyond these, the general tenor of the White Paper suggested that ministers saw market forces, rather than government intervention, as the principal stimulant of service improvements. In the subsequent absence of competition, however, it would appear that the regulation ultimately adopted to govern the passenger rail market is more extensive than that which had initially been envisaged. Indeed, in early 1998, it impacted upon the production and distribution of railway services to the extent that John Welsby, then Chairman and Chief Executive of the BRB, believed that the TOCs finished up with fewer managerial degrees of freedom than were previously enjoyed by BR under state ownership (Welsby, 1997).

Chapter two noted that the regulation established to control BT, BG and the water industry represented a form of surrogate competition in that it sought to mimic the effects of actual competition by keeping prices down and efficiency up (*The Economist*, 1995c). Surrogate competition consists of economic and social regulation and, as was the case with the utilities, both components were imposed upon the passenger rail industry. The need for economic regulation was not discussed in any detail by *New Opportunities for the Railways* (DoT, 1992a) and nothing was added in *The Franchising of Passenger Rail Services* (DoT, 1992b). In 1993, the Transport Select Committee suggested that RPI minus 'x' style regulation should be imposed upon all franchised services (*House of Commons Papers*, 1993a), but the government maintained that the market should determine the level of fares

TOCs could charge in all areas except those where they enjoyed significant market power, such as London (*House of Commons Papers*, 1993c).

Ministers' final decision on ticket price regulation was not forthcoming until after the adoption of MoC and the principle of CI and it is likely that fares policy was influenced at least in part by the outcome of the ORR and OPRAF's deliberations. Although the precise extent to which the passenger rail market would be liberalised was still unknown, it was clear that there would be significantly less scope for competition than had initially been planned. Given that a key argument underpinning the track authority model is that competition from other modes of transport does not impact sufficiently upon rail performance (see chapter three), the case for market determination of fares had been weakened considerably. Media speculation regarding the level of fares after privatisation was also becoming intense and reports predicting ticket price increases of between 50 and 130 per cent were helping to make the rail sell-off the most unpopular privatisation ever undertaken in Britain (*The Guardian*, 1993; *The Economist*, 1996b). The combination of these factors led to the announcement on May 16, 1995 of a policy to regulate fares – as the Transport Select Committee had originally recommended – across the entire network.

The decision to adopt fares regulation represented a notable reversal of a ten-year-old policy of increasing BR's ticket prices above the rate of inflation. Whilst BR was state-owned, ministers had sought to shift the burden of BR's operating loss progressively from the taxpayer to the passenger. It was claimed in 1993 that this policy would continue after privatisation (*House of Commons Papers*, 1993c), but the adoption of comprehensive fares regulation clearly limited the extent to which this would be the case (indeed, the policy was described by one commentator as "a multi-billion pound sweetener to get passenger backing for privatisation" (Barrie, 1995: 1)).

Details of the regulation are found in literature released jointly by the DoT and OPRAF (1996). As in previous divestitures, TOCs' fares are regulated by the RPI minus 'x' formula. 'X' presently stands at one (having previously been at zero). The Conservatives also created a tariff basket and only included certain fares within it, namely: unrestricted standard class return fares (which permit outward and return travel on any train), some single fares for short journeys, 'saver' fares (which, subject to certain conditions, offer a discounted rate for most journeys over 50 miles) and certain standard class season ticket fares including all weekly tickets. Some Passenger Transport Executives (PTEs) are entitled to set fares in their commuter markets and, as such, these will remain unregulated by the Franchising Director.   In London, Cardiff, Edinburgh and Greater Manchester, the Franchising Director himself takes a comprehensive approach to regulating commuter fares.   A performance incentive applies whereby a TOC's failure to meet agreed punctuality and reliability standards can result in the price cap being adjusted to RPI minus three for certain tickets.   Although the RPI minus one formula is not as stringent as it is in other utility industries (for example, the formula used to regulate BT is now RPI minus 4.5 (Office of Telecommunications, 1999)), it is still regarded by the former Rail Regulator as "radical, almost socialist, planning by a Conservative 'free market' government" (Swift, 1997c: 7).

In terms of social regulation, *New Opportunities for the Railways* noted that minimum levels of service (what became PSRs) would be required and certain quality of service standards – such as punctuality and reliability – would be expected of all operators (DoT, 1992a).   Although the imposition of PSRs was inevitable, it was not entirely clear in the market-orientated context of the White Paper how far ministers intended quality standards to be enforced specifically by regulation (see, for example, *House of Commons Papers*, 1993a). The government committed itself only to setting 'broad' objectives, leaving the Franchising Director free to determine detailed regulation for TOCs "as appropriate" (DoT, 1992a: 7).   In this sense, the White Paper might be interpreted as advocating the maintenance of quality standards through a combination of regulation and market forces depending on the operating characteristics unique to each TOC. Thus, with the exception of PSR obligations, contestable lines might have been subject only to minimal social regulation, whereas routes on which the threat of competition was remote would have had more exacting requirements imposed upon them.

As it turned out, the only piece of social regulation to vary substantially between TOCs was the PSR, each one being written according to the social, operational and market conditions particular to the services operated by the TOC it governed (see chapter four).   The remaining safeguards were based upon BR's National Conditions of Carriage (NCC) (BRB, 1996) and were applied more or less equally to all operators to reflect the high number of incontestable lines across the network.[15]   TOCs were required, as BR had been since the introduction of the Citizen's Charter in the early 1990s, to produce a 'user-friendly' summary of the NCC in the form of a 'Passenger's Charter.'[16]   The charters had to set out TOCs' commitments as regards operating punctual and reliable trains, as well as: ensuring acceptable train capacities, providing information on services, fares and facilities, meeting the needs of disabled travellers and disseminating information in advance of delays and non-emergency engineering works. In all cases, TOCs' charters had to contain provisions at least as favourable as those offered by BR. (Some operators elected to offer certain improvements over the standards aspired to by BR and a comparison in Table 6.2 of BR and Wales and West Passenger Railway's charters demonstrates this.) TOCs' performance in each area of their charters is monitored by OPRAF through customer satisfaction surveys and formal incentive regimes (OPRAF, 1997).[17] Finally, TOCs are obliged to participate in ticketing and other schemes organised by the Association of Train Operating Companies (ATOC) in order to secure the additional provision of network-wide products. Examples of such products are the National Rail Enquiries Service (NRES) and discount railcard schemes.

The imposition of economic and social regulation upon TOCs represents continuing statutory involvement in the passenger rail industry, just as it did in the utility privatisations of the 1980s. Despite a change of ownership, the absence of competition meant that the state did not simply withdraw from the affairs of the rail companies. At stake again was the *form* of government intervention rather than its existence (Thompson, 1990). As noted in chapter two, Foster (1992), when discussing the utility sell-offs, argued that the regulation adopted after privatisation was more systematic and penetrating than anything which had existed under nationalisation. Ministers addressed the constitutional loophole which had enabled them only to issue nationalised industries with instructions of a 'general character' and constructed regimes which conferred specific and detailed powers upon regulators to tackle areas of poor performance. Furthermore, the independence from government of the utility regulators has been called into question as evidence indicates that ministers sometimes used pressure to 'inform' the day to day decisions of regulatory authorities (Jenkins, 1995).

The economic and social regulation imposed upon the passenger railway shares these characteristics. The requirements are more stringent than those which governed BR in the sense that TOCs, like the utilities, can now be formally punished for failing to meet prescribed standards (see BRB, 1992, 1996; OPRAF, 1996a; 1997). Whereas any specific command to BR like "'make sure the 8.15am from Victoria runs on time' would have been legally unenforceable" (Howe, quoted in Foster, 1992: 114), the Franchising Director fines operators whose trains are delayed, too short or cancelled.

The penalties imposed on TOCs for their failure to meet NRES performance targets have confirmed the Regulator's equal willingness to enforce quality standards (OPRAF, 1997; ORR, 1997b).

Table 6.2   A comparison of key commitments in the passenger's charters of BR and Wales and West Passenger Trains Ltd

Criteria	BR (Regional)	Wales and West	Improvement?
Punctuality	90% of long distance trains to arrive within 10 minutes of schedule	90% of long distance trains to arrive within 10 minutes of schedule. To improve to 92% by 1998	Yes
Reliability	99% of services to run	99% of services to run. To improve to 99.5% by 1998	Yes
Compensation (one-off journeys)	20% of price paid for journey refunded if delayed for >1 hour	20% of price paid for journey refunded if delayed for >1 hour. Improves to 50% refund for delays >2 hours	Yes
Compensation (season tickets)	5% discount on monthly or longer season tickets if punctuality <87% or reliability <98%. 10% discount if both punctuality and reliability below these thresholds	5% discount on monthly or longer season tickets if punctuality <87% or reliability <98%. 10% discount if both punctuality and reliability below these thresholds. For annual season tickets, the above discounts rise to 7% and 14% respectively	Yes
Ticket office queueing	Maximum five minutes peak. Maximum three minutes off-peak	Maximum five minutes peak. Maximum three minutes off-peak	No
Information	Timetables at all stations. Notice of engineering work at affected stations. Notice if advertised, on-board catering is cancelled	Timetables at all stations. PA or freephone information boards at all stations by 1999. 7 days' notice of engineering work at affected stations. Advance notice if advertised, on-board catering is cancelled.	Yes
Disabled travellers	48 hours' notice for assistance at staffed stations	24 hours' notice for assistance at staffed stations	Yes

Sources: BRB, 1992; Wales and West Passenger Trains, 1997.

Neither the Rail Regulator nor the Franchising Director are protected from potential and actual ministerial interference in their affairs. Although the Regulator is officially independent from government (see chapter three), he was obliged to take into account guidance issued to him by the Secretary of State until January 1st, 1996 (House of Commons, 1993). It was under such guidance that MoC, detailed earlier in this chapter, was formulated. Even now, however, ministers still reserve the right to change his brief informally, through 'moral suasion', or formally through legislation in the same way they do with the utility regulators (Veljanovski, 1987). In 1997, for example, the Regulator signed a 'concordat' setting out a framework for co-operation and communication between his office and the government. This was followed by a request from the Deputy Prime Minister, John Prescott, for the Regulator to review his *laissez faire* position on regulating the Roscos (ORR, 1997c, 1998b). Press speculation also suggested that Prescott refused to renew John Swift's contract in 1998 because the latter had not pursued a significantly interventionist approach to regulating the railway industry (Prynn, 1999).

The Franchising Director does not operate with the same constitutional independence as the Regulator because he is required to function according to the OIG issued to him by the Secretary of State (OPRAF, 1997). In this sense, he is even more susceptible to the whim of government. On a macro level, the Labour administration has amended and rewritten the OIG (although this was in part to update OPRAF's duties), whilst on a micro level the Conservatives, particularly Brian Mawhinney, pursued policies contrary to the wishes of Roger Salmon (Grantham, 1998). The most significant example of this was the RPI minus 'x' regulation outlined above which, according to a respondent, was regarded by Mawhinney as one of his more notable achievements as Secretary of State for Transport.

One policy maker noted that he found past experience with utility regulation highly instructive when he came to construct and implement the regimes which would govern the passenger rail industry. Certainly it would appear that, as with the privatisations of BT, BG and the water industry, the Conservatives had again secured "not so much a change in the content of rules, or a departure from regulatory objectives, [but simply] an adjustment to the means of enforcement" (Hancher and Moran, 1989: 131). Given the market-orientated thrust of *New Opportunities for the Railways*, it is unlikely that the government originally intended to maintain such an extensive role for the state in the affairs of the whole passenger rail industry. Nevertheless, having failed meaningfully to liberalise the passenger rail market, ministers felt compelled to create a regulatory system to exert significant control over the privatised industry.

6.5 Conclusion

This chapter has assessed rail privatisation policy in terms of the extent to which the passenger rail market had been liberalised by early 1998, four years after BR was reorganised. It has shown that the outcome of the policy used to privatise the passenger railway differed considerably from that which had been intended in *New Opportunities for the Railways*. Despite BR's undergoing a complex restructuring exercise designed in large part to promote on-rail competition, BR's monopoly had, with relatively few exceptions, been reconstituted in the private sector. As a result, a host of regulatory mechanisms, comparable with those imposed on BT, British Gas and the water industry, were required to enforce a regime of surrogate competition capable of governing the behaviour of TOCs. Chapter two suggested that the privatisation of the utilities throughout the 1980s was as much – if not more – of an exercise in the formulation of regulatory mechanisms and institutions as it was an attempt to promote competition and reduce state control over the industries. This trend undoubtedly continued in the passenger rail industry.

A regulatory 'domino effect' developed in four stages. First, ministers' concerns regarding the consequences of mass service withdrawals resulted in continuing subsidy and PSRs. Second, the threat posed to the completion of the franchising process by on-rail competition – both from open access operations and the erosion of ticket interavailability – prompted regulation to prevent the competition ministers had originally wanted to promote (Charlton *et al.*, 1997). The regimes which were formulated to undertake this task, MoC and CI, are manifestations of ministers' realisation that on-rail competition could not be, at least in the short term, an entirely realisable outcome of rail privatisation policy. Vertical separation was efficacious when the electricity companies were privatised because the industry was profitable. Difficulties were almost certain to be encountered with the track authority model of rail privatisation because competition between train operators could threaten the viability of many services; private sector companies would simply not compete with each other for the right to lose money. The fact that this point was overlooked would seem to further illustrate just how little ministers appreciated the likely implications of vertically separating the railway industry when *New Opportunities for the Railways* was published (see chapter three). Third, economic regulation was made necessary by the re-emergence of monopoly and, finally, this was complemented by social regulation in the form of quality of service stipulations designed to provide a 'surrogate' competition regime with comparable objectives to those imposed on the utility industries in the 1980s. The likelihood of the relationship between competition and regulation in the passenger rail industry changing in years to come is discussed in the following chapter.

Notes

1.   Interviews in the field were completed by this time, almost four years after BR was initially restructured (see chapter one).
2.   The lack of ticket interavailability contributed towards the subsequent removal of the Stagecoach Rail overnight service.
3.   One respondent argued that he "certainly did not believe that on-track, head to head competition was going to happen..." However, this response contradicts his comments some years previously in documentary sources.
4.   One respondent from the DoT, when asked if policy makers had any idea at this stage how competition would be moderated, answered simply: "no".
5.   Standard single fares were £9.50 on Gatwick Express and Thameslink's trains and £8.20 on Connex South Central's – although there were actually more than 35 different fares in existence between London and Gatwick Airport.
6.   Aside from Gatwick Airport, the principal examples were Bedford, Colchester, Croydon, Luton, Milton Keynes, Peterborough, Reading, Slough, Sutton and Watford. Dedicated standard class season tickets were available from Peterborough (WAGN), Bedford and Luton (Thameslink) and from Southend (LTS Rail).
7.   Load factor requirements pertain to the amount of people south eastern commuter TOCs are supposed to carry on a train at any given time.
8.   London to Birmingham, Bristol, Coventry, Exeter, Glasgow, Leeds and Manchester; the South West to Manchester; Portsmouth to Manchester and Birmingham to Cardiff being principal examples.
9.   Apex-style fares on the railway were both invented, and promoted, by BR.
10.   When an operator introduces a dedicated ticket, he is required to compensate the other operator(s) on the affected flow because it is highly probable that passenger behaviour will change. If this change is likely to be large, the lead operator may conduct a new survey to replace the existing one. In other cases, recourse to a survey may not be necessary and the initiating operator can seek agreement from the others on the basis of an estimate.
11.   Some additional complexities, providing more opportunities for ORCATS-based competition, have recently emerged within the industry (see chapter seven).

12. Even so, interviewees' responses could not be corroborated satisfactorily with reference to timetables. For example, where services beginning in entirely different areas converge, could it be classed as an ORCATS raid if one arrives minutes before the other? Some liaison with the ORR was necessary and analytical judgements will almost certainly be open to question.
13. The ORR deals with all applications to run new services.
14. Admittedly, this would have been slight on uneconomic lines.
15. Although those operators providing services into the major conurbations are subject to some additional stipulations in certain circumstances.
16. The Citizen's Charter was the brainchild of John Major, and sought to encourage service industries to improve their standards of customer care.
17. Interestingly, the customer satisfaction surveys did not allow simple comparisons between operators because they were not standardised. In this sense, an opportunity for stimulating a degree of yardstick competition was being lost; OPRAF recognised this and uniform standards for TOCs' surveys are now being imposed.

7 Conclusions and Prospects for the Future

7.1 Introduction

The central aim of this book is to evaluate the extent to which the promotion of competition was an appropriate policy goal in the privatisation of British Rail. In pursuit of this aim, the book set out to critically evaluate the evolution, outcome and future prospects of the policy adopted to liberalise BR's market and to examine the translation of neoliberal political philosophy into practical policy measures. There are three key objectives: (a) to establish why and how the liberalisation of the passenger train market became an important goal of rail privatisation policy; (b) to assess the outcome of rail privatisation policy in terms of the extent to which the passenger rail market has been liberalised; and (c) to review the future prospects for competition developing between passenger train operators.

The preceding analysis has so far addressed the first and second of these objectives. The main findings have been that, despite the sale of BR having been considered by the Conservatives for more than a decade, neither the privatisation and liberalisation strategy advanced in *New Opportunities for the Railways*, nor the decision to adopt it, can be considered the result of a thorough exercise in policy analysis. The opportunities for, and even appropriateness of, a neoliberal agenda to promote competition between train operators – albeit inevitably compromised by the need for the state to provide continuing subsidy and demand certain performance standards in return – had not been well assessed when the White Paper was published. Despite this, private-sector interest in passenger rail franchising was for various reasons remarkably buoyant and the high degree of competition for the market affected the relationship between the passenger railway industry and the state by: a) shifting responsibility for the operation of rail services to private companies; b) initially increasing, but presenting the chance to decrease, the level of financial support paid to train operators; and c) increasing the relative importance of market, rather than state, determination of investment requirements in the privatised railway. Competition in the market, however, had largely failed to materialise by early 1998. Despite ministers' rhetoric that open access competition would begin in April 1994 and the massive restructuring of the railway industry to allow this, BR's monopoly had, with relatively few exceptions, been reconstituted in the private sector. A suite of regulatory measures, comparable with those imposed upon BT, BG and the water industry, were required to enforce a regime of surrogate competition capable of governing the behaviour of TOCs and the privatisation of BR, like the utility sales in the 1980s, was as much an exercise in the formulation of regulatory mechanisms and institutions as it was an attempt to promote competition and reduce state control over the industry.

In the context of the analysis presented in earlier chapters, it is possible to suggest two key conclusions. First, competition for the market would appear to have been a workable and successful policy option whereas competition in the market, by early 1998 at least, was less so; and second, the success of franchising seems to have occurred despite the muddled circumstances in which the track authority model was adopted whereas the failure of open access would seem to reflect them. In the context of the uncertainty which characterised the rail privatisation exercise, OPRAF's achievements, in the words of one respondent, "were quite exceptional." Had Roger Salmon and his successor, John O'Brien, failed, the franchising process might have been left uncompleted, the TOCs may have been let at significantly higher subsidy levels and private sector-driven investment in the railway could have been lower. As things stand, they managed to transfer the assets of all 25 train operators to the private sector and, provided that TOCs meet their subsidy reduction targets, the amount of competition generated in the franchising process should reduce the amount of operating subsidy to a level below that given to BR before its restructuring in 1994. Furthermore, the quality of services provided to passengers should improve by more than ministers had intended.

On the other hand, competition in the market had not, by early 1998, materialised to anything like the degree which some in the government – particularly the Treasury – had hoped. It seems that an initial failure to appreciate key aspects of British railway economics resulted in *New Opportunities for the Railways* being over-optimistic about the prospects for open access competition developing quickly around the network. John MacGregor's decision to endorse an open access regime is all the more surprising given that franchising was already a central plank of rail privatisation policy. Competition for the market is often introduced as a substitute for competition in the market where the latter is not possible (Foster, 1992) – perhaps for reasons of natural monopoly (see Demsetz, 1968) or, in this case, because an industry loses money. In the past, ministers had selected one or the other, rather than both simultaneously, and MacGregor would no doubt have been aware of this given that the Conservatives introduced competitive tendering regimes throughout the 1980s and early 1990s in many areas of the public sector (Gibb *et al.*, 1996; Pirie, 1988).

The lack of on-rail competition in the new railway industry might be regarded as a major disappointment in policy making terms given that a fundamental aim of *New Opportunities for the Railways* was to promote it. It should be remembered that vertically separating BR was directly responsible for the inflated transaction costs, and thus subsidies, currently incurred by the privatised railway industry. The Conservatives' attempts to introduce competition in the market were considerably less effective than their efforts to promote franchising and to a large extent the success of the latter is being relied upon to recapture the costs of the former. It would seem in this context that the approach adopted to privatise BR was unnecessarily complex and expensive. A different method of selling the railways, such as sectorisation or the regional model, would have been compatible with franchising (see chapter three) and might have achieved similar levels of on-rail competition at a significantly reduced cost. The history of rail privatisation policy development exposes some practical limitations of neoliberal theory and illustrates ministers' apparent failure to acknowledge some of the difficulties involved in translating philosophy into policy.

Whether or not these conclusions appear reasonable, it is certain that they can be only tentative. Whilst in some respects they confirm the speculative analyses of others such as Preston (1997) (who suggested that there would be a healthy level of competition *for* the market) and Shires *et al.* (1994a) (who argued that promoting competition *in* the market would be problematic), they are provisional in the sense that the policy to which they relate was implemented only a short time ago. Although *New Opportunities for the Railways* was published in July 1992 and BR was restructured in April 1994, most TOCs have been in private hands for only three years and the new industry structure is still, to a certain extent, 'bedding in'. To illustrate, although much on-rail competition was in 1998 being prevented by MoC and CI, these regulations have recently been relaxed to provide new opportunities for market liberalisation (OPRAF, 1999a; ORR, 1998a).

Moreover, the present Labour administration is now imposing its agenda on the rail industry and changes to its operational environment will be made as a result of impending transport legislation. OPRAF is being replaced by the Strategic Rail Authority (SRA), which will have more control over train operators and become responsible for developing a long term, coherent strategy for Britain's railways. The powers of the ORR are also being slightly redefined. It is therefore the case that further conclusions arising from this study need to be informed at least in part by a discussion about the prospects for rail competition in the foreseeable future.[1] Such conclusions will of course be unavoidably speculative, but recent events have revealed a number of trends which shed some light on possible policy outcomes.

The remainder of this chapter addresses the third objective of this book by reviewing the future prospects for competition developing between passenger train operators in the British railway industry. It also presents some overall conclusions in relation to the central aim of the study.

7.2 Future prospects: competition for the market

Speaking in late 1997 and early 1998, when interviews for this book were undertaken, respondents were confident that their involvement in passenger rail franchising would be long-term. Passenger numbers were increasing throughout the industry and, because many TOCs were still in their first year of private operation, their subsidies had not yet begun to decline (Department of the Environment, Transport and the Regions (DETR), 2000; Hope, 1997).[2] Although there had been some suggestion that certain bidders would face a tough task offsetting their future subsidy reductions (see chapter five), respondents were keen to stress that they saw no reasons to dissuade or preclude them from bidding in future franchise rounds.[3]

Several franchisees elected not to wait until 2003/04 to expand their TOC portfolios staged successful takeover/merger bids: FirstGroup, Laing and Go-Ahead bought out Great Western Holdings, M40 Trains and Victory Railway Holdings respectively and Stagecoach purchased a 49 per cent share in Virgin Trains (Morgan, 1998; *Rail*, 1999b). Media reports also suggested that initially unsuccessful bidders and other companies outside the rail industry were maintaining an interest in procuring TOCs in the future (Prynn, 1996b). The combination of these factors would suggest that key industry actors and observers shared the opinion that TOCs would continue to perform well for a number of years. If this were so, demand – and, therefore, competition – for TOCs being relet in future bidding rounds would be likely to remain high and the success of franchising would be maintained through the continued private sector operation of passenger train services, perhaps at further-reducing levels of subsidy and with increased private investment.

Since 1997/98, the aggregate number of passenger journeys made on the British passenger railway network has continued to grow (see Figure 7.1) and this growth has been accompanied by a significant increase in farebox revenues, from £2,404 million in 1994/95 to £3,089 million in 1998/98 (see Figure 7.2).[4] Such trends have led to continuing optimism regarding the future of the passenger railway industry. Further takeovers have occurred (Arriva bought out MTL in early 2000) and, significantly, the SRA announced a 'refranchising' programme in 1999. Proceedings have begun to re-let six franchises to allow a considerable lengthening of terms in exchange for heavily increased investment.[5] Six companies were shortlisted for the first 'tranche' of three TOCs, suggesting a high level of private-sector interest and confidence in the long-term success of the passenger rail industry. Some rail commentators (see, for example, James *et al.*, 1999; *Rail*, 1999c) are also optimistic about the future financial viability of TOCs and argue that recent growth rates will continue for a number of years.

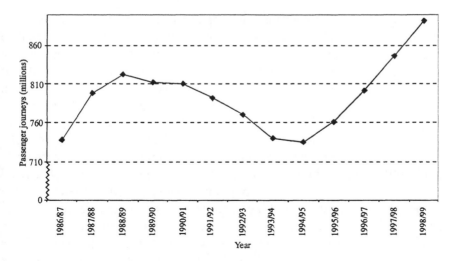

Figure 7.1   **Passenger rail journeys, 1986/87 – 1998/99**

Source: DETR, 2000.

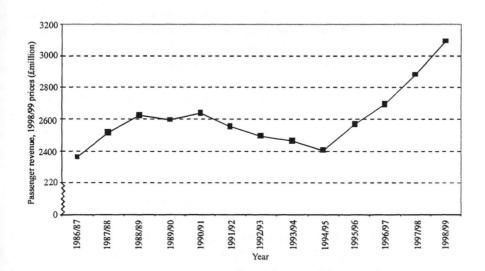

Figure 7.2   **Passenger rail revenues, 1986/87 – 1998/99**

Source: DETR, 2000.

It is not suggested here that such optimism is necessarily misplaced – indeed, it is very welcome following the gloom and uncertainty related to recession and then privatisation in the early to mid 1990s – but this section does highlight some qualifications which, it seems, are being underplayed by many in and around the rail industry. Despite the aggregate growth in passenger numbers and associated revenues, the financial performance of certain TOCs looks bleak and is unlikely to improve as the amount of subsidy they receive decreases. Should these TOCs become unprofitable, or even loss-making, the outcome of franchising – or refranchising – rounds in the future may not be as successful as optimists expect. Demand for TOCs could be lower if potential bidders, given their industry experience (or industry-watching experience), come to regard them as commercially unattractive; the government would be forced to let such franchises at more generous terms in order to secure continued private sector operation of train services and this would result in higher subsidy levels and, presumably, a reduced amount of commercially-driven investment.

It will be remembered that all TOCs need to attract more passengers in order to grow their revenue base and offset declining subsidy levels. Scope for cost-cutting does exist – operators have, for example, restructured their workforces and begun to renegotiate certain contracts – but most costs are fixed. Some TOCs, particularly South West Trains, First Great Western and LTS Rail (the first three to have been let) require only a small annual financial improvement of between 1.3 and two per cent. On the other hand, many operators need to secure more ambitious improvements of at least five per cent per annum, with some of the former Regional Railways TOCs needing up to 12 per cent (see Figure 5.1). Although the above growth figures suggest that almost all TOCs should be achieving, or coming close to achieving, their targets, this is not in fact the case. Significantly, the DETR's figures are aggregates and do not therefore take into account variations in performance between different operators.

Chapter five noted that the former InterCity TOCs are in a good position to expand their businesses, whilst Regional Railways operators could be particularly vulnerable in the future. Former Network SouthEast TOCs, although arguably having the greatest growth potential, could also be the hardest hit in a future recession because of their dependence on commuter business. The initial financial results of TOCs since privatisation generally support these assertions (see Table 7.1). Operators of InterCity-type services are performing particularly well, with First Great

Western, GNER, Virgin Trains and Gatwick Express all announcing significant pre-tax profits for 1997/98. Conversely, almost all former Regional Railways operators are beginning to encounter financial difficulties. Although the TOCs are witnessing passenger growth, this is at too low a level to offset the large reductions in subsidy they are facing (see, for example, Prism Rail plc, 1998). MTL, which until recently owned Northern Spirit and Merseyrail Electrics, managed to increase the profitability of its rail operations in 1998/99, but new owners Arriva face very large cuts in subsidy and will probably lose money on these operations this year.[6] Prism Rail has announced that its substantial fall in profits in the first half of 1998/99 was due to its Wales and West and Cardiff Railway companies incurring losses, whilst First Group has publicly written off any chance of making money from its First North Western business (Wolmar, 1999a). Anglia is currently the exception. The company, whose operations are a mix of Regional and InterCity type services, has remained in the black, although its pre-tax profits fell by 44 per cent in 1999 following a £9.3 million reduction in subsidy (see chapter five). Tellingly, former Regional Railways TOCs have begun to argue that some of their services should be cut as it will be impossible to maintain them in the face of falling subsidies:

> The rail industry is lobbying the government to allow it to cut 'unused' rural services in, it claims, a desperate attempt to avert financial disaster because subsidies are falling by almost £1bn. Measures were put in place at privatisation to protect such services, but rail companies say they are now unsustainable (Thornton and Clement, 1999: 14. Inverted commas added).

The fortunes of former NSE operators have been mixed. South West Trains and LTS Rail, with relatively generous levels of support, have both increased their profitability since privatisation. Thames Trains and Chiltern Railways have performed well although, as a respondent pointed out, this was partially expected given that both networks underwent total route modernisation shortly before they were sold. WAGN, also the recipient of many new trains, has reported a healthy profit in the last financial year (Leathley and Nelson, 1999). At the other end of the spectrum, Island Line has yet to make a profit and both Connex South Central and Connex South Eastern have remained in the red despite both franchises requiring relatively modest annual financial improvements (four per cent for South Central, 3.4 per cent for South Eastern (Glover, 1997)).

Table 7.1   TOCs' operating profits/losses (£m), 1996/97 – 1998/99*

Company	1996/97	1997/98	1998/99
InterCity			
Gatwick Express	3.25	3.54	
First Great Western	9.45	27.24	
GNER	-0.37	15.22	
Midland Mainline	1.54	4.77	
Virgin Cross Country	6.69	1.64	-8.27
Virgin West Coast	-12.8	9.9	22.63
Network SouthEast			
Chiltern Railways	0.96	2.01	
Connex South Central	-10.55	-4.66	
Connex South Eastern	-19.62	7.28	
First Great Eastern	4.78	7.42	
Island Line	-0.31	-0.62	
LTS Rail	-1.43	6.82	
Silverlink	1.38		
South West Trains	6.33	21.24	
Thameslink	-2.16	6.82	
Thames Trains	-0.77	5.53	
WAGN	-8.43	11.8	
Regional Railways			
Anglia	6.6	2.92	1.96
Cardiff Railway Company	-2.87	-1.66	
Central Trains	3.33	-6.49	
First North Western	12.52	-0.85	
Merseyrail Electrics	1.1	4.69	
Northern Spirit	-2.2	7.33	
ScotRail	-3.8	-3.06	
Wales and West	-5.19	-4.3	

* Figures for 1996/97 represent only part of the year for some TOCs and cannot always be compared meaningfully with those from following years. Certain TOCs were also in public ownership for some or most of 1996/97. Nevertheless, incipient trends are apparent as operating profit/loss figures are shown to avoid potential distortions from exceptional costs.

Source: James *et al.*, 1999.

In terms of financial viability, something of a two-tier railway seems to be developing with, on the one hand, a group of financially successful TOCs trading profitably and, on the other hand, a number of TOCs who are either already losing money or are expected to move into loss this year. Of course, it does not necessarily follow that this trend will continue in the future. The figures presented above refer to only the first (part) year or two years of private operation. Those TOCs currently experiencing significant growth could witness a slowdown or even a contraction, especially if, for example, overcrowding begins to deter customers from using their services. Conversely, many operators – including almost all former Regional Railways TOCs – are currently receiving new and/or refurbished rolling stock which will enable them to enhance both their standards and levels of service to attract more customers on to the railways. That said, there are two key factors which suggest that significant levels of growth may not be sustained by many operators over the coming years: network capacity constraints and the performance of the economy.

Capacity constraints

As chapter six showed, network capacity constraints will prevent certain operators from running more trains, especially along busy routes at the busiest times of day, regardless of regulatory restrictions. The former InterCity TOCs will be less affected by capacity constraints over the length of their franchises because most have already negotiated access rights with Railtrack which allow for frequency improvements despite current infrastructural constraints. Virgin Trains will benefit from the rebuilding of the West Coast Main Line (WCML) which is set to create a substantial number of additional trainpaths and the GNER refranchising will involve major capacity increases to the East Coast Main Line (ECML). Others, such as First Great Western, Midland Mainline and Anglia, guaranteed extra services as part of their franchise agreements when capacity was still available (although see James *et al.* (1999) for a longer term view).

The remaining TOCs will be more seriously affected. Chiltern Railways has recently been forced to cut around three per cent of its services into Marylebone because it was running more trains than the infrastructure could cope with despite the recent modernisation of the route (Thornton, 1999b). Capacity constraints will also prevent major expansion by Connex South Eastern (again, refranchising will enhance capacity on the South Central network), Silverlink, Thameslink, Thames Trains and

WAGN because of congestion in and around their respective London termini. The Regional TOCs will also face difficulties in increasing service frequencies around major provincial centres – partly as a result of increased InterCity type services – although there is considerable scope to introduce new inter-urban services between smaller population centres such as Portsmouth and Penzance and these may prove particularly lucrative if timetabled and marketed sensibly (*Modern Railways*, 1999a).

Railtrack acknowledges that congestion is a barrier to growth in the railway industry. Its 1999 Network Management Statement (Railtrack, 1999) identifies 30 'bottlenecks' around the network which are currently running at, or near, capacity. Although work to alleviate congestion is underway at 11 of these, solutions to most congestion problems will not be implemented before the current generation of seven-year franchises expire. Railtrack forecast a further 30 per cent growth in passenger numbers over the next ten years, but admitted that "even this level of growth, although unprecedented this century, is at the lower end of the range that our customers [i.e. the TOCs] aspire to achieve" (quoted in *Rail*, 1999c: 22). The company has been accused by many of being risk-averse and has faced considerable pressure from the Rail Regulator who suggested that it has behaved like a public sector utility. Although Railtrack recently revised its growth forecast to 40 per cent over 10 years and unveiled an impressive investment 'menu' potentially worth up to £52 billion (Railtrack, 2000), it may be that its previous, relatively conservative forecast reflects future trading conditions more accurately than the revised figure given the second key factor which could impact upon passenger growth across the network, namely a general economic slowdown (Prynn, 1996b).[7]

The economy

Chapter five noted that while the fortunes of many industries are tied up with the overall performance of the economy, this is especially true of the railways (Nash and Preston, 1993). The onset of a recession reduces not only the amount of rail commuters, but also impacts adversely on the demand for leisure travel as potential customers re-evaluate their expenditure priorities. Economists appear unable to decide on the likelihood of an economic downturn occurring in the near future. Shortly before the 1999 budget, many experts believed that the Chancellor's expectations for growth were far too optimistic and that the economy would stagnate over the next couple of years (*The Economist*, 1999). Some economists now believe that prospects are somewhat brighter, whilst others remain less convinced. Nevertheless, the typically cyclical nature of the British economy – particularly over the past two decades – would suggest that an economic slowdown will occur before too long (it remains to be seen whether politicians' talk about eradicating the 'boom/bust' cycle is credible) and it seems sensible to proceed on this basis.

Some commentators have argued that the effects of a future recession on the railway industry would not be as adverse as those of previous economic slowdowns. Wolmar (1999b) and Wolmar and Ford (2000), for example, suggest that a good proportion of the growth which has taken place since privatisation has been structural and will not, therefore, be eroded by a future economic downturn. This is for three main reasons. First, the 'flair' of the private sector has manifested itself through more and better-marketed services compared with those offered by BR. Second, the advent of fares capping – which replaced a policy of pricing off excess demand through above-inflation ticket price rises (see chapter six) – has improved rail's competitive position relative to that of the car especially after the introduction of the fuel tax escalator (a mechanism introduced by the Conservatives to impose a real terms annual increase in the price of motorists' fuel of five, and later six, per cent). Third, increasing road congestion is encouraging modal switch because, aggravated by delays and inconvenience, motorists will choose an alternative to car travel where one exists.

It is true that the recent growth in passenger numbers is unprecedented in the last 100 years (Railtrack, 1999). Although it is difficult to estimate the impact of exogenous influences on rail demand, it was generally assumed that elasticities with respect to GDP were around 1.5 (Owen and Phillips, 1987). The rail industry, itself taken aback by the speed of growth it has witnessed, has now commissioned revised demand forecasting models in the light of recent experience.

Yet it is unclear how far the current rate of growth can be attributed to the effects of privatisation because the 'revival' of the railway industry began around 18 months before the franchising process started (DETR, 1999). Moreover, TOCs' performance since 1996/97 has been patchy. Whereas certain operators, such as GNER and Midland Mainline, have invested heavily in service improvements and transformed their approach to customer care, others have been criticised for allowing standards to decline (Knight and Harris, 1999). Punctuality and reliability, despite initial improvements, have started declining – largely as a result of the increasing number of trains using the network – and are now little better than they were under BR (see Table 7.2). Customer complaints have risen to record levels and media reporting of railway issues has frequently been negative (Central Rail Users' Consultative Committee (CRUCC), 1999). Fares regulation, whilst protecting four key ticket types, does not control popular *SuperSaver* and 'unrestricted' return tickets and some operators, particularly Virgin, have increased the cost of these fares significantly in relation to regulated ones. Virgin's full fare return from London to Manchester, for example, rose from £96 at the time of privatisation to £141 less than three years later. In combination, these factors may not have done much to encourage large numbers of new *long-term* customers on to the privatised railway system.

The recent growth of rail passenger numbers has also taken place against a background of a seemingly inexorable rise in car ownership and use and figures suggest that the amount of car journeys made on Britain's roads could still increase by more than half over the next 25 years (DETR, 1998a). The British have tended not to buy cars to leave them sitting on the drive – despite the potential threat of traffic congestion – and may be less likely to take the train in times of recession because rail travel would represent unnecessary additional expenditure. Travel by train can still be considerably more expensive than by car despite the regulation of rail fares, particularly where a number of people are making a journey together (Leathley, 1999).[8] The fuel tax escalator narrowed the gap, although Labour has recently discontinued the mechanism and replaced it with a more *ad hoc* alternative. The escalator was proving politically unpopular and studies have shown that it was also unfairly disadvantaging certain sections of society, particularly the rural poor (Roberts *et al.*, 1999).

In short, it is probably too early to be sure that much of the current increase in patronage is structural rather than a result of the buoyancy of the economy. If it is linked to economic growth, experience suggests that passenger numbers will start to fall as the economy begins to make the transition from 'boom' to 'bust'. Yet even if the bulk of the current growth is structural and a recession causes passenger numbers only to level off rather than decline, many TOCs could still find themselves in financial difficulties in the future. Subsidies will continue to shrink after the economy slows down and passenger numbers at the point when recession starts may not be sufficient to offset the reduced government support TOCs will receive in subsequent years. Certain operators, particularly those who have relatively generous subsidies and/or have experienced greater than expected growth before recession, could well be unaffected but it is unlikely that others will be in such a happy position.

Table 7.2   Punctuality and reliability, 1992/93 – 1998/99*

	Punctuality	Reliability
1992/93	89.7	98.7
1993/94	90.3	98.8
1994/95	89.6	98.7
1995/96	89.5	98.8
1996/97	92.5	99.1
1997/98	92.5	98.9
1998/99	91.5	98.9

* The rules defining lateness were changed in April 1995 to be tightened by one minute.

Source: DETR, 2000.

Future franchising rounds

Declining or stagnating passenger numbers will almost certainly have an adverse impact on future (re)franchising rounds. Certain TOCs will of course remain attractive to bidders, especially those which currently enjoy relatively generous subsidy profiles and any which, notwithstanding potential capacity and economic problems outlined above, achieve high levels of growth throughout their franchise periods. Such TOCs will probably be let at terms more favourable to the government than their current contracts. Equally, others will probably appear less enticing and may well have to be let by government with a more generous level of financial support than that paid when the franchises expire or are relet (see also Powell, 1997). The key question is whether the relative benefits secured when letting the more attractive TOCs will be enough to offset the relative disbenefits incurred when letting those with less appeal.

There is, of course, a chance that this will happen; moreover, the premiums paid by Virgin Trains, Midland Mainline, Gatwick Express and

First Great Western (all of whom have 10 or 15 year contracts) will help stabilise the overall level of subsidy paid to the industry after 2003/04. Tough negotiation by the SRA in relation to the TOCs currently being re-franchised could bring an additional 'windfall' in certain cases. However, should a number of TOCs move into a loss-making position by the end of their franchise periods, the government may find itself having to increase, rather than continuing to decrease, the amount of financial support it pays. Although this is not to suggest that the SRA would be unable to find takers for loss-making TOCs, ministers may have to accept that there will be less competition and, as a result, it will cost more, year on year, to secure a similar level of privatised passenger services after the next franchising round. Any net gain which the state might have expected rail privatisation to deliver in the early 2000s could be delayed.

7.3 Future prospects: competition in the market

Although there was little on-rail competition in early 1998, the recent relaxation of several regulatory and operational restrictions presents a number of new opportunities for market liberalisation. The relaxation of CI involves the SRA allowing lead operators to create dedicated fares on a permanent basis (only secondary operators were originally permitted to do this – see chapter six). At first glance, such a step would seem rather drastic as it might be considered tantamount to abolishing CI altogether. Why have a compulsory inter-availability requirement if all operators can create their own dedicated fares? In practice, however, this amendment to CI will have little effect on the current trading environment. In order to create a new fare, operators must apply to, and obtain permission from, the SRA which is required by the government to view inter-availability as a key priority. A respondent from the 'shadow' SRA suggested that although he expects numerous applications, few will be sanctioned. Most additional competition for interavailable revenue is likely to be limited to ORCATS raids and that which is currently permitted by CI.

The relaxation of MoC is more noteworthy. Chapter six noted that stage one of MoC restricted competitive new entry by making virtually all of the passenger rail market incontestable. Stage two of MoC began in September 1999 and will last until at least 2002 (ORR, 1998a).[9] Following the changes, MoC will continue to be administered on a point-to-point flow basis (see chapter six), although now only 80 per cent – as opposed to 100 per cent previously – of farebox revenue will be protected on nominated flows. To illustrate, if First Great Western's Plymouth to London Paddington service raises £10 million per year, an open access rival could introduce new services on the route to compete for up to £2 million of its revenue.[10] Flows not nominated for protection will, as under stage one, be open to full competition, although, again, most of these flows will be on uneconomic lines along which there is no real prospect of new services being initiated.

As with changes to fares under CI, permission is needed (although in this instance from the Regulator as opposed to the SRA) before new services can be introduced under stage two of MoC. Unlike the SRA, the Regulator is not subject to OIG from the Secretary of State and, unless TOCs seek to run primarily abstractive trains (i.e. ORCATS raids), new services stand a good chance of being sanctioned if they can be shown to be in the consumers' interest. The potential impact of stage two, subject to the capacity constraints outlined in section 7.3, could therefore be fairly significant. With the exception of West Coast flows, which have received ongoing protection from competition in light of Virgin's investment undertakings on the route, some InterCity and many inter-urban flows have been liberalised to present a considerable number of opportunities for new inter-peak and weekend services.[11]

Complementing these regulatory changes is the fact that many TOCs are beginning to receive new rolling stock. With the notable exception of former Network SouthEast TOCs, the bulk of whose train movements are in peak hours, operators have had little spare off-peak rolling stock since privatisation because BR was unable to maintain train sets made redundant during the last recession (Knight, 1998). A hiatus of orders for new trains during the railways' lengthy divestiture served to compound this problem (*Rail*, 1998). Since 1996/97, however, many TOCs have placed substantial orders for new train sets both as part of, and in addition to, their franchise commitments (Prideaux, 2000). Many of these are now being delivered and the introduction of new trains will leave spare sets which franchisees or other open access operators can use to bolster their existing services or introduce new ones.

Attitudes to on-rail competition

It still remains to be seen how much TOCs will choose to exploit the opportunities for competition accorded by the relaxation of MoC.

Respondents were divided on this issue in 1998. Some franchisees were of the opinion that, whilst competition is usually to be encouraged, it is not yet appropriate specifically between TOCs for reasons outlined in chapter six – i.e. it cannot work effectively whilst the industry runs at a significant loss. Besides, one respondent argued, TOCs already face demanding surrogate competition, not only in the form of RPI minus 'x' and quality of service regulations, but also because the financial effects of declining subsidies/increasing premiums substantially reduce operators' overall incomes (see also Shaw, 1999). It was thought that more time was needed before properly informed decisions about open access could be made.

Other respondents were more opposed to on-rail competition in principle. Echoing arguments advanced when the track authority model was first being considered by the Conservatives (see chapter three), they argued that on-rail competition is unnecessary as TOCs already face competition with other transport modes, notably the private car:

> Of course, on-rail competition misses the point which is that rail has a pathetically small market share in most markets and that the competition is not out there wanting to use different trains, it's on the roads and that's where we have to work hard and compete.

> The idea of competition between rail companies is a bit of a distraction if you're trying to encourage more people to use trains generally... It potentially dissipates the effort if the rail operators are competing against themselves when they should actually be competing against other forms of transport.

It was further suggested that on-rail competition forces TOCs to concentrate on increasing their share of the existing market rather than seeking its *overall* growth and that this would be to the detriment of the passenger rail industry. One respondent noted that market research conducted by his company had revealed that some rail users were finding rail travel more complex following the demise of BR (although this hasn't, of course, prevented burgeoning passenger growth) and suggested that increasing on-rail competition would make matters worse since the complexities facing customers would multiply. It may well be that rail users will come to accept additional complications which arise from competition in the same way that utility customers now grapple with the liberalised telecoms, gas and electricity markets; the respondent nevertheless suggested that TOCs should focus on co-operation, rather than competition, in their efforts to provide a 'seamless' alternative to the car:

> Far more important [than competition] is co-operation between operators. We can stand or fall on the extent to which the railway operates as a single, seamless product for the public... It's imperative that operators work together... There's far more scope for that than there is for competition.

Instead of deploying rolling stock to compete with another company's services, TOCs might seek to enhance their own levels of service provision on key routes (this could involve lengthening trains instead of running additional ones); rather than omitting competitors' trains from their timetables, TOCs might include them and so on.

Examples of co-operative working have begun to develop around the network. First Great Western and Thames Trains have combined access rights to provide a new through service between Bristol and Oxford and several TOCs now take part in joint marketing schemes, particularly those initiated by extra-industry groups such as the Devon and Cornwall Rail Partnership (Pinder, 1998). Some respondents felt that such inter-TOC co-operation would increase as the industry's outlook matures after the initial uncertainty created by privatisation. Chapter six noted that whereas some TOCs initially sought to attack each other in an attempt to satisfy the egos of newly-liberated management teams, some operators had begun to eschew the superficial attractions of short-term gain in favour of a long-term growth strategy. Evidence cited by respondents in early 1998 to support this thesis was the declining popularity of ORCATS raiding.

A significant increase in co-operation between TOCs would impact considerably on the amount of on-rail competition which develops around the network in the future. If co-operation is viewed by TOCs as a desirable substitute for competition, enabling them to effectively offset declining subsidies/increased premiums, then it would become a kind of self-regulation working in addition to MoC and CI to restrict market liberalisation. The ORR (1997a) has acknowledged that extensive co-operation could negate the effects of relaxing MoC, noting that whilst the Regulator will encourage operators to compete, he cannot force them to do so.

Despite these predictions of growing inter-TOC co-operation, other respondents felt instead that more on-rail competition would take place during stage two of MoC. There were two reasons for this point of view. First, in contrast to the opinions cited above, some argued that existing co-operation around the network was exceptional and belied an immaturity which had persisted throughout much of the industry; indeed, they predicted that rivalry between many TOCs would become stronger in the foreseeable future. One respondent implied that this was because although co-operation is easy to advocate, it is difficult to achieve when sharply reducing subsidies/increasing premiums "require desperate actions." He argued that laudable long-term aims – and the logic of seeking market growth rather than maintaining market share which underpins them – might therefore fall victim to short-termism if some TOCs attempt to make a 'quick buck':

> There's little in the way, unfortunately, of co-operation... I think that's an element that's been wasted in the rail industry. There's far more options to co-operate with each other and compete against what is the real competitor, which is the car, [but] I don't think there is a maturity in the industry... There's really not been the co-operation, the maturity which one would expect, to fight the real competition which is the car.

> For the last 6-9 months I've been working very closely with colleagues to say 'we must co-operate,' but I'm getting nowhere fast. People are concerned that I will grow my market share and have a vested interest in promoting co-operation. They think I'll pinch some of [their] business... Yes, if my share goes up somebody has to decline in market share, but if the overall growth is so big why should any of us be concerned?

Just as there is emerging evidence of co-operation between TOCs, so there are examples of short-termist competition. Interestingly, and potentially reversing the trend identified in chapter six, many of these have been ORCATS raids. One TOC, which returned operating losses in its first two trading years after privatisation, has identified and implemented a novel ORCATS raiding technique at another operator's expense.[12]   In another instance, Wales and West, the former Regional Railways operator, has cut rural services to free up rolling stock to run along the West of England main line (Wales and West has not ordered any new train sets). Although the company maintains that it is responding to patterns of demand – an ostensibly valid claim, given that its branch lines are patronised so thinly – industry insiders have suggested that Wales and West is engineering an elaborate ORCATS raid in an attempt to address its worsening financial performance. The significance of the ORR's requirement that new services introduced under MoC stage two are primarily generative becomes particularly apparent given such activities.

Second, other respondents were of the view that, far from being destructive or superfluous, an increased level of on-rail competition would contribute positively to the future success of the rail industry. Much as the Conservatives argued in *New Opportunities for the Railways*, it was suggested that on-rail competition would secure market growth rather than encourage fights over market share because it would provide a spur for TOCs to provide better services for customers. Respondents referred in particular to the competition between WAGN and GNER on the Peterborough to London route (see chapter six) which, despite the arguments advanced in opposition to on-rail competition, was viewed as a success. WAGN's services have benefited not only customers – by providing a real choice of operator – but also both TOCs; whereas WAGN has increased its share of both the existing rail and overall markets between Peterborough and London (WAGN, 1999), GNER has been able to use its resultant increase in capacity to attract additional longer-distance customers and accommodate further growth from northern cities such as York and Newcastle. Although WAGN's actions were made possible through CI rather than MoC, respondents were hopeful that similar conditions might be created on other routes with the introduction of new open access services.

Some new services have been introduced since September 1999 (such as Northern Spirit's trains from Carlisle to Glasgow and Anglia's between Ipswich and Basingstoke) and several more have been proposed. GB Railways, Anglia's owner, has announced plans to run across London from Ipswich to Northampton and Romsey and the company is also in partnership with two former BR managers to introduce new services between London and Hull. Virgin will significantly expand its network after 2002, but in the meantime is considering extending its *Dorset Scot* service from Perth to Inverness (Holley, 1999). WAGN was planning to initiate services from London to Doncaster (*Modern Railways,* 1999b) but its application was turned down because of insufficient capacity on the ECML.

The sustainability of on-rail competition

Whether or not the services introduced under MoC stage two will prove financially viable is far from assured, as experience to date is mixed. Although the Peterborough to London example cited earlier has clearly been a success, other new services have foundered. First North Western has been forced to withdraw two long distance services it introduced to compete with Virgin's Blackpool/Manchester to London Euston trains because of poor loading. The Manchester-London service was particularly under-patronised, attracting only 253 passengers per week despite an available capacity of 5,040 (Thornton, 1999b). First North Western's trains might have moved into profit in the future after becoming more established, but this was unlikely owing to their relative infrequency.   Customers travelling with First North Western to and from Manchester had to choose from two services per day, whereas Virgin's could select from 21. Whilst presented in a different context, Wolmar's (1999c) argument that it is difficult to build patronage with an infrequent service is equally applicable here.

Moreover, the lack of ticket interavailability on the route exacerbated the infrequency problem because, unless they bought another ticket, customers were unable to take a Virgin train if they missed their First North Western service. Some open access services introduced under stage two of MoC could also be heavily disadvantaged by these, or similar, factors. Even if they are required to adhere to CI, new entrants are almost certain to introduce – and encourage customers to use – their own dedicated tickets and, so long as they are allowed to compete for only 20 per cent of a flow's total revenue, their services will be infrequent relative to those of the incumbent.

Furthermore, any new on-rail competition which does take place will do so against the background of the impediments to growth outlined in section 7.2. Generative new services will need to attract a large amount of long-term, structural growth against the historic trend of short-term, economically-related growth if they are to survive.   There will be some which accomplish this, particularly those designed to exploit potentially lucrative market niches (see chapter six). An example to date is Connex's Rugby to Gatwick service, which has built up a market from virtually nothing to over 100,000 journeys per month (Knight, 1998) because it greatly simplifies the journey from the south Midlands to the airport and encourages modal switch for this reason.

But such niches may be limited in number and, as a result, potential new entrants could be forced to increase the abstractive element of new service proposals in an attempt to guarantee their financial success.   The Regulator will be aware of this and no doubt seek to discourage such a trend, but in reality he could be faced with a dilemma. Despite the ORR's policy being geared towards preventing abstraction, it still has a statutory duty to promote competition where it is in the interest of passengers. These two goals may become somewhat incompatible once most lucrative niches have been filled and/or current growth levels stagnate. It will be remembered that the distinction between a generative new service and an ORCATS raid is easily blurred and that, in the words of a prominent industry regulator, "you have to make judgements."

On the one hand, the Regulator might be forced to scale down his aversion to abstraction if he wants to continue encouraging new services, because few will materialise if he refuses applications with an abstractive element larger than he is currently prepared to accept. On the other hand, however, sanctioning overtly abstractive new services could result in the financial viability of incumbents being seriously affected, particularly if they are already in difficulty because passenger numbers have failed to grow as predicted in their franchise bid. This will in turn affect the amount of competition for the market generated by future franchising rounds. Although successful new entrants might increase the value of their own businesses – and thus attract a high level of interest from bidders – badly affected incumbents would have to be re-let at far higher levels of subsidy. In 1999, the government appointed a new Rail Regulator, Tom Winsor, who is understood to be significantly less pro-market than his predecessor (Shaw, 1999). If this proves to be the case, the ORR may begin to lose its traditional enthusiasm for on-rail competition and choose to resolve the above dilemma by simply refusing to sanction most applications for competitive new services.

Perhaps the most likely outcome of MoC stage two is that, after niches have been filled, TOCs will adopt a 'defensive' rather than an 'attacking' attitude to introducing new services. In essence, this would involve incumbents identifying lines within their own networks which they think will be vulnerable to attack from new entrants and then 'protecting' them by filling spare capacity with extra trains of their own. As suggested by the theory of contestable markets (see chapter six), it would be the *threat* of competition, rather than competition itself, which forced incumbents to improve their quality and levels of service. Such an outcome has numerous advantages. It allows incumbent TOCs to expand their own markets with which they are already familiar; it minimises the cost of feasible expansion because access rights already exist (although an overall increase in train movements of more than six per cent will incur additional charges) and there is less need for extensive driver training; there will be none of the potential for ticketing and timetable confusion identified above because all new services will be provided by the same operator; and TOCs, in the absence of direct rivalry, could be more inclined to collaborate with each other. In combination, these factors could be more effective than direct competition in increasing the amount of structural growth TOCs are able to attract, thereby assisting many of them in their efforts to offset declining subsidies. Recent evidence indicates that TOCs are becoming aware of this as South West Trains has successfully fought off a threat by GB Rail to operate along the Southampton-London Waterloo corridor by introducing additional services of its own (*Modern Railways*, 1999c).

One final point to make with regard to the future prospects for on-rail competition is the likely impact of the above developments on the relationship between the passenger rail industry and the state. It will be recalled that TOCs are currently subject to surrogate competition in the form of RPI minus 'x' and various quality of service regulations specified in the Passengers' Charters and elsewhere. Although in theory an increase in the amount of competition between operators should result in a decrease in the need for regulation, this is unlikely to happen in practice. Apart from the fact that the regime originally proposed by the Conservatives – different routes being subject to different degrees of regulation depending on the level of competition they supported – would be complicated in the extreme to implement successfully, the present Labour administration is arguably less sympathetic than the Conservatives to promoting 'hands-off' policies and, in the case of the railways at least, is strengthening its control over the passenger railway industry (DETR, 1998b; Knight and Harris, 1999; Shaw *et al.*, 1998; see also Jenkins, 1999). It is extremely improbable that, even if passenger growth exceeded all expectations, capacity constraints were resolved and on-rail competition became viable across much of the network, the regulations currently governing the performance of the TOCs would be relaxed.

7.4 Promoting railway competition: an appropriate policy goal?

Competition for the market

Whilst the above analyses add a new perspective to the tentative conclusions outlined in section 7.1, they in fact do little to detract from the validity of the original statements. In terms of competition for the market, although it was suggested that the success of the 1996/97 franchising round might not be repeated in the foreseeable future, any increase in subsidy bills need not – and, indeed, should not – undermine the case for passenger rail franchising. Competitive tendering will still offer numerous advantages.

First, franchising will continue to facilitate competition for a market which, despite the impact of MoC stage two, could retain a significant element of monopoly in areas such as London.   More importantly, however, franchising will provide the government with a mechanism for the continued protection of both passengers' and taxpayers' interests (Wadsworth, 1995). If one operator's performance is poor, another can be sought after – or even, as refranchising has shown, during – a contractually specified time period.

Thirdly, franchising will also enable the government to redraw the boundaries of TOCs. It is likely that the 25 franchises designed in 1994/95 will not remain appropriate for a variety of reasons such as the completion of major infrastructural improvements or the identification of new opportunities to realise economies of scale. It was pointed out in chapter four that an optimal division of BR's operations might have involved the creation of fewer TOCs. The SRA already intends to franchise a new TOC, TransPennine Express, and has commissioned a study into the feasibility of creating a new 'WalesRail' operation. Further recasting is likely. The issue of redrawing franchise boundaries has recently been discussed by Whitehouse (1998), although the Franchising Director was aware there would be a need to reconsider the operating territories of some TOCs before letting them again in the future. As a respondent from OPRAF pointed out in 1997:

> One of the criticisms I've heard levelled against us [OPRAF] recently is 'what on earth do we think we're doing having lots of franchises finishing at the same time?' It wasn't an accident, we did it on purpose, and the reason we did it on purpose is that at the time we let these franchises we believed that the format of each of these businesses was right. In seven years' time they may be different. We wanted to give ourselves the opportunity to reconfigure some of these franchises if we thought there was a better way of getting more benefits to the passengers. It might not happen, but then again it might... So we've given ourselves the option of making sure those franchises finish at the same time so we can take the benefits of any reconfiguring if we want to.

Although any reduction in the number of franchises will obviously result in fewer competitive tenders, the amount of competition generated for each could be greater than if the current 25 are retained because potential bidders would be encouraged if improved business prospects were associated with each.

Fourthly, franchising will give ministers scope to alter rail policy in accordance with future changes to the government's wider transport and/or environmental objectives. A key criticism of the Conservatives' attitude towards rail privatisation might be that, although some major investment was secured, emphasis was placed on securing a 'cheap' rather than a quality railway.[13] From an environmental perspective, for example, the latter would have been more desirable because of its heightened potential to play a central role in effecting large and sustainable modal shift from road to rail. The sale of BR provided a real opportunity for the government to influence people's travel habits because through franchising ministers could have secured ambitious output targets at a competitive price from the private sector. Such a policy would probably have been unacceptable to the Conservatives because it would have meant significantly increasing the level of financial support to, and thus the influence of the state over, the railway industry. The new Labour administration is less preoccupied with neoliberal ideals than were the Conservatives and train operators could benefit from a public-private investment partnership in the future. The franchise renegotiations currently underway present a window of opportunity in this regard.

Ironically, it could be that a more radical neoliberal approach would offer the chance of realising a more environmentally sustainable transport policy. Numerous authors have argued that a key reason for rail's decline relative to the continued ascendancy of the private car is that the two transport modes do not compete on a level playing field (see, for example, ASI, 1983; Campbell-Bannerman, 1993; Hibbs, 1998). Although this has been the case for many decades (Shaw *et al.*, 1998), the problem was exacerbated in the 1980s by an ideological paradox in Conservative transport policy. The Thatcher administrations sought to promote individual freedom by encouraging car use, but this was achieved and maintained through what amounted to huge subsidies – i.e. state intervention – for motorists. Whilst petrol and road taxes covered the cost of road building and maintenance, they failed to take adequate account of costs incurred by externalities such as congestion, pollution, threats to safety and so on (see, for example, DoT, 1996b; Goodwin, 1993; Pearce *et al.*, 1989; Maddison *et al.*, 1996). Thus the *true* cost of motoring remained significantly higher than that which road users actually paid. At the same time the Conservatives sought to ensure that a progressively higher proportion of BR's costs were being met by its users rather than by state subsidy and, in combination, these factors hugely distorted the transport market to the benefit of road and the detriment of rail.

Recent real-terms increases in fuel duty and rail fares regulation (both of which were initiated by the Conservatives) have begun to address this imbalance, but the market distortion remains and is likely to do so for some time. It is perceived that charging motorists the true cost of using the road would be inflationary (although there is no reason that this should necessarily be the case – see Goodwin, 1993) and, to say the least, politically difficult (witness the abandonment of the fuel tax escalator). As such, it is unlikely to happen in the near future. This is unfortunate, because the long-term effect of 'levelling the playing field' between road and rail would almost certainly be significantly increased patronage for train operators. As Martin and Michaelis (quoted in Hughes, 1993: 76) point out, "if car users had to pay the full external cost, in a system which recovered the full costs of the congestion and nuisance effects of car use, they would be far more likely to take the train." The rail industry's increased revenue expectations would enable Railtrack to embark upon a far more ambitious investment programme, the train operators to order more new trains and provide more frequent services and the government to diminish its influence over the rail industry at least in terms of subsidy payable. Competition both for and in the passenger rail market would then become much more viable.

Competition in the market

Whereas franchising was and remains advantageous despite anticipated setbacks, the case for competition in the market is less convincing. In early 1998, on-rail competition was limited around the network, although more will arise because of the implementation of MoC stage two. Nevertheless, in judging whether or not it was an appropriate policy, a key question is: will the amount of on-rail competition which develops be sufficient to justify the Conservatives' method of rail privatisation and the restructuring costs/opportunity costs associated with it? Answers to this question will inevitably be speculative and also subjective, as much can depend upon differing interpretations of 'appropriateness'. One respondent pursued an ideologically dogmatic line, arguing that establishing an environment in which on-rail competition can take place was justifiable despite its cost and practical outcome. The respondent's views were based on the assumption that all competition is good and, therefore, that some competition is better than none. Another suggested that on-rail competition could only be judged appropriate if it benefited all passengers equally, but this is problematic in the sense that universal advantage is unlikely to be the result of *any* government policy. Perhaps most reasonably, it was suggested that appropriateness in this sense should be defined as a utilitarian concept to reflect the generalised circumstances in which government policies are frequently devised – will the promotion of on-rail competition result in service improvements for most passengers whilst at the same time produce a cheaper and more efficient railway for the majority of both passengers and taxpayers?[14]

Whilst on-rail competition has led to service innovations on certain lines, most improvements since privatisation have arguably had little to do with direct inter-TOC rivalry; Railtrack's station regeneration programme, rolling stock refurbishment schemes and increases in train frequencies were all enacted during stage one of MoC. It is true that competition along shared route miles and competition by emulation will have stimulated some innovations, but these kinds of competitive pressure are not exclusive to the track authority model and would have existed in a regional or sectoral rail industry too (although there would have been a need for strong regulation to ensure fair track access for all). Moreover, although MoC stage two will result in the introduction of new services, they will in the main be off-peak and/or on less busy routes. If, alternatively, the new services are defensive in nature, introduced in response to the *threat* of competition, they could bring benefits to rail users. Again, however, it is important to note that a similar outcome could have been achieved by a different method of rail privatisation, at a considerably reduced cost, through stipulating higher PSRs (or equivalent) at the time of divestiture. In neoliberal terms, although this would have meant more government involvement in terms of quality of service regulations, such intervention may have been offset by the relative reduction in restructuring costs and subsidy payments.

Yet it would be wrong to conclude that the promotion of on-rail competition *per se* is inappropriate. On a line by line basis, it has the potential to stimulate new demand and improve operational efficiency – the introduction of Connex's Rugby-Gatwick Airport service is a good example – and evidence is emerging to show that it can drive prices down (Jones, 2000). But it is not the case that the small amount of competition generated between TOCs is, or will be, sufficient to justify the adoption of a restructuring policy designed to liberalise the entire network. The track authority model has resulted in minimal direct rivalry at a cost which still outweighs that of running BR as a vertically integrated whole. Perhaps a more sensible approach to rail privatisation would have been to pursue a more simplistic method of divestiture and then evaluate the prospects for on-rail competition on a line by line basis as and when applications arose. This would have been perfectly possible in any of the methods of rail privatisation outlined in this book (although it would have required tough regulation to ensure fair access for competitors to incumbents' tracks) and still allowed the introduction of franchising.

Evidence presented in this book would support the argument that the Conservatives were mistaken to view the majority of BR's passenger services as monopolies. BR already faced competition from other transport modes, a point stressed repeatedly by critics of the track authority model before, during and after the time of privatisation. Given the distortion which currently characterises the transport market, it is crucial that a railway provides safe, fast, efficient, punctual and reliable trains in order to maximise its competitive position relative to road transport. Despite major productivity and efficiency gains in the 1980s and early 1990s, BR was arguably not achieving this at the time of its divestiture and the "management skills, flair and entrepreneurial spirit" (DoT, 1992a) of the private sector are only slowly improving the situation. As noted in section 7.3, standards of punctuality and reliability are now only marginally better than they were under BR; in addition, overcrowding is increasingly commonplace and some rural services, especially in the South West of England and South Wales, are being cut back to PSR levels (OPRAF, 1998c, 1998d, 1999b, 1999c; Ford, 1999; Thornton, 1999b). On-rail competition was supposed to help prevent such problems, but in reality it could have the opposite effect. If TOCs spend time and effort devising new services to take advantage of MoC stage two, they might devote less energy to addressing the fundamental deficiencies which pervade their day-to-day operations. So long as all TOCs are unable *routinely* to deliver fast, efficient, punctual and reliable trains, it could be that on-rail competition is an unnecessary distraction to the rail industry and a largely inappropriate policy goal. If the money spent on trying to liberalise BR's market had instead been invested in improving the quality of its network, the train operators of today – nationalised or privatised – might have found themselves far better equipped to provide a high quality service capable of attracting high levels of long-term structural growth.

Chapter three showed that the track authority model of rail privatisation was pushed by the Treasury because it wanted competition and made the erroneous assumption that vertical separation would liberalise BR's market as effectively as it had the CEGB's. Little consideration had been given to how appropriate competition would be in the railway industry, but the circumstances in which the policy was adopted precluded detailed discussion of the matter. Had the Conservatives not chosen to formulate rail privatisation policy in the context of drafting their 1992 election manifesto, their analysis might have led them to compare BR's market with those of companies other than the network industries, especially ones in which competition had been far less beneficial than free-marketeers would generally expect.

Ministers might, for instance, have considered the experience of the bus industry – where the Conservatives also sought to introduce competition for and in the market (see chapter one) – since it was privatised in 1985. Although the markets of BR and the NBC were by no means identical, they shared key characteristics such as their relative insignificance in terms of the transport market as a whole and their dependence on public subsidy to support loss-making yet socially necessary services. The chief architect of bus privatisation, Nicholas Ridley, envisaged that, as a result of his policy, the NBC would be replaced by numerous small operators in each town competing with each other to grow the bus market and improve the overall level of service to passengers. The outcome was somewhat different to that which Ridley had in mind, however. As Wolmar (1998) makes clear, the bus market was not sufficiently robust to support competition from within. Far from increasing, patronage continued to decline (passenger numbers had been falling steadily for decades), services became unnecessarily bunched along busy corridors whereas rural routes were in contrast relatively neglected, small operators went bust or sold out to larger firms and the industry is now dominated by three major players, Stagecoach, FirstGroup and Arriva (see also Knowles and Hall, 1992; Lowndes, 1997; Simpson, 1996; White, 1995).

Wolmar (1998) suggests that bus privatisation policy (and especially the attempts made by the MMC to support it) was flawed because it under-emphasised the competitive threat posed by other modes of transport. Whereas in reality the bus companies' share of the overall transport market was generally too small to support sustained competition, the regulatory authorities "insisted that competition between the bus companies was the only yardstick against which to measure the competitiveness of the market... The only recognised form of competition against the bus was other buses" (Wolmar, 1998: 171-172). Despite Ridley's efforts, the bus industry is now characterised by very little intra-modal competition, as the NBC's successor companies see the futility of 'bus wars' and for the most part respect and avoid each other's territories (Wolmar, 1998). Attempting to introduce competition into the bus market was thus a largely superfluous exercise, often creating instability and uncertainty rather than service improvements and market growth. The fact that BR's share of the overall transport market was small, and in addition that it required an annual subsidy of around £1 billion, should have alerted the Treasury to the likelihood of on-track competition having a similar impact in the rail market. Had bus and rail privatisation been considered as part of a wider neoliberal transport strategy, creating a level playing field between road and rail, liberalising the NBC and BR's markets might have been a more feasible proposition. But such a radical policy approach was always unlikely. There are, of course, both practical and political limitations to the application of theories of political economy.

7.5 Future rail policy

Whatever its view of the track authority model of rail privatisation, the Blair administration has had to review its future policy options carefully. Renationalisation was not an option as it would have involved considerable wasted expenditure. Under European law, the businesses sold outright could only be bought back at their current market values and these are significantly higher than they were at privatisation. Furthermore, the level of investment needed in the rail industry outstrips that which any UK government would be prepared to undertake. Successive administrations, both Labour and Conservative, have viewed the railways as a low priority and starved BR of investment capital and there is no reason to suppose this would change. A key benefit of privatisation is that it frees industries from public sector financial constraints, so the rail companies are able to raise their own investment capital from the financial markets. The government has also had to ensure that any changes it does implement will not significantly alter the structure of the railway. Despite the expense and complexity of the current regime, further restructuring will only create more uncertainty within the industry. As Chris Green, former InterCity Director and now Chief Executive at Virgin Trains, has pointed out, various reorganisations over the past two decades have forced British railway managers to concentrate too much on implementing new industry structures, perhaps at the expense of running the railway (Shaw, 1999).

Labour's 'third way' approach, suggesting that the answer lies in tougher state guidance rather than either nationalisation or free-marketeering, seems sensible in theory and is being welcomed by many in the industry, including some respondents.   It is hoped that the strategic vision the government is promising will contribute significantly to the future success of the railway, but it will only do so if ministers learn from the experience of the original privatisation and carefully think out their strategy first.   In the short-term, the SRA needs to concentrate on developing tougher standards of performance. Passenger's charters currently allow TOCs to run trains up to 10 minutes late and claim they are on time.   Moreover, operators can 'stretch' their timetables if they think that certain trains will be delayed, and this has resulted in advertised journey times between certain stations increasing beyond those of 100 years ago (Leake and Macaskill, 1998). The list of shortcomings in TOC regulation is considerable and will occupy the minds of SRA staff for some time to come.   In the longer term, rail policy will need to be formulated with reference to the wider context of the transport market as a whole. Although not addressed in this book, it would also seem sensible that environmental and social objectives play a key role in determining both the SRA's and the Regulator's agenda.   The effective regulation by the ORR of Railtrack will be crucial in ensuring sufficient investment in the infrastructure is forthcoming to support these wider objectives.

In terms of market liberalisation, the most appropriate course of action might be to continue with franchising – particularly given the SRA's recent innovations – but to revert to MoC stage one, at least for the time being. Further on-rail competition in the market might become viable in certain areas of the network and applications for new services could be evaluated on a case by case basis in the future.   What is certain, however, is that further research into railway competition will be essential in helping the regulatory authorities take decisions on the matter.   It was noted in chapter one that this book did not set out to undertake an exhaustive analysis of railway competition in terms of its impact upon service output.   Such research is now required.   Even if MoC stage two is dropped, pockets of on-rail competition will remain around the network and the effect of each or all of these can be measured to ascertain in detail their costs and benefits line by line.   What are the implications of on-rail competition along different types of corridors?   How does it affect the quality and frequency of services along those corridors and does it impact detrimentally on services in other areas?   What effect could on-rail competition have on local or regional socio-economic development? Finally, what is the perception of rail users towards on-rail competition? Do customers want a choice of trains between destinations or, as a respondent suggested (see section 7.3), will this give rise to unnecessary confusion and detract from rail's appeal to potential customers (see also Bradshaw, 1997b)?

The method of rail privatisation adopted by the Conservatives to liberalise BR's market has been only partially successful. Whilst franchising has much to commend it, on-rail competition is not an entirely appropriate policy goal at present. Ministers wanted to introduce on-rail competition because they thought it would bring benefits to rail passengers and taxpayers alike, but they failed to research the potential implications of the track authority model in sufficient detail before its implementation. It is the responsibility of the present government to ensure a similar mistake is not made in the future.

Notes

1. That is, until the current generation of seven-year franchises expire in 2003/04. Attempting to foretell developments beyond this point is of limited value because of the potential for circumstances to become rather unpredictable in the longer term.
2. It should be noted that published passenger journey figures do not allow a direct comparison of trends before and after privatisation. Passenger journeys are estimated from ticket sales and the post-privatisation figures include an element of double counting; a journey involving more than one operator is now scored against each operator, whereas for BR a through-ticketed journey was counted only once, irrespective of any changes made (DETR, 1999). Nevertheless, it is generally agreed that passenger numbers are rising as significant real-terms revenue increases have also been recorded by TOCs.
3. Concerns were raised about franchise length (in particular that seven years was too short given the long investment lead/recovery times) although no-one seemed to believe that this would impact on bidders' willingness to submit future tenders. Similarly, since imparting their views on long-term involvement, some respondents have sold their companies to rivals or partners who mounted takeover bids. Whilst it could be argued that this demonstrates only a short-term commitment to the industry, many of these vendors have retained employment in the railways and could, of course, bid in their own right again in the future.
4. In 1998/99 prices.
5. The TOCs concerned are Chiltern, GNER, Connex South Central, Central Trains, South West Trains and a proposed new franchise, TransPennine Express, consisting of routes currently operated by Northern Spirit. A study into the possibility of creating a new 'WalesRail' franchise has also been commissioned.
6. As part of the takeover deal negotiated by Arriva, the company can surrender its rail franchises after operating them for one full year. The franchising of the new

TransPennine Express TOC (see note five above) will presumably be made easier by this.

7. Railtrack has actually committed itself to around £8 billion of investment over the next five years and has pointed out that it cannot afford to undertake the £52 billion programme without partnership funding. Some of this may come from revenue sharing deals with TOCs under existing franchise contracts – particularly those with 15 year deals such as Gatwick Express – but it is likely that the government will have to commit substantial additional resources to the railway. This could take the form of either targeted grants – such as the £130 million Rail Passenger Partnerships scheme aimed at small projects which, despite their size, bring significant benefits – or through increased subsidy payments to TOCs. The latter would allow Railtrack to raise the track access charges it levies on the operating companies which in turn would enable it to increase its infrastructure investment.

8. Five people travelling from Plymouth to Taunton and back, for example, pay a combined fare of £92.50 by rail, compared with around £20 by road.

9. It is not known whether the Regulator will further relax MoC after 2002, but any change will be incremental in nature (ORR, 1994c) and it is safe to assume here that the regulations will remain relatively constant until 2004.

10. In certain circumstances, especially where two or more operators share a flow and none earn over 80 per cent of the revenue from that flow, open access services will not be allowed as it is deemed that some competition already exists (although this is of course severely limited by CI – see chapter six).   An example is the Thameslink/Midland Mainline flow between Bedford and London.

11. Takeovers and/or refranchising could impact upon the amount of on-rail competition which develops. For example, Virgin's proposals for the GNER franchise would remove competition between London and Glasgow/Edinburgh if successful.

12. This involved identifying a loophole in CI which enabled the creation of new dedicated flows on inter-available routes between alternative London termini. Whereas the previous flow specified only London BR as the final destination (in this case including two termini), the new flow referred to only one terminus and resulted in the manipulative operator being able to introduce its own dedicated fares to undercut the interavailable ones.

13. That is, 'cheap' in the context of the increased transaction costs associated with vertical separation.

14. There are of course problems with this concept, notably the fact that it ignores the circumstances of the disadvantaged minority.   However, because all rail users are protected by PSRs and other regulations, it is assumed that no passengers will receive a level of service *significantly* worse than before privatisation.

Appendix 1: Rail Businesses Sold/Franchised

Company and group (now trading as)	Date sold	Owner
TOC		
South West Trains	19/12/95	Stagecoach Holdings
Great Western (First Great Western)	20/12/95	FirstGroup
LTS Rail (c2c)	08/05/96	Prism Rail
InterCity East Coast (GNER)	29/03/96	Sea Containers
Gatwick Express	03/04/96	National Express Group
Network SouthCentral (Connex South Central)	12/04/96	CGEA
Midland Main Line	22/04/96	National Express Group
Chiltern Railways	25/06/96	M40 Trains
South Eastern (Connex South Eastern)	21/08/96	CGEA
South Wales and West (Wales and West)	17/09/96	Prism Rail
Cardiff Railways	17/09/96	Prism Rail
Island Line	13/10/96	Stagecoach Holdings
Thames Trains	19/10/96	Go-Ahead
CrossCountry Trains (Virgin Trains)	28/11/96	Virgin Rail Group
Great Eastern (First Great Eastern)	03/12/96	FirstGroup
West Anglia Great Northern	05/12/96	Prism Rail
Anglia Railways	05/12/96	GB Railways
Merseyrail Electrics	20/12/96	Arriva
North West Regional Railways (First North Western)	04/02/97	FirstGroup
North London Railways (Silverlink)	07/02/97	National Express Group
Regional Railways North East (Northern Spirit)	10/02/97	Arriva
Thameslink	11/02/97	GoVia
Central Trains	17/02/97	National Express Group
InterCity West Coast (Virgin Trains)	09/02/97	Virgin Rail Group
ScotRail Railways	25/02/97	National Express Group
Freight		
Red Star Parcels	05/09/95	Rald (MBO)
Rail Express Systems	09/12/95	EWS
Mainline Freight	24/02/96	EWS
Loadhaul	24/02/96	EWS
Transrail Freight	24/02/96	EWS
Freightliner	25/05/96	MCB (MBO) [1]
Railfreight Distribution [2]	13/03/97	EWS
Rosco		
Porterbrook Leasing [3]	08/01/96	MEBO
Angel Train Contracts [4]	16/01/96	Nomura/Babcock et al
Eversholt Leasing (HSBC Rail) [5]	02/02/96	Candover Partners/MBO

GoCo

Railtrack	20/05/96	Stock market flotation
Union Railways [6]	31/05/96	London & Continental Railways
European Passenger Services	31/05/96	London & Continental Railways

BRIS

DCU Birmingham (Owen Williams Railways)	25/07/95	Owen Williams
IDG Glasgow	18/08/95	Scott Wilson Kirkpatrick
Mainline Swindon (Scott Wilson Mainline)	18/08/95	Scott Wilson Kirkpatrick
Civil Engineering Design Group (CEDG York)	15/09/95	British Steel
BPE Mechanical & Electrical Engineering Consultancy (BPE Engineering)	15/09/95	James Scott (AMEC)
CEDAC (W S Atkins Rail (CEDAC))	15/12/95	W S Atkins Consultants
Powertrack Engineering (W S Atkins Power Track)	15/12/95	W S Atkins Consultants
Scotland Track Renewals	08/02/96	Relayfast (MBO)
Scotland Infrastructure Maintenance (First Engineering)	14/02/96	First Engineering (MBO)
Central Track Renewals (Centrac)	29/02/96	Tarmac
Eastern Track Renewals	15/03/96	Fastline Track Renewals (MBO)
Western Infrastructure Maintenance (Amey Railways)	25/03/96	Amey/MBO
South East Infrastructure Maintenance	02/04/96	Balfour Beatty/MBO
Eastern Infrastructure maintenance	02/04/96	Balfour Beatty
Southern Track Renewals	02/0496	Balfour Beatty
South West Infrastructure Maintenance (SWIMCO)	18/04/96	AMEC
Central Infrastructure Maintenance (GT Railway Maintenance)	19/04/96	GEC Alsthom/Tarmac
Northern Track Renewals	23/05/96	Fastline Group (MEBO)
Northern Infrstructure Maintenance (Jarvis Facilities)	18/06/96	Jarvis
Western Track Renewals	23/07/96	Relayfast (MBO)

BRML

Swindon Electronic Service Centre (ABB Daimler-Benz Transportation)	13/04/95	ABB Customer Support Services
Chart Leacon Level 5 Depot (ABB Daimler-Benz Transportation)	05/06/95	ABB Customer Support Services
Doncaster BRML Depot (ABB Daimler-Benz Transportation)	05/06/95	ABB Customer Support Services
IlFord Level 5 Depot (ABB Daimler-Benz Transportation)	05/06/95	ABB Customer Support Services
Springburn BRML Depot (Railcare)	06/06/95	Babcock/Siemens
Wolverton BRML Depot	06/06/95	Babcock/Siemens
Eastleigh BRML Depot	07/06/95	Wessex Traincare (MBO)

Central

Meldon Quarry	04/03/94	ECC Construction Materials
Special Trains Unit	31/01/95	Flying Scotsman Railways
Baileyfield Switches and Crossings Works	07/07/95	VAE-Baileyfield
Ditton Timber Treatment Works	01/09/95	The Phoenix Timber Group

OBS Services Ltd	03/10/95	European Rail Catering (MBO)
Quality & Safety Servics	10/11/95	Ingleby (805) Ltd (MBO)
Railway Occupational Health	30/11/95	Occupational Health Care
Signalling Control (UK)	01/12/95	BTR (Westinghouse Signals)
BR Telecommunications (Racal BRT)	21/12/95	Racal Electronics
Interlogic Control Engineering	04/01/96	ABB Daimler-Benz Transportation
Castleton Works (British Steel Track Products)	14/03/96	British Steel
The Engineering Link	18/03/96	Chief Policy Ltd
Interfleet Technology	22/03/96	Bromco 909 (MBO)
College of Railway Technology	29/03/96	Advicepart (MBO)
Network Train Engineering Services	01/04/96	W S Atkins (Consultants)
BR Projects	26/06/96	Addspice Ltd (MBO)
Scientifics	09/12/96	Atesta Group
British Rail Research	20/12/96	AEA Technology
Nationwide Fire Services	06/01/97	Serco
BR Business Systems	03/02/97	Sema
National Railway Supplies (including Collector's Corner)	03/02/97	MEBO/Unipart
Rail Operational Research	04/02/97	BR Projects Ltd (MBO)
Opal Engineering	13/02/97	W S Atkins (Consultants)
Railtest	14/02/97	Serco
Railpart UK	06/03/97	Unipart
BRIL	Not yet sold	

Businesses closed	
Crewe Timber Works	25/03/94
Newton Heath Concrete Works	25/03/94
Crofton Track Works, Wakefield	25/03/94
Architecture & Design	31/03/94
Haulmark	30/09/94
Brighton Fabrication Works	25/11/94
Shettlestone Fabrication Works	23/12/94
Taunton Concrete Works	02/02/95
The Grove Management School	16/02/95
Materials Technology, Derby	31/03/95
Materials Engineering Group	31/12/95
Railnews	30/10/96
First Procurement	31/12/96
British Railways Savings Co	31/03/97

Notes

1. Sale includes the promise of a subsidy totalling £75 million and a five year track access agreement with Railtrack.

2.   Ownership finally transferred to EWS on 22-11-97 after an EU enquiry.
3.   Sold on to Stagecoach for £825 million and again in 2000 to Abbey National.
4.   Sold on to Royal Bank of Scotland for £395 million.
5.   Sold on to Forward Trust for £726.5 million and again in 1999 to HSBC.
6.   Union Railways and European Passenger Services were both given to London and Continental Railways after their winning bid to build the CTRL.

Appendix 2: Mechanistic Approaches to Access Charging

Negotiated Charges required Railtrack to estimate its total future revenue requirement and then deduct anticipated income from (among other things) access charges expected to be paid from non-franchised operators. TOCs would, between them, meet the remaining 'control cost'. Meanwhile, Railtrack would have an incentive to encourage non-franchised operators onto the network – who would pay a negotiated charge – in order to increase its revenue above the control cost. This approach to charging was seen as a means "both of maximising the use of the network and of maximising financial contributions towards it – both highly desirable objectives" (ORR, 1994a: 11). However, aside from the fact that negotiations between Railtrack and non-franchised operators might fail to capture the full amount of their potential contribution, or even *dis*courage open access entry to the network, a major shortcoming of the negotiated charges regime was that it made no attempt to moderate competition. If non-franchised operators did abound, then the problems of escalating subsidy bills and/or absence of bids for franchises would have occurred.

Equalised Access Charges envisaged that all operators, whether a TOC or non-franchised, would pay the same price per unit of operation for access to a particular route. The 'unit of operation' might comprise train miles, vehicle miles or passenger revenues. Analysis undertaken by the ORR for a typical InterCity TOC showed that using train miles as the unit of operation created an almost complete barrier to entry, whilst using vehicle miles created virtually no barrier at all and would have exposed the incumbent's income in a manner similar to the negotiated charges regime. The use of passenger revenues would have been equally problematic. Because Railtrack's costs represent at least 40 per cent of all passenger revenues, train operators would have had an incentive to cease operating services which earned, on average, a margin of less than 40 per cent over direct operating costs. Such a scenario would have required detailed timetable specifications (in considerable excess of those included in PSRs) to prevent this happening, thus, as the Regulator pointed out, entrenching inflexibility instead of removing it.

Access Deficit Charges represented a different approach to the above models. The charges would contain some of the risks a TOC might face from competition by requiring new entrants to compensate incumbents for their reduced capacity to cross-subsidise services. This type of charge was first considered in the railway industry in 1991, when the Virgin Group expressed a desire to run services from London to Edinburgh in competition with British Rail (*House of Commons Papers*, 1992d). However, the calculation of an access deficit charge would have raised problems of practicality because of the extreme difficulty in identifying the incidence and extent of cross-subsidy within any given TOC. This approach could, therefore, have resulted in regulatory capture and created artificially high barriers to market entry if TOCs deliberately over-estimated the likely effects of competition on their businesses.

Appendix 3: Duplicated Routes

Route	Competition ?	Operator(s)
Barking/Upminster to Benfleet/Southend	No	LTS Rail
Birmingham to Edinburgh	No	Virgin Trains
Birmingham to Leamington Spa	Yes	Central Trains, Virgin Trains, Wales and West
Birmingham to Stafford	Yes	Virgin Trains, Central Trains
Birmingham to Smethwick	No	Central Trains (Centro)
Birmingham to Worcester	Yes	Central Trains, Wales and West
Cardiff to Cheltenham/Birmingham	Yes	Wales and West, Virgin Trains
Cardiff to Radyr	No	Valley Lines
Clapham Junction to Staines	No	South West Trains
Didcot to Worcester	Yes	Thames Trains, First Great Western
Edinburgh to Perth	Yes	Virgin Trains, ScotRail
Gatwick to Barnham	No	Connex South Central
Glasgow to Carlisle	Yes	Virgin Trains, ScotRail
Glasgow to Edinburgh	Yes	ScotRail/Virgin Trains
Glasgow to Motherwell	Yes	ScotRail (SPT)/Virgin Trains
Glasgow to Dalmuir	No	ScotRail (SPT)
Glasgow to Newton	No	ScotRail (SPT)
Glasgow to Springburn	No	ScotRail (SPT)
Leeds to Bradford	Yes	First North Western, Northern Spirit
Liverpool to Chester/Ellesmere Port	Yes	Merseyrail Electrics, First North Western
Liverpool to Hunts Cross	Yes	Merseyrail Electrics, Central Trains
Liverpool to Manchester	Yes	First North Western, Northern Spirit, Central Trains
Liverpool to Preston	No	First North Western
Liverpool to Wigan	No	First North Western
London to Beckenham Junction	No	Connex South Central/Eastern
London to Birmingham	Yes	Virgin Trains/Silverlink, Chiltern Railways
London to Clapham	Yes	Connex South Central/Eastern, South West Trains
London to Croydon	Yes	Thameslink, Connex South Central, Connex South Eastern

London to Epsom	Yes	South West Trains, Thameslink
London to Exeter	Yes	First Great Western, South West Trains
London to Glasgow	Yes	Virgin Trains, GNER
London to Havant/Portsmouth	Yes	Connex South Central, South West Trains
London to Herne Hill	Yes	Thameslink, Connex South Eastern
London to Reading	Yes	First Great Western, Thames Trains, Virgin Trains, South West Trains
London to Leeds/Wakefield	Yes	GNER, Midland Main Line
London to Southend	Yes	LTS Rail, Great Eastern
London to Stevenage	Yes	GNER, WAGN
London to Streatham	Yes	Thameslink, Connex South Central
London to Sutton	Yes	Thameslink, Connex South Central
London to Wimbledon	Yes	Connex South Central, South West Trains
London to Ashford	No	Connex South Central/Eastern
London to Aylesbury	No	Chiltern Railways
London to Bromley	No	Connex South Eastern
London to Broxbourne	No	WAGN
London to Cambridge	No	WAGN
London to Canterbury	No	Connex South Eastern
London to Catford	No	Connex South Eastern
London to Charlton	No	Connex South Eastern
London to Dartford	No	Connex South Eastern
London to Dover	No	Connex South Eastern
London to Finsbury Park	No	WAGN
London to Horsham	No	Connex South Central
London to Lewisham	No	Connex South Eastern
London to Maidstone	No	Connex South Eastern
London to Margate/Ramsgate	No	Connex South Eastern
London to Minster	No	Connex South Eastern
London to Orpington	No	Connex South Eastern
London to Peckham/Denmark Hill	No	Connex South Central/Eastern
London to Penge	No	Connex South Central/Eastern
London to Rochester/Chatham	No	Connex South Eastern
London to Sevenoaks	No	Connex South Eastern
London to Twickenham	No	South West Trains
Loughborough to Chesterfield	Yes	Central Trains, Midland Mainline
Manchester to Bristol	Yes	Wales and West, Virgin Trains
Manchester to Chester	No	First North Western
Manchester to Leeds	No	Northern Spirit
Manchester to Sheffield	Yes	First North Western, Northern Spirit, Central Trains
Manchester to Stafford/Birmingham	No	Virgin Trains

Manchester to Rochdale	No	Northern Spirit
Manchester to Wigan	No	First North Western
Milton Keynes to Rugby	Yes	Virgin Trains, Silverlink
Norwich to Great Yarmouth	No	Anglia
Preston to Blackpool	Yes	First North Western, Northern Spirit, Virgin Trains
Surbiton to Guildford	No	South West Trains
Wakefield to Castleford	No	Northern Spirit
Wakefield to Sheffield	Yes	Midland Mainline, Northern Spirit
Wimbledon to Effingham Junction	No	South West Trains
York to Leeds	Yes	Virgin Trains, Northern Spirit
York to Sheffield	Yes	Virgin Trains, Northern Spirit
York to Selby	No	Northern Spirit

Bibliography

Abbott, J (1984) 'A disposition to dispose' *Modern Railways* Vol. 41, pp. 289-293

Adam Smith Institute (1983) *The omega report: transport policy* Adam Smith Institute, London

Adamson, M; Jones, W and Pratt, R (1991) 'Competition issues in privatisation: lessons for the railways' in Banister, D and Button, K (eds) *Transport in a free market economy* Macmillan, London

Aglietta, M (1979) *A theory of capitalist regulation* New Left Books, London

Ashford, N (1991) 'Neoliberalism' in Ashford, N and Davies, S (eds) *A dictionary of conservative and libertarian thought* Routledge, London

Association of Train Operating Companies (1998) 'Examples of excellent value fare deals' Personal communication

Atkinson, R and Savage, S (1994) 'The Conservatives and public policy' in Savage, S; Atkinson, R and Robins, L (eds) *Public policy in Britain* MacMillan, London

Banister, D and Button, K (1993) *Transport, the environment and sustainable development* Spon, London

Banister, D (1998) *Transport policy and the environment* Spon, London

Barry, N (1983) 'Review article: the new liberalism' *British Journal of Political Science* Vol. 13, pp. 93-123

Barry, N (1987) *The New Right* Croom Helm, London

Batchelor, C (1997) 'First test of competition on railways coming up' *Financial Times* May 8, p. 6

Baumol, W (1982) "Contestable markets: an uprising in the theory of industrial structure" *American Economic Review*, Vol. 72 (1) pp. 1-15

Beesley, M (1981) *Liberalisation of the use of the Telecommunications network* HMSO, London

Beesley, M and Littlechild, S (1983) 'Privatization: principles, problems and priorities' *Lloyds Bank Review* 149, July, pp. 1-20

Beesley, M and Littlechild, S (1989) 'The regulation of privatized monopolies in the United Kingdom' in Beesley, M *Privatization, regulation and deregulation* Routledge, London

Bishop, M and Kay, J (1988) *Does privatisation work?* London Business School, London

Bowdery, J (1994) *Quality of service in the regulated industries* Centre for the Study of Regulated Industries, London

Boyson, R (1971) *Goodbye to nationalisation* Churchill Press Limited, London

Bradley, I (1985) *The strange rebirth of liberal Britain* Chatto & Windus, London

Bradshaw, W (1991) *A review of policies for the future of Britain's railways* Paper presented to the Railway Study Association, 13 November, London

Bradshaw, W (1996a) 'The privatization of railways in Britain' *Japan Railway and Transport Review* September 1996, pp. 15-21

Bradshaw, W (1996b) 'The real costs of rail privatisation' *Public Transport Information* September/October 1996, pp. 8-9

Bradshaw, W (1997a) 'Competition in the rail industry' *Oxford Review of Economic Policy* Vol. 13 (1) pp. 93-102

Bradshaw, W (1997b) Untitled letter to Office of the Rail Regulator, October 31

British Broadcasting Corporation (1996) *Off the rails* Panorama documentary

British Railways Board (1962) *The reshaping of Britain's railways. Part two: maps* HMSO, London

British Railways Board (1981) *Rail policy: a statement by the British Railways Board of its policies and potential for the 1980s* British Rail Publications, London

British Railways Board (1992) *The British Rail passenger's charter* BRB, London

British Railways Board (1996) *National conditions of carriage* BRB, London

Brittan, S (1984) 'The politics and economics of privatisation' *Political Quarterly* Vol. 55, pp. 109-128

Brown, K (1989) 'BR chairman warns of risks in rail break-up' *Financial Times* October 17, p. 10

Buchanan, J; Rowley, C; Breton, A; Wiseman, J; Frey, B; Peacock, A; Grimond, J; Johnson, N; Judge, K; Legage, H; Grant, R; Whitely, P; Niskanen, W and Ricketts, M (1978) *The economics of politics* Institute of Economic Affairs, London

Burns, P; Crawford, I and Dilnot, A (1995) 'Regulation and redistribution in utilities' *Fiscal Studies* Vol. 16 (4) pp. 1-22

Campbell-Bannerman, D (1993) *Levelling the tracks – using rail privatisation to right an historical imbalance* The Bow Group, London

Central Rail Users' Consultative Committee (1999) *Annual report 1998/99* CRUCC, London

Central Statistical Office (1992) *Financial statistics No. 368, December 1992* HMSO, London

Central Statistical Office (1995) *Financial statistics No. 395, March 1995* HMSO, London

Central Trains Ltd (1997) *Under a fiver, under a tenner – Go* Central Trains Ltd, Winchester

Channon, P (1988) 'Speech to the conference' in Redwood, J *Signals from a railway conference* CPS, London

Chapman, C (1990) *Selling the family silver: has privatisation worked?* Hutchinson, London

Charlton, C; Gibb, R and Shaw, J (1997) 'Regulation and continuing monopoly on Britain's railways' *Journal of Transport Geography* Vol. 5 (2) pp. 147-153

Clarke, J (2000) 'Selling the freight railway' in Freeman, R and Shaw, J (eds) *All change. British Railway Privatisation* McGraw-Hill, Maidenhead

Conservative Party (1970) *Campaign guide* Conservative Central Office, London

Conservative Party (1974) *Policy points number 4* Conservative Central Office, London

Conservative Party (1976a) *The right approach: a statement of Conservative aims* PY 5119, Conservative Political Centre, London

Conservative Party (1976b) *Britain doesn't have to go steadily downhill: this is the right approach* PY 5175, Conservative Central Office, London

Conservative Party (1977) *Campaign guide* Conservative Central Office, London

Conservative Party (1979a) *Contact brief – the economic outlook* August/September, Conservative Political Centre, London

Conservative Party (1979b) *The Conservative manifesto 1979* Conservative Central Office, London

Conservative Party (1983) 'The challenge of our times' in The Times, *Guide to the House of Commons* Times Books, London

Conservative Party (1984) *Election brief* Conservative Central Office, London

Conservative Party (1987) 'The next moves forward: the Conservative Manifesto 1987' in The Times, *Guide to the House of Commons* Times Books, London

Conservative Party (1992) *The best future for Britain: The Conservative manifesto 1992* Conservative Central Office, London

Conservative Party (1996) *Privatisation: creating competitive, world-class companies* Unpublished information document, Conservative Research Department, London

Conservative Research Department (1968) *Report of the policy group on nationalised industries* Conservative Research Department, London

Cormack, J and Pigott, N (1997) 'The great railway sale is over!' *The Railway Magazine* April, pp. 20-25

Curwen, P (1997) 'The end of the line for British Rail' *Public Money and Management* Vol. 17 (4) pp. 55-67

Demsetz, H (1968) 'Why regulate utilities?' *Journal of Law and Economics* Vol. XI, October, pp. 55-65

Department of the Environment, Transport and the Regions (1998a) *Developing an integrated transport policy: Factual background* DETR, London

Department of the Environment, Transport and the Regions (1998b) *Developing an integrated transport policy* DETR, London

Department of the Environment, Transport and the Regions (2000) *Bulletin of rail statistics* Quarter 3 1999/2000, DETR, London

Department of Transport (1992a) *New opportunities for Britain's railways* Cmnd 2012, HMSO, London

Department of Transport (1992b) *The franchising of passenger rail services: a consulation document* Department of Transport, London

Department of Transport (1993a) *Railway privatisation: passenger rolling stock* Department of Transport, London

Department of Transport (1993b) *Gaining access to the railway network: the government's proposals* Department of Transport, London

Department of Transport (1994) *Britain's railways: A new era* Department of Transport, London

Department of Transport (1996a) *Rail privatisation programme: sales completed or agreed/franchises awarded as at 27 June 1996* Personal communication

Department of Transport (1996b) *Transport. The way forward* Department of Transport, London

Department of Transport and Office of Passenger Rail Franchising (1996) *New rail fare policy* Unpublished press release, May 15

Dodgson, J (1989) *Privatising Britain's railways: lessons from the past?* Discussion Papers in Economics, Number 59, University of Liverpool

Dodgson, J (1994) 'Railway privatization' in Bishop, M; Kay, J and Mayer, C (eds) *Privatization and economic performance* Oxford University Press, London

Dnes, A (1993) 'Franchising passenger rail' *Scottish Journal of Political Economy* Vol. 40 (4) pp. 420-433

Doe, B (1998) 'Service please' *Modern Railways* Vol. 55 (601) p. 668

Dynes, M (1992) 'Critics may slow BR sell-off plans' *The Times*, October 26, p. 3

Eccleshall, R (1994) 'Liberalism' in Eccleshall, R; Geoghegan, V; Jay, R; Kenny, M; MacKenzie, I and Wilford, R *Political ideologies: an introduction* Routledge, London

The Economist (1919) 'Nationalisation' March 22, pp. 472-473

The Economist (1991) 'Rifkind tries to build a model railway' March 30, pp. 27-28

The Economist (1993) 'On the right tracks' January 23, p. 20

The Economist (1995a) 'Disgusted' March 11, pp. 25-26

The Economist (1995b) 'How to privatise' March 11, p. 15

The Economist (1995c) 'Incredible' March 11, p. 126

The Economist (1996a) 'Liberalism defined' December 21, pp. 19-21

The Economist (1996b) 'A great train cash' January 21, p. 20

The Economist (1999) 'Pot luck' March 13, pp. 38-41

Electricity Association (1998) *Electricity industry review 2* Electricity Association, London

Else, P (1996) 'Subsidy requirements in a restructured rail network: with particular reference to British Rail' *Transport Policy* Vol. 3 (1/2) pp. 13-15

Economic Research Centre (1993) *Report of the ninetieth round table of transport economics, held in Paris on 4th-5th February 1993 on the following topic: Privatisation of railways* European Conference of Ministers of Transport, Paris

Farnham, D and Horton, S (1993) *Managing the new public services* Macmillan, London

Financial Times (1992a) 'Delay over BR sell-off proposals denied' January 13, p. 6

Financial Times (1992b) 'BR sell-off likely to take 10 years' July 18, p. 4

Financial Times (1996) 'Acquisitions drive FirstBus: comment' November 26, p. 26

Ford, R (1995) 'Franchising timescale vague' *Modern Railways* Vol. 52 (562) p. 399

Ford, R (1999) 'Straw men are no push-over' *Modern Railways* Vol. 56 (607) 229-230

Foster, C (1992) *Privatization, public ownership and the regulation of natural monopoly* Blackwell, Oxford

Foster, C (1994) *The economics of rail privatisation* Centre for the Study of Regulated Industries, London

Fowler, N (1977) *The right track: a paper on Conservative transport policy* CPC 612, Conservative Political Centre, London

Freeman, R (1993) 'Opportunities for the private sector' Speech given to Financial Times Conference *Economics of rail privatisation*, London, November 22

Freeman, R and Shaw, J (2000) *All Change. British railway privatisation* McGraw-Hill, Maidenhead

Friedman, M (1962) *Capitalism and freedom* University of Chicago Press, London

Friedman, M (1980) *Free to choose* University of Chicago Press, London

Gamble, A (1994) *The free economy and the strong state: the politics of Thatcherism* Macmillan, London

Gibb, R; Lowndes, T and Charlton, C (1996) 'The privatization of British Rail' *Applied Geography* Vol. 16 (1) pp. 35-51

Gibb, R; Shaw, J and Charlton, C (1998) 'Competition, regulation and the privatisation of British Rail' *Environment and Planning C: Government and Policy* Vol. 16 (6) pp. 757-768

Glaister, S and Travers, T (1993) *New directions for British Railways? The political economy of privatisation and regulation* Institute of Economic Affairs, London

Glover, J (1997) 'The franchised railway' *Modern Railways* Vol. 54 (584) p. 273-277

Goodwin, P; Hallett, S; Kenny, F and Stokes, G (1991) *The new realism* Transport Studies Unit, University of Oxford

Goodwin, P (1993) 'Efficiency and the environment: possibilities of a green-gold coalition' in Banister, D and Button, K (eds) *Transport, the environment and sustainable development* Spon, London

Graham, C and Prosser, T (1988) 'Rolling back the frontiers? The privatisation of state enterprises' in Graham, C and Prosser, T (eds) *Waiving the rules: the constitution under Thatcherism* Open University Press, Milton Keynes

Grantham, A (1998) *Privatisation and reorganisation: case studies in rail policy implementation* Unpublished PhD thesis, University of East Anglia

Gray, J (1995) *Liberalism* Open University Press, Buckingham

Gray, M and Ramanadham, V (1994) 'The UK experience in regulation' in Ramanadham, V (ed) *Privatization and after: monitoring and regulation* Routledge, London

Great North Eastern Railway Ltd (1997) *Great leisure travel* GNER, York

Green, D (1987) *The New Right - the counter revolution in political, economic and social thought* Wheatsheaf, London

Grimstone, G (1990) 'The British privatisation programme' in Richardson, J (ed) *Privatisation and deregulation in Britain and Canada* Dartmouth, Aldershot

Gritten, A (1998) *Reviving the railways: a Victorian future?* Centre for Policy Studies, London

The Guardian (1995) 'Railway chief answers jibe by Major' February 25, p. 6

The Guardian (1997a) Independents fume as British Gas gets price cuts go-ahead' September 3, p.18

The Guardian (1997b) 'Half of all electricity customers could switch their suppliers' September 16, p.18

Gylie, M (1984) 'Alternative way to run railways' *Transport* January/February, pp. 16-17

Hancher, L and Moran M (1989) 'Introduction: regulation and deregulation' *European Journal of Political Research* Vol. 17, pp. 129-136

Hansard (1983a) Vol. 44, Col. 37w, June 27

Hansard (1983b) Vol. 47, Col 175w, October 27

Hansard (1984) Vol. 55, Col. 19w, February 27

Hansard (1985) Vol. 74, Vols 5-6, February 25

Hansard (1986) Vol. 102, Col. 1169, October 22

Hansard (1988a) Vol. 138, Cols 668-689, July 28

Hansard (1988b) Vol. 140, Cols 177-183, November 8

Hansard (1990) Vol. 181, Col. 606, November 26

Hansard (1992a) Vol. 211, Cols 971-986, July 14

Hansard (1992b) Vol. 213, Cols 1160-1233, October 29

Hansard (1993a) Vol. 216, Cols 771-889, January 12

Hansard (1993b) Vol. 218, Cols 156-255, February 2

Hansard (1993c) Vol. 225, Cols 585-727, May 24

Hansard (1993d) Vol. 236, Col. 859, August 4

Hansard (1993e) Vol. 225, Cols 411-412w, May 24

Hansard (1995) Vol. 256, Col 53w, March 6

Hardin, R (1993) 'Liberalism: political and economic' *Social Philosophy and Policy* Vol. 10 (2) pp. 121-144

Harper, K (1995) 'Rail privatisation running late' *The Guardian* September 6, p. 18

Harris, N and Godward, E (1997) *The privatisation of British Rail* The Railway Consultancy Press, London

Harrison, A (1982) 'Liberalising telecommunications' *Public Money* Vol. 1 (1) pp. 15-20

Hayek, F (1944) *The road to serfdom* Routledge Kegan Paul, London

Hayek, F (1960) *The constitution of liberty* Routledge Kegan Paul, London

Hayek, F (1976) *Law, legislation and liberty* Routledge Kegan Paul, London

Hayes, M (1994) *The New Right in Britain – an introduction to theory and practice* Pluto Press, London

Heald, D (1983) *Public Expenditure* Martin Robertson, Oxford

Heald, D and Steel, D (1981) 'Nationalised industries: the search for control' *Public Money* Vol. 1 (1) pp. 13-19

Heath, A, Jowell, R and Curtice, J (1985) *How Britain votes* Pergamon Press, Oxford

Helm, D (1987) 'RPI minus X and the newly privatised industries: a deceptively simple regulatory rule' *Public Money* Vol. 7 (1) pp. 47-51

Helm, D (1996) 'Putting the railways back together again: rail privatisation, franchising and regulation' in Beesley, M (Ed.) *Regulating utilities: a time for change?* Institute of Economic Affairs, London

Helm, D and Thompson, D (1991) 'Privatised transport infrastructure and incentives to invest' *Journal of Transport Economics and Policy* Vol. 25 (3) pp. 231-246

Henshaw, D (1991) *The great railway conspiracy* Leading Edge, North Yorkshire

Hibbs, J (1998) 'Review: A new deal for transport – analysis of the transport white paper (Cm 3950)' *Public Money and Management* January/March, pp. 70-72

Hillman, J and Braeutigam, R (1989) *Price level regulation for diversified public utilities* Kluwer Academic Publishers, Boston

Holley, M (1999) 'London-Inverness motorail trains start running in March' *Rail* No. 348, January 13 - 26, p.6

Hope, R (1983) 'I see Serpell as a stimulus to change... not an axeman's charter' *Railway Gazette International*, April, pp. 273-274

Hope, R (1997) 'Franchise operators confident of growing revenue' *Railway Gazette International* November, pp. 779-783

House of Commons (1981) *Transport Act 1981* HMSO, London
House of Commons (1993) *Railways Act 1993* HMSO, London
House of Commons Papers (1992a) Session 1992-1993, 246-V, Appendix 137, pp. 302-304
House of Commons Papers (1992b) Session 1992-1993, 246iii, November 4, pp. 39-65
House of Commons Papers (1992c) Session 1992-1993, 246-ii, November 4, pp. 27-39
House of Commons Papers (1992d) Session 1992-1993, 246-i, October 29, pp. 1-25
House of Commons Papers (1992e) Session 1992-1993, 246-viii, November 25, pp. 185-218
House of Commons Papers (1992f) Session 1992-1993, 246-ix, November 25, pp. 219-245
House of Commons Papers (1992g) Session 1992-1993, 246-iii, November 4, pp. 46-68
House of Commons Papers (1993a) Session 1992-1993, 246-I, April 20
House of Commons Papers (1993b) Session 1992-1993, 246-xxii, February 10, pp. 727-746
House of Commons Papers (1993c) Session 1992-1993, 685, May 19
House of Commons Papers (1996) Session 1996-1997 HC39-i, October 28, 1996
Howe, G (1994) *Conflict of Loyalty* MacMillan, London
Howe, G; Joseph, K; Prior, J and Howell, D (1977) *The right approach to the economy: outline of an economic strategy for the next Conservative government* PY 5139, Conservative Political Centre, London
Hughes, P (1993) *Personal transport and the greenhouse effect: a strategy for sustainability* Earthscan, London
Irvine, K (1987) *The right lines* Adam Smith Institute, London
Irvine, K (1988) *Track to the future* ASI (Research) Ltd, London
James, T; McHardy, J; Schmid, F and Scott, J (1999) *Report of the findings of the BBC/ARRC British railway model* BBC, London
Jenkins, S (1995) *Accountable to none: the Tory nationalization of Britain* Penguin, London
Jessop, R (1997) 'Survey article: the regulation approach' *The Journal of Political Philosophy* Vol. 5 (3) pp. 287-326
Johnson, P (1978) *Britain's on the road to serfdom* Conservative Political Centre, London
Jones, I (2000) 'SRA should reconsider benefits produced by on-rail competition before opening its chequebook' *Transit* May 5
Jones, I; Marks, P and Willis, C (1993) *Franchising passenger rail services* National Economic Research Associates, London

Joseph, K (1976) *Stranded on the middle ground?* Centre for Policy Studies, London

Joseph, K and Sumption, J (1979) *Equality* Murray, London

Kay, J and Silberston, Z (1984) 'The new industrial policy – privatisation and competition' *Midland Bank Review* Vol. 8, Spring, pp. 8-16

Kay, J and Thompson, D (1986) 'Privatisation: a policy in search of a rationale' *Economic Journal* Vol. 96 (1) pp. 18-32

Kay, J and Vickers, J (1988) 'Regulatory reform in Britain' *Economic Policy* Vol. 7, pp. 286-351

Kennedy, D (1995) *Competition in the British rail industry* Regulatory Brief 6, Chartered Institute of Public Finance and Accountancy, London

King, D (1987) *The New Right – politics, markets and citizenship* Macmillan, London

Knight, S (1998) 'Economic slowdown could hit train profits' *Rail* No. 346, December 16 - 29, pp. 30-33

Knight, S and Harris, N (1999) '"We're in the dock together," John Prescott tells National Rail Summit' *Rail* No. 352, March 10 - 23, p.6

Knill, C and Lehmkuhl, D (1998) 'An alternative route of legal integration: The Community's railways policy' *European Integration Online Papers* Vol. 2 (3) pp.1-18 http://eiop.or.at/eiop/texte/1998-003a.htm

Knowles, R (1989) 'Urban public transport in Thatcher's Britain' in Knowles, R (ed) *Transport policy and urban development: methodology and evaluation* Transport Geography Study Group, Institute of British Geographers, London

Knowles, R (1998) 'Passenger rail privatization in Great Britain and its implications, especially for urban areas' *Journal of Transport Geography* Vol. 6 (2) pp. 117-133

Knowles, R and Hall, D (1992) 'Transport policy and control' in Hoyle, B and Knowles, R (eds) *Modern Transport Geography* Belhaven Press, London

KPMG (1996) *Review of CAPRI/ORCATS Systems description – 22 February, 1996* KPMG, London

Labour Party (1996) *Consensus for change: Labour's transport strategy for the 21st century* Labour Party, London

Landale, J (1993) 'Meacher tries to scare would-be rail investors' *The Times* October 5, p. 12

Leadbeater, C; Brown, K; Stephens, P and Thompson, F (1989) 'Issues privatisation cannot resolve' *Financial Times* July 1, p. 6

Leake, J and Macaskill, M (1998) 'Trains were faster in the last century' *Sunday Times* May 3, pp.8-9

Leathley, A (1999) 'Extra drivers for train crisis' *The Times* February 25, p. 8

Leathley, A and Nelson, F (1999) 'Rail firms must help little-used services' *The Times*, p. 28

Letwin, O (1988) *Privatising the world: a study of international privatisation in theory and practice* Cassell, London

Lewis, R (1971) 'How to denationalise' in Boyson, R (ed) *Goodbye to nationalisation* Churchill Press Ltd, Enfield

Leyshon, A (1992) 'The transformation of regulatory order – regulating the global economy' *Geoforum* Vol.23 (3) pp. 249-267

Lindblom, C (1977) *Politics and markets* Basic Books, New York

Lipietz, A (1993) 'The local and the global: regional individuality or regionalism?' *Transactions of the Institute of British Geographers* Vol. 18 (1) pp. 8-18

Littlechild, S (1983) *The regulation of British Telecommunications' profitability* Department of Industry, London

Littlechild, S (1993) 'New developments in electricity regulation' in Beesley, M (ed) *Major issues in regulation* IEA, London

Lowndes, T (1997) *Privatisation, rural railways and community development* Unpublished PhD thesis, University of Plymouth

Madison, D; Pearce, D; Johansson, O; Calthrop, E; Litman, T and Verhoef, E (1996) *Blueprint 5: The true costs of road transport* Earthscan, London

Marsh, D (1991) 'Privatization under Mrs Thatcher: a review of the literature' *Public Administration* Vol. 69, Winter, pp. 459-480

McLachlan, S (1983) *The National Freight buyout* MacMillan, London

Michalak, W (1994) 'The political economy of trading blocs' in Gibb, R and Michalak, W (eds) *Continental trading blocs: the growth of regionalism in the world economy* John Wiley, Chichester

Midland Main Line Ltd (1997a) *Chatsworth day out* Midland Main Line Ltd, Winchester

Midland Main Line Ltd (1997b) *Low fares for small groups: 4-sight* Midland Main Line Ltd, Winchester

Mitchell, J (1990) 'Britain: privatisation as myth?' in Richardson, J (ed) *Privatisation and deregulation in Canada and Britain* Dartmouth, Aldershot

Modern Railways (1980a) 'Differing views on private investment in BR' Vol. 37 (379) p. 146

Modern Railways (1980b) 'Minister speaks on private investment' Vol. 37 (380) p. 195

Modern Railways (1980c) 'Privatisation – slowly and by degrees' Vol. 37 (384) p. 386

Modern Railways (1981a) 'Privatisation becomes denationalisation' Vol. 38 (391) p. 147

Modern Railways (1981b) 'Independence for Southern Region?' Vol. 38 (391) p. 147

Modern Railways (1988) 'Railtalk' Vol. 45 (481) pp. 505-506

Modern Railways (1995) 'Why take a franchise?' Vol. 52 (562) p. 386

Modern Railways (1998a) 'Infrastructure maintenance out to tender' Vol. 55 (594) p.145

Modern Railways (1998b) 'Chiltern carries off railway Oscar' Vol. 55 (596) pp. 294-295

Modern Railways (1999a) 'Wales and West plans Penzance-Portsmouth' Vol. 56 (606) p. 157

Modern Railways (1999b) 'WAGN sets sights on Doncaster' Vol. 56 (606) p. 157

Modern Railways (1999c) 'SWT battles GB' Vol. 56 (606) p. 161

Monopolies and Mergers Commission (1980) *British Railways Board: London and South East Commuter Services* HMSO, London

Moore, J (1983a) *Speech to the annual conference of the stockbrokers 'Fielding Newson Smith'*, November 1, Press release, Conservative Central Office, London

Moore, J (1983b) 'Why privatise?' in Kay, J; Meyer, C and Thompson, D (eds) *Privatisation and regulation: the UK experience* Clarendon Press, Oxford

Moore, J (1985a) 'The success of privatisation' in Kay, J; Meyer, C and Thompson, D (eds) *Privatisation and regulation: the UK experience* Clarendon Press, London

Moore, J (1985b) *Speech to the Canford Cliffs branch of the Poole Conservative association* Press Release, November 16, Conservative Central Office, London

Morgan, O (1998) 'Full steam ahead on rail takeovers' *Financial Mail on Sunday* April 26, p. 9

Mountford, R (1996) 'Roscos: Private sale of the year' in *Privatisation Yearbook, 1996* HMSO, London

Mueller, D (1979) *Public choice* Cambridge University Press, London

Nash, C (1990) *Role of rail in future transport policy* Transport and society discussion paper No. 12, Rees Jefferys Road Fund, Oxford

Nash, C (1993) 'Rail privatisation in Britain' *Journal of Transport Economics and Policy* Vol. 27 (3) 317-322

Nash, C and Preston, J (1992) *Barriers to entry in the railway industry* Working Paper 354, Institute for Transport Studies, University of Leeds

Nash, C and Preston, J (1993) 'Franchising rail services' in Harrison, A (ed) *From hierarchy to contract* Transaction Books, Oxford

Nash, C and Preston, J (1994) Railway performance – how does Britain compare? *Public Money and Management* Vol. 14 (4) pp. 47-53

National Audit Office (1996) *The award of the first three passenger rail franchises* The Stationery Office, London

National Audit Office (1998) *The flotation of Railtrack* The Stationery Office, London

Nelson, F (1997) 'City wipes £250m off rail operators' shares' *The Times*, March 15, p. 32

Newman, S (1984) *Liberalism at wits' end* Ithaca, New York

Niskanen, W (1971) *Bureaucracy and representative government* Aldine Atherton, Chicago

Office of Passenger Rail Franchising (1996a) *Passenger rail industry overview* OPRAF, London

Office of Passenger Rail Franchising (1996b) 'Franchise Director awards first passenger rail franchise' News Release, December 19

Office of Passenger Rail Franchising (1997) *1996-97 annual report* OPRAF, London

Office of Passenger Rail Franchising (1998a) *1997-98 annual report* OPRAF, London

Office of Passenger Rail Franchising (1998b) 'New counts show surge in London traffic' News Release, March 26

Office of Passenger Rail Franchising (1998c) 'Franchising Director calls for action on poorly performing services' News release, May 11

Office of Passenger Rail Franchising (1998d) 'Action plans demanded from train operators' News release, August 13

Office of Passenger Rail Franchising (1999a) Personal communication

Office of Passenger Rail Franchising (1999b) *Bulletin. Performance of the passenger railway network, 20th September 1998-12th December 1998* OPRAF, London

Office of Passenger Rail Franchising (1999c) *Bulletin. Performance of the passenger railway network, 13th December 1998-31st March 1999* OPRAF, London

Office of Telecommunications (1996) *Annual report, 1995* HMSO, London

Office of Telecommunications (1999) *Future developments in the competitiveness of UK telecommunications markets: A Consultative Document issued by the DGT* http://www.oftel.gov.uk/pricing/prc799/htm

Office of the Rail Regulator (1994a) *Summary of responses* Unpublished information document

Office of the Rail Regulator (1994b) *Competition for railway passenger services: a consultation document* ORR, London

Office of the Rail Regulator (1994c) *Competition for railway passenger services: a policy statement* ORR, London

Office of the Rail Regulator (1996) *Annual report 1996-97* ORR, London

Office of the Rail Regulator (1997a) *New service opportunities for passengers: a consultation document on the development of the competitive framework for passenger rail services* ORR, London

Office of the Rail Regulator (1997b) 'Rail regulator announces further fines for train operators as calls go unanswered' News Release, October 23

Office of the Rail Regulator (1997c) 'Rail Regulator and Government agree framework for co-operation and communication' News Release, November 6

Office of the Rail Regulator (1998a) *New service opportunities for passengers: a policy statement* ORR, London

Office of the Rail Regulator (1998b) 'Regulator to review regulation of rolling stock companies' News Release, January 21

Owen, A and Phillips, G (1987) 'The characteristics of railway passenger demand' *Journal of Transport Economics and Policy* Vol. 21 (3) pp. 231-253

Pangalos, P (1995) 'Profit warnings test nerves of investors' *The Times*, December 20, p. 24

Parris, H (1965) *Government and the railways* Routledge and Kegan Paul, London

Pearce, D; Markandya, A and Barbier, E (1989) *Blueprint for a green economy* Earthscan, London

Peck, J and Tickell, A (1994) 'Jungle-law breaks out: neoliberalism and global-local disorder' *Area* Vol. 26 (4) pp. 317-326

Pirie, M (1988) *Privatization* Wildwood House, London

Pinder, D (1998) 'The Devon and Cornwall rail partnership and sustainable tourism in south west England' in Blacksell, M; Matthews, J and Sims, P (eds) *Environmental management and change in Plymouth and the South West* University of Plymouth, Plymouth

Powell, T (1997) *The prospects for the franchised railway* Save Our Railways, London

Preston, B (1980) *The impact of the motor car* Brefi Press, Dyfed

Preston, J (1996) 'The economics of British Rail privatization: an assessment' *Transport Reviews* Vol. 16 (1) pp. 1-21

Preston, J (1997) *The privatisation of passenger rail services* Transport Studies Unit, University of Oxford

Prideaux, J (2000) 'Trains: the rolling stock companies' in Freeman, R and Shaw, J (eds) *All change. British railway privatisation* McGraw-Hill, Maidenhead

Prism Rail plc (1998) *Interim report, 1998* Prism Rail plc, London

Prynn, J (1996a) 'BR scraps bid plans' *The Times*, July 10

Prynn, J (1996b) 'British Rail on track for full privatisation' *The Times*, August 22

Prynn, J (1999) 'Get tough lawyer set for key rail role' *Evening Standard* March 23, p.35

Rail (1998) 'Test runs for Britain's first new passenger train in 1,064 days' No. 330, May 6-19, p. 6

Rail (1999a) 'Silverlink justifies 'heritage' Class 121 'bubble car' repaints' No. 349, January 27 - February 9, p. 20

Rail (1999b) 'FirstGroup eyes up rail rivals for takeover bid' No. 353, March 24 - April 6, p. 19

Rail (1999c) 'Congestion is a barrier to growth' No. 354, April 7 - 20, pp. 22-23

Rail Privatisation News (1997) 'ORCATS tempts revenue raiders' May 15, p.4

Railtrack (1998) *Great Britain passenger railway timetable* Railtrack, London

Railtrack (1999) *1999 network management statement for Great Britain* Railtrack, London

Railtrack (2000) *Network management statement 2000* Railtrack, London
Railway Gazette International (1998) 'Early sales yield huge profits' April, p. 209
Ranelagh, J (1991) *Thatcher's people* HarperCollins, London
Redwood, J (1988) *Signals from a railway conference* Centre for Policy Studies, London
Ridley, N (1991) *My style of government* Hutchinson, London
Roberts, D; Farrington, J; Gray, D and Martin, S (1999) 'The distributional effects of fuel duties: the impact on rural households in Scotland' *Regional Studies* Vol. 33 (3) pp. 281-288
Rovizzi, L and Thompson, D (1992) 'The regulation of product quality in the public utilites and the citizen's charter' *Fiscal Studies* Vol. 13 (3) pp. 74-95
Royal Commission on Environmental Pollution (1994) *Transport and the environment* HMSO, London
Saunders, P (1991) *What difference has water privatisation made: Consumers, shareholders and voters* Working paper No. 80, Centre for Urban and Regional Research, University of Sussex
SBC Warburg (1996) *Railtrack share offer: mini prospectus* SBC Warburg, London
Segall, A 'Optimistic chancellor pins faith on growth' *Daily Telegraph* June 12, p. 5
Senker, P (1989) 'Ten years of Thatcherism: triumph of ideology over economics' *Political Quarterly* Vol. 60 (2) pp. 179-189
Serpell, D (1983) *Railway finances: report of a committee chaired by Sir David Serpell* HMSO, London
Shaw, J (1999) 'What about the competition?' *New Statesman* April 9, pp. xx-xxi
Shaw, J; Charlton, C and Gibb, R (1998) 'The competitive spirit re-awakens the ghost of railway monopoly' *Transport Policy* 5 (1) pp. 37-49
Shires, J; Preston, J; Nash, C and Wardman, M (1994a) *Rail privatisation: the economic theory* Working Paper 419, Institute for Transport Studies, Leeds
Shires, J; Preston, J; Nash, J and Wardman, M (1994b) *Rail privatisation: the practice. An analysis of seven case studies* Working Paper 420, Institute for Transport Studies, Leeds
Simonian, H (1996) 'Warning signals come on in rail sell-off' *Financial Times* August 2, p. 6
Simpson, B (1996) 'Deregulation and privatisation: The British local bus industry following the Transport Act 1985' *Transport Reviews* Vol. 16 (3) pp. 213 - 223
Smithers, R (1993a) 'BR managers shun idea of privatisation buyouts' *The Guardian*, October 30, p. 6
Smithers, R (1993b) 'Climbdown over rail sell-off plan' *The Guardian* January 20, p. 3

Smithers, R (1994) 'Fears grow of cuts to rail services after privatisation' *The Guardian* December 15, p. 8

Starkie, D (1984) 'BR – privatisation without tears' *Economic Affairs* October - December, pp. 16-17

Starkie, D (1993) 'Train service co-ordination in a competitive market' *Fiscal Studies* Vol. 14 (2) pp. 53-64

Stephens, P (1989) 'BR sell-off moves on to the sidings' *Financial Times* October 26, p. 10

Stephens, P and Brown, K (1989) 'BR sell-off 'not a high priority'' *Financial Times* October 13, p. 1

Stittle, J (1996) 'The use of modern equivalent asset values in UK rail privatization' *Public Money and Management* January-March, pp. 59-64

Swift, J (1997a) *Encouraging leisure use of rail* Speech given to the Association of Charter Train Operators' National Conference, October 7

Swift, J (1997b) *Competition in rail* Unpublished draft paper, ORR, London

Swift, J (1997c) *Regulating the railway in the public interest* Address to the Railway Study Association sessional meeting at the London School of Economics, June 11

Thaler, R (1988) 'The winner's curse' *Journal of Economic Perspectives* Vol. 2 (19) pp. 191-202

Thameslink (1997) *Seasons are changing for the better from 24 November 1997* Thameslink, London

Thatcher, M (1993) *The Downing Street years* HarperCollins, New York

Thompson, G (1990) *The political economy of the New Right* Pinter, London

Thornton, P (1999a) 'Prescott urged to tear up rail map' *The Independent* February 3, p. 17

Thornton, P (1999b) 'Train service axed as subsidies fall' *The Independent* April 19, p. 11

Thornton, P and Clement, B (1999) 'Station with only two passengers points way to cull of branch lines' *The Independent* May 1, p. 14

The Times (1993) 'Tory rail revolt fizzles out' November 3, p. 11

The Times (1995) 'Buses make good trains' December 21, p. 28

Tomkins, R (1992a) 'Tories redraw post-election plans for BR sell-off' *Financial Times* March 4, p. 7

Tomkins, R (1992b) 'More of the same for BR' *Financial Times* July 3, p.9

Tomkins, R (1992c) 'Rail sell-off rules may be eased' *Financial Times* December 8, p. 16

Tomkins, R (1993) 'BR sell-off attracts few would-be buyers' *Financial Times* July 21, p. 1

Tomkins, R and Smith, A (1992) 'Timetable slows for BR sell-off' *Financial Times* November 24, p. 12

Tonts, M and Jones, R (1996) 'Rural restructuring and uneven development in the Western Australian wheatbelt' in Lawrence, G; Lyons, R and Montaz, S (eds) *Social change in rural Australia* Central Queensland University, Rockhampton

Transport 2000 (1989) *Rails for sale? The privatisation of British Rail* Transport 2000, London

Truelove, P (1991) 'Movement towards the privatisation of British Rail' in Button, K and Pitfield, D (eds) *Transport Deregulation: an international movement* MacMillan, London

Turton, B (1992) 'British Rail passenger policies' *Geography* 77 (1) pp. 64-65

Veljanovski, C (1987) *Selling the state: privatisation in Britain* George Wiedenfeld and Nicolson, London

Veljanovski, C (1989) 'Privatisation: monopoly money or competition?' in Veljanovski, C (ed) *Privatisation & competition: a market prospectus* Institute of Economic Affairs, London

Vickers, J and Yarrow, G (1988) *Privatization: an economic analysis* The MIT Press, Cambridge

Virgin Rail Group Limited (1997) *Hot lines* Virgin Rail Group, London

Wadsworth, B (1994) 'British railways case study' in Kopicki, R and Thompson, L (eds) *Best methods of railway restructuring and privatisation* CFS Discussion Paper Series # 111, World Bank, Washington, D.C.

Waghorn, T (1905) *The effect of railway competition on railway dividends* William Clowes and Sons Ltd, London

Wales and West Passenger Trains Ltd (1998) *Our passenger's charter* Wales and West, Cardiff

Webster, P (1988) 'Channon lists five options on BR sell-off' *The Times*, October 24, p.1

Welsby, J (1997) 'What next in UK railways?' in Beesley, M (ed) *Regulating utilities: understanding the issues* IEA, London

Welsby, J and Nicholls, A (1999) 'The privatisation of Britain's railway: an inside view' *Journal of Transport Economics and Policy* Vol. 33 (1) pp. 55-76

West Anglia Great Northern Railway (1997) *Season tickets from Peterborough to London: a classic clip from WAGN* West Anglia Great Northern Railway, London

West Anglia Great Northern Railway (1999) Personal communication

White, M and Smithers, R (1993) 'BR privatisation rethink likely' *The Guardian* August 28, p. 8

White, P (1995) 'Deregulation of local bus services in Great Britain: an introductory review' *Transport Reviews* Vol. 15 (2) pp. 185-209

White, P (1998) 'Rail privatization in Britain' *Transport Reviews* Vol. 18 (2) pp. 109-130

White, P and Farrington, J (1998) 'Bus and coach deregulation and privatisation in Britain, with particular reference to Scotland' *Journal of Transport Geography* Vol. 6 (2) pp. 135-141

Whitehouse, A (1998) *Making tracks: Setting the SRA in motion* ATOC, London

Whitelegg, J (1993) *Transport for a sustainable future: the case for Europe*, Belhaven, London

Williams, C (1992) *Can competition come to the railways?* Centre for the Study of Regulated Industries, London

Wiltshire, K (1987) *Privatisation: the British experience* Longman Cheshire, Melbourne

Wintour, P (1993) 'Government concession on rail sell-off dismissed as 'a fraud'' *The Guardian*, October 28, p. 8

Wolmar, C (1996) *The great British railway disaster* Ian Allen Publishing, Shepperton

Wolmar, C (1998) *Stagecoach: A classic rags to riches tale at the frontiers of capitalism* Orion Books, London

Wolmar, C (1999a) 'Why a rail showdown could be good news' *Rail* No. 351, February 24-March 9, pp. 20-21

Wolmar, C (1999b) 'The wrong kind of capitalism?' *New Statesman* April 9, pp. iv-v

Wolmar, C (1999c) 'The future of subsidised services must be debated' *Rail* No. 356, May 5-18, pp. 20-21

Wolmar C (2000) 'Creating the passenger rail franchises' in Freeman, R and Shaw, J (eds) *All Change. British Railway Privatisation* McGraw-Hill, Maidenhead

Wolmar, C and Ford, R (2000) 'Franchising the passenger railway' in Freeman, R and Shaw, J (eds) *All Change. British Railway Privatisation* McGraw-Hill, Maidenhead

Wright, M and Thompson, S (1994) 'Divestiture of public sector assets' in Jackson, P and Price, C (eds) *Privatisation and economic performance* Oxford University Press, Oxford

Yarrow, G (1994) 'The economics of regulation' in Ramanadham, V (ed) *Privatization and after: monitoring and regulation* Routledge, London

Young Conservatives (1976) *Young Conservatives' key policy statement* YC 5136D, Young Conservatives, London

Zahariadis, N (1995) *Markets, states and public policy: privatization in Britain and France* University of Michigan Press, Ann Arbor

Zahariadis, N (1996) 'Selling British Rail: an idea whose time has come?' *Comparative Political Studies* Vol. 29 (4) pp. 400-422

Index